Panic on the Pacific

PANIC on the PACIFIC

How America Prepared for a West Coast Invasion

BILL YENNE

REGNERY
HISTORY

Regnery History™ is a trademark of Salem Communications Holding Corporation; Regnery® is a registered trademark of Salem Communications Holding Corporation

Cataloging-in-Publication Data on file with the Library of Congress

ISBN 978-1-62157-497-2

Published in the United States by
Regnery History
An imprint of Regnery Publishing
A Division of Salem Media Group
300 New Jersey Ave NW
Washington, DC 20001
www.RegneryHistory.com

Manufactured in the United States of America

10 9 8 7 6 5 4 3 2 1

Books are available in quantity for promotional or premium use. For information on discounts and terms, please visit our website: www.Regnery.com.

Distributed to the trade by
Perseus Distribution
250 West 57th Street
New York, NY 10107

CONTENTS

PART THREE: WHAT MIGHT HAVE BEEN

*Any time war breaks out between Japan and the United States,
I shall not be content merely to capture Guam and the
Philippines and occupy Hawaii and San Francisco. I am
looking forward to dictating peace to the United States in the
White House in Washington, DC.*
—Admiral Isoroku Yamamoto, Commander in Chief, Imperial
Japanese Navy Combined Fleet, (January 24, 1941, as released
by the Domei news agency on December 17, 1941)

*The [Japanese] could have landed anywhere on the coast,
and after our handful of ammunition was gone, they
could have shot us like pigs in a pen.*
—Major General Joseph Warren Stilwell, Commander, Western
Defense Command Southern Sector, (December 11, 1941)

*The contention that the United States cannot be invaded is as
much a myth as that the Maginot Line could not be taken, or
that Pearl Harbor or Singapore are impregnable...it will be for
us to say when, where and how we will strike.*
—*The Japan Times*, in an item broadcast over short wave,
(January 9, 1942)

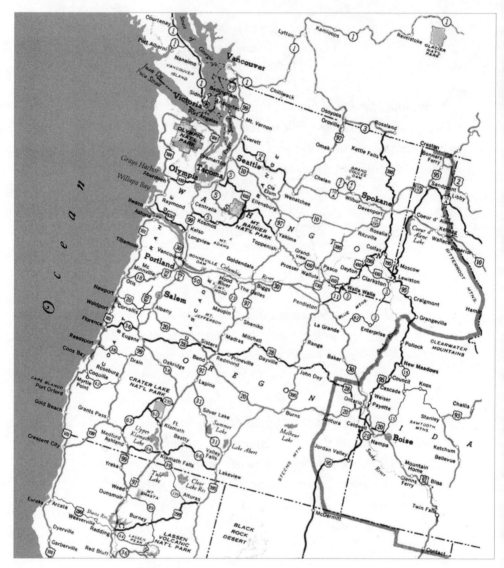

The Pacific Northwest and its Highway Grid (1941) *Library of Congress*

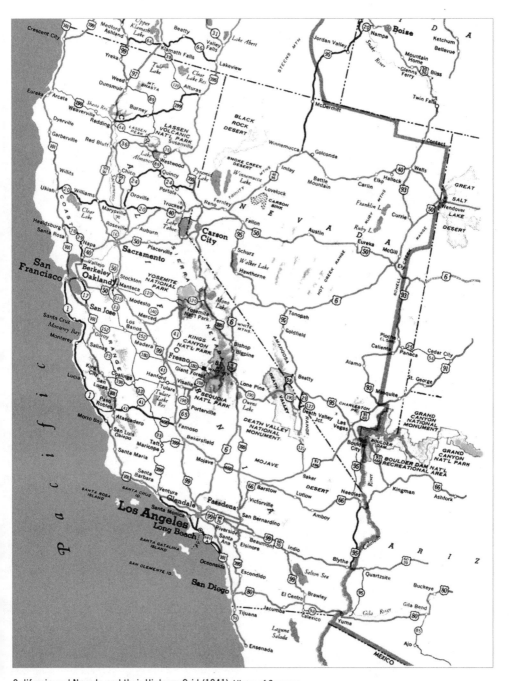

California and Nevada and their Highway Grid (1941) *Library of Congress*

INTRODUCTION

Brigadier General Henry Harley "Hap" Arnold, the future commanding general of the U.S. Army Air Forces (the precursor of the U.S. Air Force) in World War II, was on the front lines of the potential Pacific War before such a thing could have been imagined by most. As the commander of the 1st Wing at March Field, California, he well knew and understood the potential threat faced by the people of the Pacific Coast. His concerns were summarized in comments published in the *Los Angeles Times*, on January 12, 1936:

"Forty high-speed bombers, launched from a carrier off this coast, could in a few minutes completely demoralize the Los Angeles area by the simple expedient of bombing the exposed siphons or the Los Angeles Aqueduct in Owens Valley.... In so doing these enemy planes need not even approach the air defenses of Los Angeles, yet the havoc created by such a well-directed attack would be far more effective than if they dropped their bombs on the very heart of the city. Some 2 million people are absolutely dependent on Los Angeles' water supply," he wrote, and "a one-minute rain of bombs" could force the evacuation of Los Angeles and make the area as arid "as it was when Cabrillo first sighted this coast [in 1542]."

In 1936, the thought that such a thing would happen, or indeed that it even *could* happen, was considered a far-fetched fantasy. But then, there were a lot of things which were about to happen, or *almost* happen, during World War II, which seemed beforehand as unimaginable. Prior to the spring of 1940, for instance, the thought of a German conquest of virtually all of non-fascist Western Europe in a little more than a month and a half was seen as impossible—a ridiculous proposition. Then suddenly, the specter came to life. The rapid, decisive defeat of France, one of the world's preeminent powers, numbed the world. In the summer of 1940, a German invasion of the United Kingdom, untouched by cross-Channel invaders since 1066, seemed inevitable.

Fear and bleak gloominess fell upon that land and her people, who knew how little they could throw up against the blitzkrieging legions of Nazi Germany if they made it ashore. The people of southern England scanned the English Channel horizon with worried eyes. The people held their breath and did what they could with what they had to prepare.

A great deal has been written about the German invasion of Britain in 1940 that never came. Operation Sea Lion, and the efforts to defend against it, remain an indelible part of the historical memory of Britain's wartime era.

It set a somber precedent that was revisited by the people of the West Coast of the United States a year and a half later. Worried, they looked westward toward the vastness of the Pacific, squinting at the horizon for signs of a Japanese invasion armada.

From December 1941 and well into 1942, the same fear and the same bleak gloominess felt in England fell upon the Pacific Coast and its people who knew how unprepared they were to fight the Imperial Japanese Navy—the same force that had just reached thousands of miles across the ocean to cripple the U.S. Pacific Fleet at Pearl Harbor in a few hours—and the Imperial Japanese Army, which was conquering large swaths of Southeast Asia and humbling proud European colonial powers.

Neither invasion ever came, and there are many who insist that neither ever *could have* come, but, in those fearful times, you'd have made no headway trying to persuade someone in Dover or Hastings in 1940, or to someone in Santa Barbara, California, or Astoria, Oregon, in 1941 to be less fearful. The sky seemed to be falling, and there was no way to stop the enemy. Fearful Americans looked out to a once peaceful ocean where Japanese submarines now roamed, torpedoing freighters and shelling the shoreline. Paranoia descended upon the land. Rumors ran rampant, and a cold dread gripped those who were charged with protecting a no longer peaceful Pacific Coast and the people they were charged with protecting.

PROLOGUE

Dreadful Sunday

Decември 7, 1941, arrived as a quiet Sunday morning on the West Coast. It didn't stay that way for long. In the early afternoon, in Washington, D.C., Secretary of the Navy Frank Knox told President Franklin Roosevelt that a message from Hawaii had reached the Mare Island Naval Shipyard north of San Francisco. It read: "Air Raid Pearl Harbor. This is no drill." The message had arrived at 10:58 a.m. California time, 7:58 a.m. Hawaii time.

Knox told Roosevelt that the attack was in progress even as they spoke.

Secretary of State Cordell Hull was scheduled to meet that afternoon with Japanese ambassador Admiral Kichisaburo Nomura and special envoy Saburo Kurusu to discuss the American trade boycott of Japan. Roosevelt phoned Hull and told him to say nothing to the Japanese diplomats.

The president next called his press secretary, Steve Early, and told him to issue a statement to the wire services, and Early got the Associated Press, United Press, and the International News Service on a three-way call. At 2:22 p.m. Eastern Time, the first bulletins went out, reading "Washington—White House Announces Japanese Wave Attacked Pearl Harbor." Within minutes, the radio networks were interrupting their regular broadcasts with the news.

The NBC Blue Network got the story in its most graphic form. A reporter with KGU, the NBC affiliate in Honolulu, had gone up to the roof of the *Honolulu Advertiser* Building with microphone in hand and telephone in the other and had called NBC with the first eyewitness account to reach the mainland. "This battle has been going on for nearly three hours.... It's no joke, it's a real war."

By now, and over the course of the coming hours, additional bulletins flooded in, telling of the simultaneous Japanese air strikes against the Philippines and Thailand. Both Hong Kong and Wake Island were also under attack.

"Japanese parachute troops are reported in Honolulu," CBS reported. "They have been sighted off Harbor Point. At least five persons have been reported killed in the city of Honolulu. The Japanese dive bombers have been making continuous attacks, apparently from a Japanese aircraft carrier. A naval engagement is reported in progress off Honolulu. And there's one report that a Japanese warship is bombarding Pearl Harbor. Aerial dogfights are raging in the skies over Honolulu itself."

Neither the naval battle off Honolulu nor the repeated radio reports about the Japanese paratroopers on the ground in Honolulu were true, but there was no immediate clarification, and in the days following, speculation fed a bonfire of anxiety that would rage beyond control.

═══

In San Francisco, author and radio personality Upton Close, who was described by NBC as their "expert on the Far East," opened his radio commentary Sunday afternoon by saying "there's more behind this than meets the eye."

He had picked up his phone, called the Japanese Consulate in San Francisco and asked to speak with Consul General Yoshio Muto. Instead, he was connected with Kazuyoshi Inagaki, who identified himself as the Consul's secretary and who told Close that the Pearl Harbor attack came as a "complete surprise" to the consulate staff and that the first that he and Muto knew about it came in American radio bulletins.

"That may prove to be true," Close speculated. "It is very possible that there is a double-double cross in this business.... It is possible that this is a coup engineered by a small portion of the Japanese Navy that has gone fanatic.... It might be possible for the Japanese government to repudiate this action, to repair the injury to America."

Though he was nurturing a conspiracy theory, he went on to accurately recall that in 1931, when the Japanese Kwantung Army had launched its offensive against the Chinese in Manchuria, the Japanese government in Tokyo had no advance knowledge of the action. Indeed, Close had verified this at the time by phoning the Japanese foreign office and speaking to the chagrinned diplomats.

◗━━

Inside Japan's consulate in San Francisco at 2622 Jackson Street, Muto and Inagaki were busily shoveling sensitive documents into fireplaces. The flames burst out of control and the fire department had to save the building.

That afternoon, Close reported, "Here on the Pacific coast where there are more Japanese than anywhere else, so far we have no word whatever of anything untoward having happened. I think we can take the word of the local San Francisco Consulate General that the Japanese community has been totally surprised by this action, and so far there is no indication here whatsoever that any sabotage has broken out or that any Japanese spies or saboteurs were warned in time to go into action."

He reported that in Los Angeles, County Sheriff Eugene Biscailuz had "taken charge" of the city's Little Tokyo district and "gathered up a number of volunteers and they have set up a volunteer watching post, and they're watching the Japanese, but they haven't had any reason to do anything. And people on both sides of the fence there are remaining calm and decent, which is certainly good news."

At 4:10 p.m., the Jack Benny Program on NBC Red was interrupted on California affiliates with news of civilians reporting for volunteer duty, and to issue a warning about avoiding "hysteria."

Many of the 9.7 million people of the Pacific Coast States wondered what they *should* be doing. The immediate fear was of air raids. The images from the newsreels of the London Blitz the previous year, the firestorms and devastation wrought by German bombs during the Battle of Britain, were deeply ingrained in the minds and imaginations of Americans. For those on the Pacific Coast, knowing that the Japanese had projected their airpower as far as Hawaii clearly suggested that they *could* reach Washington, Oregon, or California.

It was assumed that the best form of civil defense against air raids was a blackout—turning off all lights in the evening so as not to aid enemy bombardiers in identifying cities, bridges and other targets. Throughout the West, lights were ordered to be turned off at 11:00 p.m. Likewise, civilian radio stations went off the air, because aircraft could use radio waves to locate cities, though most people did not realize that this was why the radio was suddenly silent on the night of December 7. It was unnerving. It was *scary*.

At 6:56 p.m., the sky was already getting dark in Seattle when radio station KIRO, announced that "in the states of Oregon, Washington, and California...every farm house, every light of any kind in that area must be out by eleven o'clock. To test your blackout, you will have plenty of time between the hours of seven and eleven...to make arrangements to get heavy black paper to seal your windows, or heavy drapes or something.... No lights are to be used on automobiles and no lights whatever are to be shown anywhere on the Pacific coast in the states of Oregon, Washington, and California until thirty minutes after daylight."

As the sun rose on Monday morning, those in urban areas well knew that it had been an imperfect blackout. Many had not gotten the word that there would be a blackout and large sections of downtown areas, with their lighted neon signs, had remained bathed in their usual glow. In San Francisco, master switches plunged neighborhoods into darkness while Market Street blazed brightly. William Harrelson, the general manager of the Golden Gate Bridge District, ordered his bridge into darkness shortly after 6:00 p.m., but he turned the lights back on an hour later to prevent automobile accidents.

In the San Fernando Valley north of Los Angeles, the Lockheed Aircraft factories, including the air terminal in Burbank went dark, but they were merely patches of darkness in a twinkling sea. In many places, streetlights were on individual timers and had to be turned off individually. There had been no prior planning to get this job done, and it was still not completed by morning.

Civil Defense volunteers swung into action, but most people were simply confused by the well-intentioned air raid wardens. The Associated Press reported that a woman in San Francisco phoned the police to report "a crazy man prowling about my place shouting 'Lights out.'"

In the composing rooms of the newspapers, typographers reached for the largest fonts they had to set the headlines that screamed "WAR," and readers stripped the newsstands as soon as the morning papers appeared.

"Japan has asked for it," read the editorial in the *Los Angeles Times*. "Now she is going to get it. It was the act of a mad dog, a gangster's parody of every principle of international honor."

The editorial writer at the *San Francisco Chronicle*, agreed, reflecting that "If war had to come, it is perhaps well that it came this way, wanton, unwarned, in fraud and under a flag of truce."

In many cases, it was only when they got their hands on the morning newspapers that many people learned the details of the would-be blackout, and the reason why the radio stations had gone mysteriously off the air.

In Portland, *The Oregonian* pointed out that the state's coastal residents awoke to the "grim realization that the mouth of the Columbia

River is the closest mainland point to Japan." At Fort Stevens, near Astoria, the U.S. Army outpost guarding the mouth of the Columbia, Colonel Clifton Irwin ordered his 18th and 249th Coastal Artillery Regiments to "fire on any enemy ship in sight." None were seen.

Shortly after 9:00 a.m. on December 8, most Pacific Coast radio stations went live to Washington to cover Franklin Roosevelt's speech to a joint session of Congress. Roosevelt announced that the attack on Pearl Harbor was "a day that would live in infamy," and he asked Congress for a declaration of war.

On the West Coast, the most disconcerting thing about the war so far had been air raid sirens blaring indiscriminately during the night. No bombs had fallen *yet*, but there was real worry that the false alarms might soon become real ones.

⋗

Lieutenant General John Lesesne DeWitt was commander of the Fourth Army and of the Western Defense Command at the Presidio in San Francisco. He was the military commander responsible for the entire Pacific Coast, and he was hardly a voice of calm reassurance to a worried population. He set the tone on December 9 during a Civilian Defense Council meeting at San Francisco's City Hall. DeWitt believed that civilians were not taking the threat seriously enough and considered the city's failure to achieve a complete blackout for two nights running as a dereliction of duty.

He told San Francisco's leaders that their city contained "more damned fools...than I have ever seen," and accused them of "*criminal apathy*."

The Japanese were out there and they were coming, he insisted. "If I can't knock these facts into your heads with words," he shouted, "I will have to turn you over to the police and let them knock them into you with clubs."

A United Press correspondent diligently took notes as DeWitt warned that San Francisco had *already* been visited by Japanese aircraft the night before. So far, the city had been lucky, but "death and destruction are likely to come to this city at any moment.... Unless definite and stern action is taken to correct last night's deficiencies, a great deal of destruction will come. Those planes were over our community. They were over our community for a definite period. They were enemy planes. I mean *Japanese* planes. They were tracked out to sea."

He took credit for the fact that nobody had been killed.

The first fatality had been the truth.

PART ONE

Peaceful Coast

ONE

Three States on the Eve of War

O n December 7, 1941, the three westernmost of the forty-eight states became a de facto theater of World War II. Together, Washington, Oregon, and California encompass around three hundred thousand square miles, a vast area larger than any country in Europe, yet in 1941, this was a remote and largely empty land. The three states of the Pacific Coast were home to just 7 percent of the United States population, while the five mid-Atlantic states, with just a sixth of their area, were then home to 27 percent of all Americans.

For a century, the Pacific Coast's allure as a land of opportunity had drawn pioneers westward, and in the 1940s, it was *still* a place where population growth was driven by transplants from other states farther east. Indeed, in 1941, the governors of Oregon, Washington, and California had been born in Kansas, Minnesota, and Utah respectively.

The story of the Pacific Coast in the first half of the twentieth century was the story of *two* distinct regions—one that was urban, and a much larger one that was distinctly rural. Unlike the thickly settled areas of the country east of the Mississippi River, the population in the Pacific Coast states was highly concentrated. Around 5.5 million of their 9.7 million people lived in just four metropolitan areas—San Diego County, Los Angeles County, the San Francisco-Oakland Bay Area, and the Seattle-Tacoma metro area around Puget Sound. Without its metro areas, California had fewer people than Massachusetts, which has only 5 percent of California's land area. Without the people who lived in the Puget Sound region, Washington would have ranked as thirty-fifth among the states in terms of population. Without the people within the Portland city limits, Oregon was only slightly larger in population than Rhode Island.

California was the most populous state on the Pacific Coast, while Oregon was the most rural. Washington and Oregon led the nation in forest products, while California accounted for 70 percent of the fruits and vegetables produced in the country. The Golden State was also second only to Texas in oil production.

Seattle, San Francisco, and Southern California were leading ports and centers of shipbuilding. Southern California led the nation in aircraft manufacturing, with Seattle-based Boeing and Buffalo, New York's Curtiss vying for second place. San Francisco, where Montgomery Street was known as the "Wall Street of the West," was the region's financial hub. And Hollywood, of course, was the movie capital of the United States (and, for that matter, the *world*).

⊃➡

The Great Depression struck the West Coast less harshly than other parts of the country. In fact, California had become the refuge for tens of thousands of migrants, especially those from the prairies, where a series of severe droughts over the course of more than six years had turned millions of acres of farmland into what was known as the "Dust Bowl."

In the 1930s, the West benefitted from dramatic public works programs, including hydroelectric dam-building projects, including the massive Hoover Dam on the Colorado River, which in due course would supply electricity to Southern California, and on the Columbia River the Grand Coulee Dam, the Bonneville Dam, and nine others that helped transform the economies of Oregon and Washington.

Politically, the Pacific Coast was fickle. Oregon and Washington had followed the election of Democrat governors with Republicans in 1938 and 1940 respectively, and California, which had elected nine Republican governors in a row, in 1938 elected Democrat Culbert Olson, a Utah-born Mormon turned atheist who refused to say "so help me God" when he was sworn into office.

One worry united these governors—that the National Guard in their states might be federalized and under the authority and command of the U.S. Army. What they did not realize was that they were soon themselves to be subordinated to a de facto military governor: Lieutenant General John Lesesne DeWitt, U.S. Army.

TWO

The General:
John Lesesne DeWitt

oday, the man who commanded the West Coast when it was a theater
of war is somewhat of an enigma. Though he was once recognized
as the most powerful single figure on the Pacific Coast, and though
he was one of the highest-ranking general officers in the U.S. Army in
1941, he has never been the subject of a biography, and he is rarely mentioned, even in passing, in general histories of World War II. Aside from
his regrettable role in the infamous internment of Japanese-Americans,
even seasoned students of World War II history know little of him.

When I inquired about DeWitt at the visitor center of San Francisco's
Presidio—for 218 years a military post, but now under National Park
Service administration—I received blank stares. Though we were standing, literally across a parking lot from DeWitt's wartime headquarters,
no one on duty could recall having heard his name. As I explained who
he was, and why they *should* know about him, they chuckled as though
I was describing a fictional character. When I contacted the museum at

Quartermaster Corps headquarters at Fort Lee, Virginia, where DeWitt served four years as Quartermaster General of the U.S. Army, I learned that mine was one of just a handful of inquiries that they had received about DeWitt in more than three decades.

When he arrived at the Presidio, one month short of turning sixty, DeWitt was nearing the end of a career that had taken him into the upper reaches of the U.S. Army. As the commander of the Fourth Army, he was one of four men commanding field armies and wore the three stars of a lieutenant general. Technically, he was outranked only by General George Catlett Marshall, the four-star Chief of Staff of the Army.

DeWitt had been in or around the Army all his life. Born at Fort Sidney, Nebraska, on January 9, 1880, he was the son of Captain Calvin DeWitt, an Army surgeon who had served in the Civil War, each of whose three sons were born at different Army posts on America's Western frontier. He attended Princeton University, as his father had done, but left in 1898 to accept a regular Army commission, and was soon serving in the Philippines. By the age of twenty-five, he was married, with a son, and had already risen to the rank of lieutenant colonel. In July 1918, he was a full colonel serving in France at the headquarters of General John J. Pershing's American Expeditionary Force as the G-4, that is, the head of logistics and supply, for the First American Army.

After the war, DeWitt returned to a series of staff jobs at U.S. Army headquarters in Washington, but while he appeared to be on a postwar career fast track, he lacked—aside from his early experiences as a young officer in the Philippines and in the Mexican punitive expedition before World War I—significant combat command experience, which might be why he was assigned to command the 1st Battalion of the 1st Infantry Regiment for two years. Promoted to brigadier general, he served as commander of the 1st Brigade of the 1st Infantry Division and in 1928 became assistant commandant of the General Staff College at Fort Leavenworth.

In 1930, DeWitt received his second star and became Quartermaster General, where, among other tasks, he was charged with organizing official pilgrimages for the wives and mothers of servicemen who had been killed in action during the Great War. Through October 1933, DeWitt and the Quartermaster Corps sent nearly seven thousand women to visit war cemeteries, most of them in France.

In early 1937, DeWitt returned briefly to the Philippines to serve as commander of the U.S. Army's Philippine Division, a unit that included the famous Philippine Scouts. This brief posting served to put a "combat" command on DeWitt's resume, though there was no actual combat to command. He returned stateside later that same year to become commandant of the Army War College in Carlisle, Pennsylvania.

When DeWitt assumed command of the United States Fourth Army—and, concurrently, the Ninth Corps Area and the Western Defense Command—at the Presidio in 1939, war was already underway in Europe and in China.

The Fourth Army was not a tactical field army, but one of four geographic defense commands, collocated with other administrative units. Of the four American armies, only the Fourth could not trace its lineage to a field army that had been active in World War I. Within the Ninth Corps Area, essentially a service command district, DeWitt had two subsidiary field corps headquarters: the III Corps at the Presidio of Monterey and the IX Corps at the Presidio of San Francisco.

In 1940, he commanded a series of training exercises that had been planned prior to his coming to San Francisco. The first two had General DeWitt cooperating with Admiral James Richardson, the commander of the U.S. Navy's Pacific Fleet Battle Force at San Diego. The first, in January, involved eight thousand U.S. Army troops that were landed, with naval support, between Monterey Bay and Point Conception. Two more, held in May and August in Washington, involved a much larger contingent of personnel and were conducted mainly at Fort Lewis. The latter was a disaster from DeWitt's perspective. "The use of cover was generally poor," he complained to the press from his desk at the Presidio. "Troops disclosed their positions by too much movement, and, when most men took off their coats and exposed their white undershirts, exposure was complete."

Meanwhile, the U.S. Army conducted the largest field exercise in American peacetime history in Louisiana. While what became famous as "The Louisiana Maneuvers" demonstrated that the U.S. Army had embraced mechanized warfare, the maneuvers in the Pacific Northwest demonstrated to DeWitt only the shortcomings of his own force.

DeWitt's vision of contemporary warfare was colored by nostalgia for the Old Army, the Army he remembered from his boyhood in cavalry posts on the Plains. Even as the world's armies were embracing mechanization and Germany's panzer divisions were showing the power of armored formations he told the Associated Press on August 28, 1940, that "I believe the day is far in the future when the horse cavalry will not be needed in our Army. Horse cavalry gives the commander fire power of a type that is invaluable. It is mobile fire power par excellence." He didn't see that sort of dash in the men with white t-shirts.

Initially, all three of DeWitt's commands, Fourth Army, Western Defense Command, and Ninth Corps Area, operated with the same staff. By 1941, though, each now has its own staff, all of which answered to DeWitt. This new command structure was the sort of bureaucratic arrangement that suited DeWitt's administrative background and his organizational disposition. Described as aloof and distant, DeWitt preferred his contact with civilians to be through spokesmen, and made few contacts with local and state government officials outside the Presidio gates.

"We don't know him very well in Los Angeles," wrote Tom Treanor, a columnist with the *Los Angeles Times*. "He visits us frequently, but he does not make speeches nor does he call press conferences nor go on the radio. He comes down and sees his generals and those officials with whom the Army has liaison and then goes back to San Francisco. He gives orders and expects to have them executed." Even to the governors of California, Oregon, and Washington, he remained something of a mysterious authority figure, but he was also the single most important man on the Pacific Coast.

THREE

An Army Before Dawn

W hen General DeWitt first stepped onto the parade ground of the Presidio on December 5, 1939, and smelled sea air blowing softly through the eucalyptus, he might have found it easy to believe that the wars engulfing Europe and China would never come his way.

Most officers of DeWitt's generation, indeed, most Americans, still held fast to the idea that two vast oceans separated the United States from any conceivable threat. As Mark Skinner Watson wrote in his book *Chief of Staff: Prewar Plans and Preparations*, after the First World War, various factors including a desire to curtail public spending and a suspicion of the way the United States entered the Great War—prompted Congress to reduce the size of the U.S. Armed Forces considerably. They "underwent an almost continuous weakening from 1918 onward for a decade and a half. The fluctuation in numbers from 1922 to 1936 was small, but the deterioration in equipment was continuous in that the 1918 surplus, used up rather than replaced, was not only increasingly obso-lescent but increasingly ineffective owing to wear and age."

Watson points out that, in the 1930s, the U.S. Navy was permitted, "by a cautious increase in appropriations," to make a start a new ship-building program, adding that the U.S. Army was "less favored, presum-ably because there was a continuing public confidence, shared by the White House and Congress, in oceans as a bulwark and a belief that the Navy could safely be thought of not merely as the traditional 'first line of defense' but as the only really necessary line of defense for the time being."

Army Chief of Staff General Douglas MacArthur observed in 1934 that "in many cases there is but one officer on duty with an entire bat-talion; this lack of officers [has] brought Regular Army training in the continental United States to a virtual standstill...Stocks of materiel [are] inadequate even for limited forces...such as they are, manifestly obso-lescent. The secrets of our weakness are secrets only to our own people."

The Army's personnel strength bottomed out at 133,949 men in 1927, and had reached only 267,767 by the time that France fell to the Germans in June 1940. This was despite a 1937 plan for an emergency defensive command known as the Initial Protective Force that contemplated a Regular Army of 280,000 men and a National Guard of 450,000 men. When the National Guard was federalized at the end of 1940, it contained only about 200,000 men with limited training.

Four years after succeeding MacArthur as Chief of Staff, General Malin Craig complained in his June 1939 annual report that "the problem encountered on my entry into office was the lack of realism in military war plans...Time is the only thing that may be irrevocably lost, and it is the thing first lost sight of in the seductive false security of peaceful times."

Another simmering issue within the Army concerned the future of airpower. There were many visionary aviators, like Henry Harley "Hap"

Arnold, who promoted and often over-promoted the transformative power that air forces would have on warfare. They advocated an independent air force, potent enough to take the fight to an enemy and, through sustained aerial bombardment, cripple his war industries and undermine his public morale. The airmen even saw airpower as having the potential to replace the Navy as the country's first line of defense.

Representing a traditional and contradictory doctrine within the U.S. Army establishment were generals like Craig and DeWitt, the latter who, in 1940, asserted that airpower should be used "as if it were artillery." Craig, similarly, thought that the Army should not invest too heavily in airplanes because they would inevitably become obsolescent. Cost was everything, so the Army, over the objections of the Air Corps, preferred the Douglas B-18 Bolo as a strategic bomber because, although it had a shorter range and a lighter payload, was half the price of a Boeing B-17 Flying Fortress.

As we know in retrospect, the B-18 became a footnote in aviation history, while the Flying Fortress, of which more than twelve thousand were eventually built, is rightly remembered as one of the half dozen greatest American military aircraft, and for shouldering so much of the weight of the successful strategic air campaign that destroyed the Third Reich's war economy.

The Army was similarly shortsighted about ground force technology. Watson wrote "alongside the 1918 tanks at U. S. Army posts until 1938 lay the 1918-type antitank weapons.... The M-1 semiautomatic rifle (Garand), which greatly increased infantry fire power and which was developed by Army Ordnance persistence as a replacement for the pre-1917 Springfield, came from the factories so slowly in 1941 that training plans had to be adjusted to its delivery."

At the Military Establishment Appropriation Bill hearings in 1941, the issue of anti-aircraft weapons came up. The Battle of Britain and "The Blitz" were fresh memories, and they had provided stunning examples of the potential damage that could be wrought by a sustained aerial bombardment campaign and the attendant need for an effective air defense system that included interceptor aircraft (or, to use the parlance of the time "pursuit planes"), radar, and anti-aircraft artillery.

"I should like to do something to quiet the alarm about our…vulnerability to aircraft attack," Massachusetts Senator Henry Cabot Lodge told Craig's successor, General George Marshall. "People will say that this bill carries only 138 90mm guns, while they have 5,000 around London, and the War Department will be accused of being negligent."

"Facilities for the manufacture of antiaircraft equipment are limited," Marshall replied. "What is necessary for the defense of London is not necessary for the defense of New York, Boston, or Washington. Those cities could be raided…but…continuous attack…would not be practicable unless we permitted the establishment of air bases in close proximity to the United States."

While Marshall was correct about the lack of a threat to East Coast cities, he might have been less sanguine had he used Seattle, San Francisco, and Los Angeles as examples and recalled that Japan was in possession of aircraft carriers that *could* be placed "in close proximity to the United States."

When World War II had begun in Europe in 1939, American public opinion was strongly opposed to American involvement. Most voters recalled the sacrifices made in World War I, and did not want to become involved again. The strong isolationist sentiment continued to prevail into 1940, but after France fell to the Germans, and Britain came under air attack, there came a sobering willingness, championed by President Roosevelt, to consider rearming for "National Defense." Countering the mood that had prevailed for two decades, he called for a robust build-up of American military strength though the acquisition of new equipment, especially aircraft, and an increase in personnel strength.

A key aspect of the latter was the Selective Training and Service Act of 1940, which established America's first peacetime draft. It was enacted in September, the same month that Nazi Germany, Fascist Italy, and Imperial Japan signed the Tripartite Pact, bringing all three into the alliance that became known as forming the Rome-Berlin-Rome-Tokyo Axis.

By June 1941, the law had allowed the Army to expand to 1.5 million men. On paper, this was impressive, but 42 percent were draftees whose enlistments expired in October, and 20 percent were members of the National Guard. As for training, the Army was still making do with aging and obsolete equipment and a logistical infrastructure built for an army of one hundred fifty thousand.

FOUR

DeWitt's Army

The U.S. Army of 1941 was a work in progress—and nowhere more so than in DeWitt's Western Defense Command and its Ninth Corps Area. It encompassed not only Washington, Oregon, and California, but Idaho, Montana, Nevada, Utah, and the Alaska Territory. His first priority was protecting the 1,300 miles of coastline from southern California to northern Washington and the nearly six-thousand-mile coastline of Alaska.

Most of the fixed gun emplacements on the Pacific Coast dated back to around the turn of the century. These thick, concrete gun bunkers and pillboxes built by the U.S. Army Corps of Engineers between 1895 and 1905 were manned by the Coastal Artillery Corps, which had been separated from the Field Artillery Corps in 1901, and which maintained its own bureaucracy through individual coast artillery districts.

The coastal guns were seen by strategic planners as the U.S. Army protecting U.S. Navy facilities so that the latter could conduct offensive operations at sea. It was never imagined that most of the U.S. Navy's Pacific Fleet could be taken off line in a single attack—especially not by an *air* attack as was to happen in December 1941. Such a thing was just *impossible*.

The Ninth Coast Artillery District within the Ninth Corps Area was commanded by Brigadier General Henry Burgin, and included five locations. In California, Fort MacArthur at San Pedro guarded the entrance to Los Angeles Harbor, while Fort Rosecrans protected San Diego Harbor. The 6th Coastal Artillery Regiment at Fort Winfield Scott in the Presidio protected San Francisco Bay. In Oregon, Fort Stevens, near Astoria, covered the mouth of the Columbia River, while Fort Worden, near Port Townsend, guarded Washington's Puget Sound.

Each location had two or three batteries, including decades-old ten-inch and twelve-inch guns, 1920s vintage sixteen-inch guns, as well as six-inch rifled guns on "disappearing" carriages that could pop up to fire, then retract out of sight for reloading. In 1940, the Army finally started building casements to protect the sixteen-inch guns from air attack.

As formidable as they were, the fixed coastal guns could do nothing beyond defending access to a harbor or a river at a narrow choke point. They would be useless in protecting the remaining coastline against an invader. To do that would have required mobile forces, including infantry and field artillery, supported by air and naval power that were in short supply.

❧

"With but few exceptions our seacoast batteries are outmoded and today are woefully inadequate," wrote Major General Joseph Green, head of the Coast Artillery Corps in a May 31, 1940, memo to Chief of Staff Marshall. "Nearly every battery is outranged by guns aboard ship that are of the same caliber. More alarming than this is the fact that every battery on the Atlantic Coast, and all but two of the batteries on the Pacific Coast, have no overhead cover so are open to attack from the air."

The Coast Artillery Corps did have some mobile guns. As of December 1941, however, they were concentrated in just six regiments equipped with 155mm guns, and one regiment equipped with eight-inch railroad guns. But most of these were not on the Pacific Coast.

In 1935, the U.S. Army and U.S. Navy had agreed to begin coordinating their efforts toward preparations for coastal defense through a plan published as *Joint Action of the Army and the Navy*, but very little practical work had been done toward implementation of the plan before Pearl Harbor. For its part, the U.S. Navy would later install harbor nets and booms, and plant contact mines and detection devices in outer harbor approaches, but most of this work occurred after 1941.

Air defense was the U.S. Army's responsibility, but despite ambitious plans, there had been little improvement since 1937, when the Army had a grand total of 135 three-inch antiaircraft guns, divided between five understrength regiments, to protect the Pacific Coast. In March 1941, the Army told the Coast Artillery Corps that it had no antiaircraft guns (fixed or mobile) for General Green's harbor defense modernization program.

Within the Western Defense Command, the only dedicated Regular Army antiaircraft regiment was the 78th Coastal Artillery at Fort MacArthur. Antiaircraft troops from the 101st Coastal Artillery Brigade of the Minnesota National Guard, including the 216th Coast Artillery Regiment, were moved to Camp Haan in Southern California in 1941. Less than a week before the attack on Pearl Harbor, Battery B of the 216th moved to San Francisco. It and the newly formed IV Anti-Aircraft Command took over Aquatic Park on the north waterfront west of Fisherman's Wharf, and established their headquarters in a former bathing casino, a few hundred feet down the hill from General DeWitt's residence at Fort Mason.

Along with its antiaircraft batteries, the Army deployed barrage balloons. Anchored to the ground, these large unpowered blimps floated several hundred feet above a potential target. The idea was that the cables would snarl the propellers and damage the wings of low-flying aircraft.

❦

The regular U.S. Army forces within DeWitt's Fourth Army/Western Defense Command area were divided into sector commands. On the coastline, the Northwest Sector, Washington and Oregon, was commanded by Major General Kenyon Joyce at Fort Lewis, near Tacoma, Washington. The Southern Sector, which included California, was under the leadership of Major General Joseph Warren Stilwell, the future commander of American forces in the China-Burma-India Theater, and a man who had served previously as United States military attaché to China during the Japanese invasion in 1937.

Each sector contained a field corps headquarters and a single Regular Army infantry division. The IX Corps headquarters, containing the 3rd Infantry Division, now led by Major General John Porter Lucas, had moved to Fort Lewis from the Presidio of San Francisco in 1940. Major General Walter Wilson led III Corps at the Presidio of Monterey, which contained the 7th Infantry Division, based at Fort Ord, a former artillery training facility just north of Monterey.

Also on the Pacific Coast were two divisions that consisted primarily of National Guard troops and recent draftees. The men of the recently activated 40th Infantry Division at Camp San Luis Obispo, California, were mostly California National Guardsmen with a few from Nevada and Utah. The 41st Infantry Division at Fort Lewis was mainly a Washington National Guard unit, with additional troops from Oregon, Idaho, and Montana. At Camp Murray, adjacent to Fort Lewis, were elements of the 153rd Infantry Regiment and antiaircraft units of the 206th Coastal Artillery Regiment, both from the Arkansas National Guard.

At the end of 1941, both divisions were led by new commanders. Major General Ernest Dawley assumed command of the 40th in September, and

Major General Horace Fuller had taken over the 41st after the sudden death of Major General George White at the end of November. The headquarters of the 35th Infantry Division was also at Fort Lewis, but it was without its operational units, who were members of the Kansas, Missouri, and Nebraska National Guard.

None of DeWitt's four divisions were near full strength, even with the draft and the National Guard mobilization. The majority of the troops that were in the service had been on active duty for less than a year, and, because of widespread shortages of munitions and materiel, the levels of training and equipment left much to be desired. *Los Angeles Times* reporter John Cornell, who visited the 40th Infantry Division at Camp San Luis Obispo in April 1940, reported 9,700 men at the post, including 3,300 from Southern California, and that the division was seriously under strength. Amazingly, in an environment where there was supposed to be some pretense about maintaining military secrecy, he got these numbers through official channels. Discipline also seemed to be lax, and Cornell was able to report this as well. He observed that to some of the servicemen, San Luis Obispo had "the advantage of offering [easy] week-end furlough jaunts" to Los Angeles.

Two months later, when the 7th and 40th Infantry Divisions went on maneuvers at Fort Hunter-Liggett, seventy miles north of San Luis Obispo, Cornell was there to observe the "mock wars." He noted that the authorities had to "warn children, hikers, and picnickers from wandering" onto the mock battlefield. The mood was still relaxed. The war must have seemed a long way off.

In June 1941, American military leaders assumed that if the United States entered the war, the troops would be deployed to Europe and all of the tactical and logistical planning was geared toward this. Though there was widespread revulsion about the harsh conduct of Japan's war machine in China, there was little in the way of practical planning for a war against Japan, except in defense of the Philippines. Beyond the hypothetical, there was even less serious thought given to combat on the Pacific Coast. In August, nevertheless, there was a training exercise that war-gamed the possibility of an enemy invasion, starting with an enemy seizure of the Hawaiian Islands before an attack on the West Coast of the continental United States. Even Chief of Staff Marshall and Secretary of War Henry Stimson flew in to observe.

To add realism to the exercise, even DeWitt himself—commanding the "Blue," or defending, force—was not told where the "Red" invaders would land until April 9, the day before the mock invasion. The target was the Puget Sound area, and DeWitt flew to Fort Lewis to take command.

The exercise went as scripted, with IX Corps holding the invaders at bay until III Corps could arrive from California by road and rail. Despite a surprise Red capture of Blue light tanks, which caused some uneasy moments, the defenders won the nine-day campaign. George Marshall reported that he had seen "tremendous improvement" in the Fourth Army since the "Battle of California" war game in June. DeWitt had praise for his men after both exercises, On August 22 after the Battle of Washington, he told reporters that "definitely and positively, the troops of the Fourth Army, their spirit, willingness to do, determination…cannot be excelled by any troops in the world today."

When the media pointed out how poorly equipped his men were, DeWitt bristled, explaining acerbically that "it is recognized by everyone that the shortage of equipment exists because it has been necessary for the War Department to establish priorities for many items so as to equip quickly certain divisions for very definite and logical reasons. There can be no justification for criticism of that action."

⬤━━

During the exercises, DeWitt's airpower had been limited to observation planes, but he did have an air force, however small, and it looked pretty good, at least on paper. Within the geographic boundaries of the Fourth Army and Western Defense Command were parts of two of the U.S. Army Air Forces (USAAF)'s numbered air forces. In Oregon and Washington, within Fourth Army jurisdiction, were parts of the Second Air Force, with headquarters at Fort George Wright, near Spokane, and a bailiwick that extended all the way to Kansas and into the turf of the Second Army. The Fourth Air Force was based at Hamilton Field in California and its responsibilities extended all the way to Texas and Oklahoma.

For those concerned about the possibility of enemy air attacks on the West Coast, these two air forces did not provide much in the way of security. In their book, *Guarding the United States and its Outposts*, Stetson Conn, Rose Engelman, and Byron Fairchild wrote that even after the war began, the Second and Fourth Air Forces, except for a small number of aircraft assigned to the II and IV Interceptor Commands, "were there primarily for the training of units, and they had only a secondary and very subordinate mission of providing an air defense and an attacking force along the Pacific front."

For themselves, the two interceptor commands were burdened by abnormally long and convoluted lines of communication. Brigadier General Carlyle Wash's II Interceptor Command was located at Fort Lawton within the Seattle city limits, 230 air miles from Second Air Force headquarters, while its handful of interceptors were based at Paine Field, twenty miles north of Seattle.

The Fourth Air Force at Hamilton Field was less than an hour's drive north of San Francisco, although its commander, Major General Jacob Fickel, maintained his own headquarters office at the Presidio near DeWitt's. Fickel's IV Interceptor Command component of the Fourth Air Force was *not* headquartered at Hamilton Field, but 420 air miles to the south, at March Field, near Riverside, in Southern California—although its commander, Brigadier General William Ord Ryan, maintained a command office and an Aircraft Warning Service office at the Presidio.

The latter arrangement might have been fine in facilitating Ryan's interaction with the two other officers, but the distance to March Field, over which communications was by way of commercial telephone lines, posed obvious problems for command and control in a combat situation.

Nor was there much in the way of actual air assets. At the end of November 1941, between them, the Second and Fourth had only 140 pursuit planes, including P-40s, then the standard USAAF fighter, along with obsolescent P-36s and other older types—and not all of these were based on or near the Pacific Coast. The USAAF believed that bombers would provide an effective defense against an approach enemy fleet—and invasion force—but the two West Coast air forces could muster only about one hundred of the inadequate B-18s, a handful of B-17s, and a few B-25 medium bombers. Meanwhile, the air defense mission had been largely ignored. There had been some air defense exercises during 1937 and 1938, but these tapered off in 1939 because of a shift in policy from air defense to offensive action against the airfields from which the attackers would operate. Neither Germany nor Japan had aircraft with sufficient range to reach the United States from their respective homelands, but because of Germany's prewar involvement in Latin American commercial aviation, American planners assumed that if air attacks against the United States materialized, they would originate from captured airfields within the Western Hemisphere.

The threat from carrier-borne aircraft was downplayed despite the fact that Japan had six aircraft carriers in 1939 and more on the way. Furthermore, the allocation of interceptor units, like antiaircraft artillery units, was tilted more toward the densely populated Eastern Seaboard between Boston and Norfolk rather than on the Pacific Coast, which was vulnerable to attack by Japanese naval airpower. A report issued by the Army Air Board in June 1939 dictated that air defense strategy was to "provide in the United States (zone of the interior) the necessary close-in air defense of our most vulnerable and important areas, to include, where necessary, reasonable protection against off-shore carrier attacks. These forces are not intended to repel a mass air attack or to afford air protection to our entire coastline, but are designed to limit the effectiveness of air raids upon our exposed vital areas."

Radar was in its infancy when World War II began, but it had proven its worth during the Battle of Britain. In the United States, the state of the art systems were the mobile Signal Corps Radar Model 270 (SCR-270) and its fixed location counterpart, the SCR-271. They were capable of detecting aircraft at a range of one hundred miles if they were at twenty thousand feet. However, if aircraft came in at one thousand feet, the radar would not detect them until there were within just twenty miles range.

The radar system had been declared operational in the summer of 1941, but relatively few had been deployed, and the procedures for their use were not formalized. The SCR-270s installed in Hawaii, for example, operated only for a few hours each day. On the Pacific Coast, the SCR-270s were at only ten sites and not yet functioning when the war began.

━

As the Armed Forces did not have the manpower to watch over the coastlines and inland infrastructure, so, beginning in May 1941, the federal government moved to recruit civilians to fill in the gaps. To watch the skies, the Aircraft Warning Service (AWS), was established as an adjunct of the Army's Ground Observer Corps. The AWS would involve a network of spotters who were trained to observe and to pass visual sightings to a filter center, which processed the data and passed it on to the USAAF. On the Pacific Coast, this information would be routed to controllers at the IV Interceptor Command for action.

Civilians were also organized for a variety of emergency response roles under the Office of Civilian Defense (OCD), which was created by presidential decree inside the Office of Emergency Management (OEM), an organization roughly analogous to the present Federal Emergency Management Agency. The OCD depended to a much greater degree on volunteers than OEM. It grew so large that it became independent of OEM in early 1942. Though the federal OCD office was a brainchild of President Roosevelt, and he its champion, Civilian Defense had already been embraced by most of the states, especially on the coasts.

Before the war, the national OCD provided the familiar red, white, and blue triangle Civilian Defense logo—designed by Charles Coiner of the N.W. Ayer Advertising Agency—as well as truckloads of World War I-vintage doughboy helmets painted white, but the organization and recruiting of Civil Defense volunteers were the responsibility of state and local agencies. Their success varied from locality to locality.

In New York, Mayor Fiorello La Guardia's support for the idea of organizing for Civilian Defense earned him the job of titular director of Roosevelt's federal agency, while he remained as mayor. After the war began, however, and as the OCD budget mushroomed, Congress became insistent that a full-time leader was needed. In January 1942, Roosevelt appointed Harvard Law School Dean James Landis as OCD's executive director and La Guardia's eventual successor.

In 1940, as mayor of Seattle, Arthur Langlie had created the city's Home Defense Committee at the urging of City Councilman John Carroll. After attending an American Municipal Association conference where city-wide blackouts were discussed, Carroll had been convinced, and in turn he convinced Langlie.

In Oregon, Governor Charles Sprague moved lethargically, prodded by snippy editorials in Portland's *Oregon Journal*, a rival to Sprague's own *Oregon Statesman*. Finally, the governor reactivated the State Council of Defense for Oregon, which had existed during World War I. As "coordinator" for the newly reconstituted organization, Sprague picked Jerrold Owen, an Army officer in the First World War who was well-connected within the American Legion. Sprague kept the directorship for himself. In California, Culbert Olson had the same idea, making himself chairman of the State Council of Defense while picking a military man, Brigadier General Joseph Donovan, to run the operation.

Within it, the Office of Civilian Defense formed a Ninth Regional Defense Board with headquarters in San Francisco, numerically designated to correspond to the Army's Ninth Corps Area on the Pacific Coast. Intended to foster interagency cooperation, it consisted of representatives of local governments of the region, such as those from police and fire departments, and the attorneys general of each western state. For example, California's attorney general Earl Warren represented the latter at meetings in San Francisco, while Mayor Fletcher Bowron of Los Angeles represented the region's mayors on the board.

Meanwhile, other civilians had already been recruited into a service called the State Defense Forces, better known as the State Guards or Home Guards, which were created to replace federalized National Guard units in the home defense role. After the Guard was federalized in September 1940, Congress amended the National Defense Act of 1916 to permit, even encourage, the states to form such units to act as guards for sensitive locations and facilities.

"There can be no argument as to the importance of protecting our plants against sabotage, but I am convinced that the use of soldier guards is an expensive and not particularly efficient expedient," observed General Marshall in an October 1941 memo. "Soldiers are not trained as watchmen and are generally younger and more impulsive than is desirable for men on such special duty.... I am sure that military units should be kept as an emergency reserve under the Corps Area commanders."

In theory, the State Guards were to have been trained and equipped by the U.S. Army, but just as there was little military manpower available for guard duty, there was even less available for training guards. As for equipment, the federal government loaned some stocks of World War I-surplus Enfield rifles to the State Guards. Another problem was manpower. Recruits had day jobs and were mostly over draft age, and the federal government did not allow its civilian employees to join such units.

The Army would have been incapable of sustaining a comprehensive program of site security. Though the War Department's ambitious prewar plans called for the creation of fifty-six military police battalions for duty in the continental United States, only three such battalions existed by September 1941. Eventually, to close this gap, the Army developed plans to give military police training to one of the three infantry regiments in each of National Guard divisions. It is difficult to see how this would have done anything but diminish the combat power of these infantry divisions.

The ability of local authorities to defend against sabotage loomed very large in the mind of General DeWitt. A window into this thinking is provided by Victor Hansen, a young officer who had come to the Army seven months earlier by way of the ROTC program at UCLA, and who had joined DeWitt's staff at the Presidio a month later. He was part of the Fourth Army G-3 (or operations) staff and a member of DeWitt's War Plans Division. As such, he was involved in the planning for protection of civilian installations and infrastructure.

In a 1976 interview conducted by Amelia Fry of the Bancroft Library regional oral history office, Hansen recalled that DeWitt "was very much concerned with the possibility of sabotage. He was concerned with the effects of sabotage and particularly how civilian agencies would assume their responsibility.... However, the planning for...civilian protection in the event of enemy attack or...sabotage...was quite inadequate. The military plans...were inadequate unless they were tied into civilian plans"—and coordinated with them, which they were not.

◗▬

The future Secretary of Defense Donald Rumsfeld famously said, "You go to war with the army you have, not the army you might want." The Army—or, more precisely, the part of it commanded by DeWitt— was small and top-heavy with administrative units at the expense of operational units. Its harbor defense guns were powerful, but outdated, and covered just four locations on a 1,300-mile coastline. Its airpower was badly organized and poorly equipped, and the embryonic Civilian Defense organization was inadequate. On the ground, DeWitt had just four underequipped and undermanned divisions to guard more than three hundred thousand square miles of territory that was separated from the main part of the United States by a thousand miles of narrow roads and vulnerable rail lines. In short, if war came, he would face a daunting defensive challenge.

FIVE

A Distant, Vulnerable Land

Making a defense of the Pacific Coast states extremely challenging would be the fact that they were largely isolated from the rest of the country.

Thanks to radio and railroads, and to the ubiquity of Hollywood movies, the Pacific Coast *seemed* close for the majority of Americans, most of whom lived east of the Mississippi, but it was, in fact, a distant land. In 1941, less than a decade had passed since it had first been possible to drive all the way from coast to coast on a paved road, and those that existed by 1941 were narrow and often precarious.

At the time, few Americans had ever traveled farther than five hundred miles from home, and fewer still had traveled coast-to-coast. Most people who did took the train, but that often meant an uncomfortable trip of several days (moderated only if you could afford a sleeping compartment). In the air, the Douglas DC-3, the first modern airliner to make a significant impact on American air travel, was still new, and those traveling cross country by air needed to make multiple stops as they traveled.

Travel took so long because the distances involved were immense. The highway distance from Minneapolis-St. Paul to Seattle was around 1,700 miles. From St. Louis, it was more than two thousand miles to San Francisco or Los Angeles. New York was far closer to Chicago, or even San Antonio, than cities on the Mississippi River were to the West Coast.

For those who drove, some of the routes took motorists across vast deserts where services, and even sources of water, were few. Water bags hanging on cars as a precaution in case of boiled over radiators were still a common sight on western highways as late as the 1950s. The mountain passes through the Rockies and the Sierra Nevada were steeper, higher, and more treacherous than those on any major road east of the Mississippi. The premier roads in the national highway grid were those of the U.S. Highway System, some of which were superseded two decades later by the Interstates, and some of which still exist. Outside of urban areas, there were virtually no U.S. Highways west of the Mississippi that were wider than two lanes and there were still occasional segments that were not yet paved. Indeed, it had been less than a generation since many of the routes were wagon trails.

In 1941, there were few continuous transcontinental roads, and those that existed were widely separated. Of the major east-west U.S. Highways, only three crossed into Washington, and all three—Route 2, Route 10, and Route 10A—were in steep and rugged country that was often impassible in the winter. Of the roads into Oregon, Route 20 and Route 30 crossed contiguously from Idaho and were, from a military point of view, a single-road choke point.

In California, there were seven major options. Routes 40 and 50 crossed the Sierra Nevada near Lake Tahoe, but winter snow in the mountain passes could bring motor traffic to a standstill. (This *still* happens on modern Interstate 80.)

In the south, three U.S. Highways came out of the Arizona desert and passed over the Colorado River and through more than one hundred miles of inhospitable Mojave Desert before reaching any major population center. Route 80 crossing at Yuma, Route 60/70 crossing at Blythe, and the as-yet-famous Route 66 crossing at Needles each presented a potential invader with a chokepoint at which the loss of a bridge in the middle of nowhere could shut down east-west traffic indefinitely. The remaining major crossings, Route 6 and Route 91, north and south of Death Valley, were even deeper into the middle of nowhere.

When the first Transcontinental Railroad was completed in 1869, there was already a network of more than fifty thousand miles of railroad *east* of the Mississippi. By 1941, there were *still* only a half dozen transcontinental lines that connected the West with the rest of the country.

Of the transcontinental main lines coming into California, two were operated by the Southern Pacific, one from New Orleans via El Paso, crossing the Colorado River at Yuma, while the other ran to San Francisco from St. Louis via Salt Lake City, crossing the Sierra Nevada north of Lake Tahoe. The West's biggest railroad, the Southern Pacific, had long been controversial because of its nearly total control of the lines in California's agriculturally rich Central Valley and in the farming country of western Oregon. Its only major rival in California was the Atchison, Topeka & Santa Fe Railway, known universally as the "Santa Fe," which operated one line into California which generally paralleled Route 66 from Chicago to Los Angeles via Kansas City and Barstow.

The smaller Western Pacific had a line that ran from Salt Lake City to San Francisco, crossing into California substantially north of the Southern Pacific main line and passing through the steep and narrow Feather River Canyon.

The Union Pacific Railroad, the traditional rival of the Southern Pacific, operated one route into Southern California across the empty desert of southern Nevada (passing through a little known town of eight thousand people called Las Vegas) and another route to Portland, by way of the Oregon side of the Columbia River Gorge.

The three major northern transcontinental railroads ran roughly parallel routes across the northern tier of the United States from St. Paul to Seattle, through Montana, and by way of Spokane. From north to south, they were the Great Northern Railway, the Northern Pacific Railway, and the Chicago, Milwaukee, St. Paul & Pacific (also known as the Milwaukee Road).

Through the Washington side of the Columbia Gorge, the Spokane Portland & Seattle Railway, a joint venture of the Great Northern and Northern Pacific, connected Spokane with the Pacific Ocean at Astoria via Portland.

In Canada, transcontinental roads and railways passed through the canyon of the Fraser River. The canyon, nearly three hundred miles of vertical cliffs on either side of the river, affords virtually the only connection between the Pacific Coast's Vancouver, British Columbia, and the rest of the country. The main lines of Canada's two transcontinental railroads, the Canadian National and Canadian Pacific, as well as Canada Route 1, passed through this canyon. It should also be added that in 1941, much of Route 1 in British Columbia remained unpaved.

Because so few lines carried all of the rail traffic in and out of the Pacific Coast states and British Columbia, it would have been possible, at least theoretically, for an invader to shut most or all of them down for an extended period of time, and to render many of the crossings unusable for up to a year.

Within the Pacific Coast States, there was a comprehensive network of rail lines and highways, albeit within roughly one hundred miles of the coastline. The two principal north-south U.S. Highways were Route 101 and Route 99. The former passed from San Diego through Los Angeles and San Francisco to Port Townsend, Washington, following the coast or inland valleys. Route 99 ran from Mexico to Canada through the major agricultural valleys of California, Oregon, and Washington, serving all three state capitals, as well as Los Angeles, Portland, and Seattle. California had just completed its State Route 1, which hugged the Big Sur coastline between Carmel and Morro Bay.

In and around San Diego, Los Angeles, San Francisco, and Seattle, there were road and interurban transit systems comparable to those of any metropolitan area east of the Mississippi. California led the nation in automobile registrations, with a car for every three persons, and had already begun to embrace the "car culture" that would become iconic in the coming decades. In 1940 Los Angeles completed its first two "stop-free express highways" between downtown Los Angeles and the San Fernando Valley, which are considered to be the first "freeways." Outside the populated areas between San Diego and San Francisco, and between Portland and Seattle, however, it was a different story, especially in terms of the north-south routes over which General DeWitt's forces would need to move to meet any invasion. The Achilles heel of the north-south transportation corridor lay between Northern California and Oregon, where the Southern Pacific main line, as well as Route 99, passed through the Siskiyou and Cascade mountain ranges, where it was as vulnerable as the highways and railroads that crossed the Rockies or the Sierra Nevada. On the coastline north of Eureka, Route 101 was in very rural country. Of the bridges that made it a viable route, many had been recently constructed, and were exposed to attack from the ocean.

The Pacific Coast states were, in many ways, just as isolated as they had been at the end of the nineteenth century, connected by a tenuous lifeline to the east.

PART TWO

On the Frontier of a Great War

SIX

The Sudden Darkness of Fear

On December 8, on the morning after Pearl Harbor, a front-page editorial in the *San Francisco Chronicle* called for unity of purpose, and an end to the ongoing debate over isolationism, noting that "by the act of Japan, America is at war. The time for debate has passed and the time for action has come. This action must be united and unanimous. 'Politics is adjourned.' From now on America is an army with every man, woman and child in it, all joined by the one end of victory."

Each of the three Pacific Coast governors issued statements calling for calm, and preparing their citizens for the unknowns that were sure to flow from the confused circumstances of the war in which they now found themselves.

"The State of Washington is on the frontier of a great war," said Governor Arthur Langlie. "We do not know what the future holds in store for us. We do not know what trials we must go through or what sacrifices we will be called upon to make. We do know what is at stake.

We know that our country, our liberties and our very homes are threatened. We are individually and as a nation being called upon to make good our pledge of allegiance to flag and country."

Oregon governor Charles Sprague, who was also the editor and publisher of Salem's *Oregon Statesman*, as well as the director of the State Council of Defense for Oregon, used a front page editorial published in an "Extra" edition of his own newspaper on Sunday. "We are at war," Sprague wrote. "Well, we have been at war before and have acquitted ourselves honorably. We will do so again. We are all Americans in this war of defense."

Sprague sent a telegram to President Roosevelt promising the "full support of the human and material resources of the State of Oregon." He also proclaimed an "unlimited emergency."

In Sacramento, though, Governor Culbert Olson downplayed the immediate threat. He postulated in his official statement that "I do not believe that even with the sudden and almost unbelievable attack on Hawaii that we may anticipate any immediate and similar attack on our coast. I feel that the unexpected move should be regarded as requiring the perfection and completion of all civilian protection plans which have been proposed for just such a situation."

"You know the seriousness of the situation," San Francisco's mayor, Angelo Rossi, told a packed meeting at City Hall, taking on a more urgent tone. "This is a real emergency...We won't fail. We are doing all in our power to protect lives and property and ultimately to win any conflict we are forced into." In his official declaration, he appealed "to all citizens of San Francisco to remain calm and resolute in this emergency."

Fear of enemy bombers striking at night gripped the states of the Pacific Coast. Blackouts were imposed almost immediately—and while haphazard at first—soon became an obsession of many people.

As the skies darkened on December 8th, Brigadier General William Ord Ryan of the IV Interceptor Command in San Francisco ordered the city to be blacked out. The erratic blackout extended seventy-five miles inland to the USAAF supply depot at McClellan Field near Sacramento, and from Santa Rosa in the north to San Jose in the south. In Southern California, the order called for blackouts as far inland as Las Vegas and Boulder Dam.

Meanwhile, Brigadier General Carlyle Wash of the II Interceptor Command ordered a blackout from the Canadian border to Roseburg, Oregon. In Portland, Mayor Earl Riley reported receiving orders directly from DeWitt himself not to allow any nighttime lights to be "left burning which cannot be turned out in 60 seconds." It was the same story from British Columbia, where the coast was ordered to be blacked out.

In Seattle, where John Carroll's Home Defense Committee was supposed to have engineered a plan for seamless city-wide blackouts, things turned rough. On the night of December 8, many downtown stores left their lights on, just as they had on December 7. A short time after 11:00 p.m., when the blackout was supposed to begin, nineteen-year-old Ethel Chelsvig paused outside the Foreman & Clark clothing store on Pike Street near Fourth Avenue, where the lights were still blazing.

"Are you going to stand by while these lights threaten the very life of our city?" She shouted to passers-by. Gradually a crowd formed as she explained that her husband, Raymond Chelsvig, was a sailor aboard the destroyer USS *Kane*, and he was fighting the Japanese while the store owners ignored the blackout. Soon, she began shouting to the crowd, "Break them! Turn them out!"

It took just one to start things moving. One man broke out the neon lights in the Weisfield & Goldberg Jewelers clock, and soon windows and neon were being smashed all around. The lighted letters in the Foreman & Clark sign were being broken one by one when an employee arrived to turn off the rest. As reported in both the *Seattle Times* and the *Seattle Post-Intelligencer*, the window smashing continued, with a crowd of more than one thousand spreading toward Fifth Avenue in one direction, and Third in the other. The police soon arrived, but when they formed lines in front of stores, rocks and other objects were thrown over their heads, and they had to call for backup. Eventually, the police were joined by the fire department and 150 civilian air raid wardens.

Before they were finally dispersed by police, the rioters paused briefly to sing "God Bless America." There were six arrests, including a defiant Mrs. Chelsvig. According to the *Seattle Times*, she told police "This is war.... One light in the city might betray us." She was charged with disorderly conduct and later paid a fine of twenty-five dollars.

After the "Blackout Riot," the Seattle City Council passed a blizzard of ordinances to prevent future disturbances. They banned congregations of five or more on sidewalks or streets and the sale of alcohol during blackouts. Given that cars were required to drive without lights, speed limits were reduced to 15 mph during blackouts. Nevertheless, as was the case in other cities down the coast, crashes and fender-benders increased dramatically. One motorist drove his car into the Duwamish River during a blackout.

In Southern California, where a strict blackout was declared by the 11th Naval District within a fifteen-mile radius of San Pedro, including the ports of Los Angeles and Long Beach, the darkness turned deadly on the night of December 8. Benito Montez of Wilmington, just north of San Pedro, was struck and killed by a car driven by Harry Davis, becoming the first fatality of World War II on the Pacific Coast.

In San Francisco, the first victim of the confusion wrought by the blackout was twenty-seven-year-old Marie Sayre. On that same evening of December 8, she and her husband were driving to Oakland. As their car passed onto the First Street approach to the Bay Bridge, Home Guardsman Albert Rownd called for the vehicle to stop. He had been ordered to stop any car with its lights on and instruct the driver to turn them off. The guardsman shouted, but Donald Sayre did not hear him. Rownd opened fire and a bullet struck Mrs. Sayre in the back, lodging near her spine. Amazingly, she survived and lived until 1968.

Even as Marie Sayre was being wheeled into surgery, and as downtown Seattle was rumbling and rioting, the Pacific Coast experienced the first intrusion into its air space by enemy aircraft—or so everyone was led to believe.

At 1:45 a.m. on December 9, General Ryan, downing coffee at his IV Interceptor Command headquarters, was handed a bulletin. As he later explained, "the controller at the board of command detected planes about which we knew nothing.... We are sounding warnings when the detection signals on our board call for them." Ryan notified General DeWitt, who phoned Mayor Rossi personally. Reports were circulated that "army authorities" had "authenticated" the report. Estimates of the number of aircraft ranged between thirty-five and fifty, but in the confusion, the sources of the estimates were unclear.

Radio station KFRC reported at 1:51 that it had been ordered off the air, and other stations were shut down at the same time. Traffic on both the Golden Gate Bridge and Bay Bridge was halted and the bridges were blacked out, but the huge neon signs along San Francisco's Market Street and the streets to the south remained illuminated. At the Port of Oakland, a glitch in the system would not allow the lights to be shut off, so Home Guard troops shot them out with their rifles. It would not have mattered. It was a clear night and the Bay Area lay beneath a bright moon.

The *San Francisco Chronicle* reported that "Confusion prevailed... Fire sirens screamed, and police cars raced through the streets warning residents to turn out their lights."

After the sun rose on Tuesday, December 9, and the "all-clear" siren had sounded, Ryan spoke to the media in time to be quoted in the morning papers. "There was an actual attack," he confirmed. "A strong squadron was detected approaching the Golden Gate. It was not an air raid test. It was the real thing. The planes came from the sea and turned back.... Some of the planes got into the Golden Gate then turned and headed southwest [over San Francisco].... I don't think there's any doubt they came from a carrier, but the carrier would have moved after they were launched and they would rendezvous at another spot."

When someone asked whether his interceptors had gone up to meet the intruders, Ryan replied, "You don't send planes up unless you know what the enemy is doing and where they are going. And you don't send planes up in the dark unless you know what you are doing."

Ryan's admission that the IV Interceptor Command knew neither what the enemy was doing—aside from flying over the West's second largest city—nor what the command itself was doing, did little to allay concerns.

Later in the day, the top brass, the military leaders upon whom the defense of the Pacific Coast rested, met reporters at a meeting of the Civil Defense Council at San Francisco's City Hall. General DeWitt was there, looking lean and almost brittle next to the round-faced Vice Admiral John Wills Greenslade, the newly appointed commandant of the Twelfth Naval District in San Francisco.

"By the grace of God, we were saved from a terrible catastrophe," Greenslade said nervously. "If bombs had fallen, damage would have been worse than anything I can imagine. When the time comes, be ready."

But all eyes were on DeWitt.

No one comprehended the extent of the shock of Pearl Harbor upon the man with the three stars on each shoulder. He knew that the extent of the damage done was far greater than had been revealed to the news media and general public. He was desperately afraid of suffering the same level of ruin within his area of responsibility, the same humiliating defeat. It came as no surprise to DeWitt when both Lieutenant General Walter Short, whose job in Hawaii was analogous to DeWitt's on the West Coast, and Pacific Fleet commander Rear Admiral Husband Kimmel were relieved of duty on December 17 for having their forces in Hawaii "not on the alert." It was clear that Short's career was now unsalvageable, and DeWitt did not want that to happen to him.

As the highest ranking American military officer on the Pacific Coast, DeWitt was the man of the hour at the December 9 City Hall conference. He was the man to whom many would look in this time of crisis for leadership, inspiration, reassurance, and confidence. With the right words and the right attitude, he could have calmed innumerable fears, quashed countless rumors, and established a mood of calm across the entire West Coast. He had many examples from which could have drawn: Winston Churchill's unshakable resolve, Franklin Roosevelt's buoyant confidence, George Marshall's rock-solid steadiness, and even Douglas MacArthur's overly eloquent optimism.

DeWitt instead took a tone that was strident and hectoring. He warned that "death and destruction are likely to come" if the people of the Pacific Coast did not heed his warnings, and take his orders seriously. His voice rose and quavered, as he scolded his audience, telling them that they were "damned fools" for not sharing his concerns.

Instead of speaking of shared goals and common purpose, he accused those to whom he spoke of "criminal apathy." It was as though he believed himself to be the only one who truly understood the gravity of the situation.

"The people of San Francisco do not seem to appreciate that we are at war in every sense," he exhorted. "I have come here because we want action and we want action now. Unless definite and stern action is taken to correct last night's deficiencies, a great deal of destruction will come. Those planes were over our community. They were over our community for a definite period. They were enemy planes. I mean Japanese planes."

He said, "if I can't knock these facts into your heads with words, I will have to turn you over to the police and let them knock them into you with clubs."

DeWitt seemed flustered when someone asked why the Japanese aircraft had not dropped bombs and why there had been no attempt to shoot them down.

"I say it's none of [your] business." He continued, "San Francisco woke up this morning without a single death from bombs," he continued. "Isn't that good enough?"

That *was* good, but was it really *enough*—especially after DeWitt had warned them that "death and destruction" were likely at any moment, especially after DeWitt had accused the civilians of neglecting their duties?

In that morning-after meeting, DeWitt had been handed an opportunity to set the tone for the public reaction to the enemy threat against the Pacific Coast and he had done so, but in so doing he had inspired an atmosphere of apprehension rather than of assurance. His fearfulness was palpable, and it was contagious. DeWitt had been handed an opportunity for greatness and he had let it slip from his grasp. His three stars may have given him authority, but did not instill confidence.

SEVEN

The Unthinkable Realization

The blackout riot in Seattle and the other mishaps notwithstanding, panic did not ensue on much of the West Coast. The *Los Angeles Times* reported that the city remained calm "as the shadow of war fell upon her. But through it all, through the first day of tension, there was a stiff jawed lack of hysteria."

The report was the same from Portland, where *Oregonian* reporter Earl Pomeroy, later a famous history professor at the University of Oregon, wrote that "there was no hysteria. There were no demonstrations. But there was emotion—a mounting anger born of the conditions under which the United States had been attacked, a gnawing kind of anger which found release in a fervently expressed desire for full vengeance."

The newspapers published the Office of Civilian Defense rules for "what to do in case of an air raid." These included recommendations to "keep cool. Don't lose your head. Do not crowd the streets; avoid chaos; prevent disorder and havoc.... The chance you will be hit is small."

The West Coast papers began running public service articles instructing people on what to do in the event of different attacks. In the case of poison gas, for instance, residents in foggy San Francisco, were reassured that poison gas decomposes on contact with water. In the case of incendiary attacks, the word was that "if water is applied too rapidly, an explosion is likely." Shovels came out across the Pacific Coast as individuals began working on backyard bomb shelters. In the cities, Civil Defense officials inspected basements in downtown buildings for possible designation as public shelters.

In Sacramento, Bertram Brown of the State Department of Public Health issued orders to increase the levels of chlorine in drinking water as a precaution against sabotage or a possible biological weapons attack.

Across town, California governor Culbert Olson, who chaired his own State Council of Defense, called for another ten thousand volunteers for Civil Defense and the Home Guards. In San Francisco, Mayor Rossi called for volunteers to report to police stations to sign up. By mid-day on December 8, around one thousand had already done so. Among them was a housewife named Hazel Shive, who announced that "I am ready to go to work. I can do anything from driving a truck to handling a gun."

In Los Angeles, her words were echoed by eighteen-year-old Madeline Evans, a volunteer ambulance driver, who told the *Los Angeles Times* that "I'm ready to go now if I can be of any help. I've been studying for seven months preparing for just such an emergency." Los Angeles county sheriff Eugene Biscailuz ordered the mobilization of another ten thousand for his own Major Disaster Committee.

Various accounts show substantial numbers of women volunteering. Indeed, in many cases, more women came forward than men. Men, of course, were able to enlist in the armed forces, and they did so in droves during December 1941.

With the recently completed hydroelectric projects an obvious target for enemy action, Secretary of the Interior Harold Ickes contacted General Marshall to ask that regular U.S. Army troops be assigned to protect the Grand Coulee Dam in Washington, the Shasta Dam in Northern

California, and the Boulder Dam on the Nevada-Arizona border, which supplied so much power to the California electrical grid.

Along with the Army and the Navy to protect the West Coast, there were the separate state Civil Defense organizations and their parallel State Guards, which functioned as a substitute for the federalized National Guard units. These guards, both formal organized units and volunteers, took up their posts, watching potential infrastructure targets, such as bridges, tunnels, shipbuilding plants, commercial radio stations, dams, power plants, oil wells, hospitals, and airfields—as well as scanning the skies for the sight or sound of enemy aircraft.

With so many federal and state entities leaping into action, there was an inevitable hodgepodge of blurred and overlapping interjurisdictional lines. Even as Governor Olson asserted his authority as director of Civil Defense in California, Attorney General Earl Warren announced that citizens should call *his* office "in the event of need of outside civilian assistance to prevent civilian disorder of any kind." In San Francisco, the California Home Guards protected the Bay Bridge, but the U.S. Army guarded the Golden Gate Bridge, the southern end of which was inside the Presidio.

The Coast Guard came ashore, and in a precursor to conditions in our own time, began searching baggage at the San Francisco airport. Home Guards were deployed to the numerous aircraft factories throughout Southern California—but these private factories, as well as the likes of the Southern Pacific Railroad, Bethlehem Shipbuilding, and Pacific Telephone & Telegraph were using their own guards and instituting ID checks at their facilities. The Army's 11th Cavalry at Camp Lockett near the Mexican border rode out to look after the dams in the system that supplied water to San Diego.

Shortly after Pearl Harbor, Victor Hansen of DeWitt's G-3 planning staff informed his commander that prewar G-3 studies "had disclosed... hazardous deficiencies, particularly in the local fire protection services [because of jurisdictional issues].... [F]ire fighters or their trucks would not cross municipal or county boundaries [even if they were the closest units to the scene of the fire].... The same problems existed in the law enforcement agencies."

During the first week of the Pacific war, as he cancelled leaves and furloughs for U.S. Army personnel, and put the Coast Artillery on round-the-clock alert, DeWitt assigned Hansen as the War Department representative on the Ninth Regional Defense Board of the Office of Civilian Defense.

While DeWitt remained at his headquarters in San Francisco, the commander of his army on the ground in California, Major General Joe Stilwell was putting hundreds of miles on his command car. This was because the field units within Stilwell's Western Defense Command Southern Sector were scattered from one end of the state to the other.

Stilwell's only Regular division, the 7th Infantry Division, was at Fort Ord, 150 miles from where his 40th National Guard Infantry Division was stationed. In turn, Fort Ord was only about a half hour drive from the Presidio of Monterey, which was the headquarters of the III Corps, the umbrella for the 7th and the 40th, but Monterey is more than one hundred miles from the Presidio of San Francisco, and mainly over narrow, winding roads. In time of emergency, which was now certainly the case, Stilwell would also theoretically have access to the newly reactivated 2nd Marine Division at Camp Elliot near San Diego—but lines of command, communication, and cooperation were by no means clear.

Stilwell's own sector headquarters was located near neither Monterey nor San Francisco, but nearly *500 highway miles away* in the four-story, Mission Revival-style California Hotel in San Bernardino. As was the case with General Ryan, whose office was a similar distance from his IV Interceptor Command at March Field, communication was by way of commercial telephone lines, which ran through remote open country offering ample opportunity to any saboteur wishing to cut them. Indeed, Hansen's G-3 team had discovered that the telephone junction in Los Angeles, if sabotaged "could knock out all the communications of the whole West Coast." Of course, a Route 66 motor hotel, even with ideal communications, was not the most secure location for Stilwell's headquarters.

The saving feature was that Stilwell was only about eighty miles from the Ports of Los Angeles and Long Beach, where the harbor defenses were also under his command.

On December 7, Stilwell had been at his house in Carmel, just outside Monterey. He and his wife had been holding an open house for junior officers from Fort Ord, when he received the phone call from San Francisco at about 3:00 p.m.

He noted in his diary that he was told the Japanese fleet was twenty miles to the south and only ten miles off the California coast, so he phoned Major General Charles White, the 7th Infantry Division commander at Fort Ord, ordering him to send a reconnaissance patrol down California Route 1 toward Big Sur. White had taken command of the division four months earlier from Stilwell himself.

Driving up to San Francisco the next day to meet with DeWitt, Stilwell confided in his diary that he found the Fourth Army headquarters "kind of jittery." Throughout the ensuing weeks, his diary pages frequently mention a "sinking feeling" that permeated the mood of the Army from San Francisco to San Diego. He learned what DeWitt knew about the full magnitude of the damage done in Hawaii, and he felt a palpable sense of panic in DeWitt's manner and mood. He also learned the details of the initial Japanese landings in the Philippines, and of DeWitt's fear that it could happen on the Pacific Coast. Indeed, it was that night DeWitt believed Japanese aircraft flew over the city, and the following day that, as Stillwell returned to San Bernardino, that DeWitt unleashed his tirade about unpreparedness at San Francisco's City Hall.

On December 10, there was another presumed Japanese incursion, this time in Los Angeles. At around 8:15 p.m., an "Army spokesman," presumably from Ryan's command, informed the Associated Press that there were enemy aircraft in the "general locality" of the city.

"This is serious," the spokesman insisted. "We cannot divulge exactly what is taking place, but it is serious enough to impose vigorous blackout precautions. That is all we can say at this time."

And on December 11, it happened once again in San Francisco.

Stilwell was in San Diego that day, paying a visit to Brigadier General E. R. Mittelstadt, former Adjutant General of the California National Guard and now with the 79th Brigade of the 40th Infantry Division. While he was in Mittelstadt's office at Balboa Park, Major Frank "Pinky" Dorn, Stilwell's aide and public affairs man took a phone call from the Fourth Army headquarters. The room went silent as Dorn repeated what he had been told.

"The main Japanese battle fleet is 164 miles off San Francisco," Dorn explained, adding that DeWitt had ordered a general alert of all units. It was reported that the enemy was operating with thirty-four warships, including a number of aircraft carriers.

"I believed it, like a damn fool," Stilwell told his diary, "and walked around the room trying to figure what to do. I imagined a wild rush up to Frisco with all available troops, and the first thing to do seemed to be to inform the Marines at Camp Elliott. So we dashed out and barged in, and saw [Major General Clayton] Vogel [the commanding general of the Second Marine Division], a calm, solid citizen who.... agreed at once to play ball and do anything I told him.... The first reaction to that news was like a kick in the stomach—the unthinkable realization that our defenses were down, the enemy at hand, and that we not only had nothing to defend ourselves with, but that time was against us. We could not ship the ammunition in time, nor could we evacuate the three million people in this area."

It was not until the end of the day that Stilwell learned, in a phone call to Colonel Thomas Hearn, chief of staff of the III Corps, that the report was a false alarm. Fourth Army headquarters attributed it, however, to a "usually absolutely reliable source."

Two days later, however, it happened yet again, with DeWitt's headquarters reporting "reliable information that attack on Los Angeles is imminent," and discussing another "general alert."

The news had reached the Los Angeles Police from the Aircraft Warning Service (AWS) at 7:35 p.m. and Ryan's office ordered a blackout five minutes later. At 7:41 p.m., radio station KFI, under instructions from the FCC, announced that the IV Interceptor Command had extended the blackout from the Coast to Bakersfield and as far inland as Las Vegas.

Los Angeles Police Chief Clemence Horrall had already ordered the city's 8,702 air raid wardens on duty for the first time. By 8:00 p.m., streetlights were going out across Los Angeles, and the May Company department store on Wilshire Boulevard, having announced that it would stay open until 9:30 every night for Christmas shoppers, shut its doors. The *Los Angeles Times* called it a "City of Shadows."

Tonight, the urgency of the wardens, the nervousness in Horrall's manner, and the narrative defined by DeWitt combined to heighten Angelinos' anxieties.

Across Southern California on December 11, people who had remained calm earlier, began to follow the example set by people in Seattle on December 8, and break neon signs. On the vast network of streets and highways drivers were slowed to a snail's pace, but emergency rooms were still filling with pedestrians struck by cars during the blackout. In Inglewood, John Marvel, a seventy-nine-year-old pedestrian, was struck and killed, while in San Diego, a Consolidated Aircraft Corporation worker was fatally injured in a head-on collision with a blacked out truck. The Los Angeles Receiving Hospital system reported that four of its hospitals had treated eighty-six injured pedestrians.

Some people covered their headlights with Christmas wrapping paper because it was near at hand. In many cities, the practice of motorists covering their lights with blue paper or blue cellophane became widespread, but police departments insisted that this was unacceptable and it was officially prohibited. In San Francisco, Police Chief Charles Dullea had gone so far as to caution drivers not to touch their brakes while stopped to prevent brake lights from coming on, and to keep their doors closed because of interior lights.

The "all clear" was announced in the Southland around 11:00 p.m., but the damage was done. The next day, General Ryan, still smarting from the San Francisco air raid fiascos, tried to walk back the actual threat, implying that the public had *overreacted* to the AWS bulletin—this after DeWitt's tantrum over San Francisco's *underreaction*.

In his diary, Stilwell's own reaction to Ryan's about face on his blackout order was that "the higher the headquarters, the more important is calm. Nothing should go out unconfirmed." Presumably he conveyed that to Ryan's headquarters verbally.

At 6:45 p.m. on the same night as the Los Angeles debacle, 300 miles to the north in Monterey and Santa Cruz Counties, local police received what turned out to be an erroneous evacuation order. They set about vigorously removing everyone living within one thousand yards of the beaches for a distance of nearly forty miles around the shoreline of Monterey Bay. Between seven thousand and ten thousand people were moved inland to churches and theaters. Most went calmly, and the Red Cross was enlisted to help move invalids. The all-clear was sounded at 8:00, and, as people filtered home to resume their interrupted evenings, officials began finger pointing. The police claimed that the U.S. Army had ordered the evacuation, but the military refused to take the blame, writing it off to the "overzeal" of local police. Though Generals DeWitt and Ryan had hardly distinguished themselves as reliable sources of information, the War Department, in order to avoid confusion, issued an edict to the media that "news concerning all military operations, including air raid warnings, in the continental United States will be released through the four field armies."

Public safety, meanwhile, was handled differently from jurisdiction to jurisdiction. In San Francisco, Police Chief Dullea and Max Lilienthal of the Civil Defense Council announced that they had worked out a plan to evacuate all 680,000 civilian residents of their city; though a mass evacuation during a blackout in a city surrounded on three sides by water would be no easy thing to do. But Western Defense Command had already made clear the threat. On December 14, General DeWitt told the *Los Angeles Times* "emphatically" that, unlike the apparent false alarm in the Southland, "every blackout in San Francisco has been genuine, based on official military information."

Stilwell noted that when it came to southern California "the plain truth is that it is not possible to evacuate three million people east, over waterless desert, and there would have been frightful casualties if a general exodus had started. What jackass would sound a general alarm under the circumstances? The [Fourth] Army G-2 [intelligence officer] is just another amateur, like all the rest of the staff."

It was not until the day after Christmas that DeWitt finally calmed down long enough to release a statement admitting that "evacuation should not be undertaken except under conditions where continuous bombing can be expected and the military situation on the Pacific Coast as present does not justify such a contingency."

Meanwhile, the Ninth Regional Defense Board had reached a similar conclusion on the basis of practicality. As Victor Hansen recalled, the Board had "prepared some very elaborate evacuation plans. They prepared some plans that showed that it was not possible to evacuate people in case of an attack, or even in case of an earthquake—primarily an attack. In other words, they'd just have to stay put."

On December 12, the morning after the great Los Angeles blackout debacle, General Ryan met with Attorney General Earl Warren, whose office was in San Francisco, and he followed up with an order that "no blackout shall be undertaken by any city or county except on direct orders from Regional Controllers in San Francisco and Los Angeles information centers of the IV Interceptor Command."

Los Angeles mayor Fletcher Bowron went on the record to tell the media that this was exactly what he had done the night before. Bowron explained that he had "ordered city police officials to attempt to black out Los Angeles on orders from IV Interceptor Command."

At 7:20 p.m. that very night, Ryan's command ordered the longest blackout to date over the San Francisco Bay Area, snarling traffic as far away as Napa. Highways, streetcars, and rail lines shut down. All access to the Bay Bridge and Golden Gate Bridge was cut off and guards enforced the closures with fixed bayonets. In San Mateo, Eva Lyons and J. H. Harris were killed in a collision. Mrs. Lyon's husband was badly injured.

There was some window smashing in San Francisco and Oakland, but in general, the mood was festive that night. People dismounted from buses or streetcars and continued their journeys on foot. Some gathered in darkened bars and restaurants and sang songs—and occasionally forgot to pay their tabs. Cub Scouts who were meeting at St. Francis Community Church passed their time singing Christmas carols. In movie theaters, the films continued to run and many patrons sat through their film a second time before heading into the night.

⋗━

Then DeWitt cancelled the Rose Bowl.

Though without martial law, DeWitt was not technically a military governor, his edicts carried such weight that the Pacific Coast's civilian governors felt compelled to agree to whatever he wanted to do.

On December 13, DeWitt sent a memo to Governor Culbert Olson insisting that "the Pasadena Tournament of Roses Parade and the Rose Bowl football game scheduled for New Year's Day be not held, and that all preparations should be abandoned for reasons of national defense and civilian protection." In turn, the governor sent a telegram to the organizers in Pasadena, conveying the message and adding that he agreed because of the "congestion of the State highways over a large area."

The morning after DeWitt's telegram to Olson, Tournament of Roses organizing committee president Robert McCurdy and some of his people drove north to demand a meeting with DeWitt himself. The general was adamant. Perhaps he threatened, certainly he cajoled, and, ultimately, he prevailed. Late that night, Captain Robert Robb, DeWitt's public affairs officer, issued a terse statement announcing that the Rose Bowl was cancelled, adding that McCordy and his organization "agreed to cooperate 100 percent with General DeWitt."

Paul Zimmerman, the *Los Angeles Times* sports editor, reported that the news came as a stunning surprise to both Oregon State and Duke University, who were scheduled to play in the annual classic. Two-thirds of the game's tickets had already been sold, but, as the *Times* put it, the Rose Bowl tickets "usually worth their weight in gold... [were] now only scrap paper."

DeWitt also pulled the rug from beneath the Pro Bowl in Los Angeles and the annual East-West game in San Francisco, as well as horse racing from Bay Meadows in San Mateo to Santa Anita in Southern California.

"DeWitt was a peculiar individual," Victor Hansen observed when recalling how the Rose Bowl incident came about. "Among my other duties assigned me was to get the mail that went to General DeWitt, letters complaining about protection of this and protection of that, and all the screwball plans that people had.... We got one from someone in Portland, Oregon, who said they were going to have a big gathering in the [Portland Metropolitan Exposition Center], where there would be many thousands of people gathered. It would be an ideal time for sabotage, and 'they are going to get in there and blow these people up, and you're going to have to account for this.' DeWitt saw that letter and he said, 'Well, this can happen.' So what does he do? He puts out a directive that dispenses with large gatherings. Hence, the Rose Bowl game [was] played at Duke [in North Carolina], rather than in Pasadena."

⬤━

Despite the presence of the Ninth Regional Defense Board and a plethora of volunteers, Civilian Defense remained inefficient at best, fading from the priority list after the lights came back on.

Chief Dullea said that he had formed a volunteer air raid warden organization in San Francisco numbering sixteen thousand, but when First Lady Eleanor Roosevelt, now serving as assistant director of the Office of Civil Defense, visited the city on December 10, she asked

Theodore Roche, vice chairman of the San Francisco Civil Defense Council how many wardens were trained.

"None," he said meekly.

The next day, Mayor Rossi took personal charge of Civil Defense in his city.

"That's my sworn duty!" Rossi insisted emotionally. "I want to make it very clear that this is my responsibility. I accept it and I'm going to do the job.... I expect this committee and every citizen to give full cooperation."

That same day, President Roosevelt announced that San Francisco Bay was to become one of eight Defensive Sea Areas in the United States in which the Navy was fully in charge of granting and monitoring access. Puget Sound, the mouth of the Columbia River, and San Diego were also on the list. The harbors of Los Angeles and Long Beach were not.

During December, up and down the coast, Civil Defense leaders met to sort out rules to be published for blackout behavior, especially on the streets. Many jurisdictions adopted a $500 fine or time in jail for blackout violations.

In Los Angeles, School Superintendent Vierling Kersey announced a requirement for all children to carry name tags in case "youngsters should be separated from their parents" during an air raid. Unspoken officially was the grisly prospect of having to identify bodies.

A meeting of Civil Defense officials took place in Los Angeles, at which Army and USAAF representatives were conspicuously absent. The Los Angeles County Defense Council was being organized under the chairmanship of County Sheriff Eugene Biscailuz in an attempt to coordinate the Civil Defense efforts of the myriad of agencies. Biscailuz told the conferees that "if the job that we face was one resulting from an earthquake, or disastrous flood, we would be at it a few days and then be about our regular business, but this may take a number of years."

In Southern California, the town of Altadena cancelled its annual "Christmas Tree Lane" for the first time in twenty-one years, but in Exposition Park, the public Christmas lights went on, albeit with attendants "ready to douse the electric decorations." The Defense Council approved lighted decorations elsewhere with the same caveat. In San Francisco, a Fillmore Street flower shop put up a sign announcing "Buy your candles here. Complete blackout tonight." They were just guessing, but it was a good bet.

The Los Angeles City Council appropriated money for a new type of air raid siren—described by *Los Angeles Times* columnist Tom Treanor as an "instrument of appalling noises." However, when the 276 sirens were tested in Los Angeles County, people complained that they could not hear them. San Francisco announced that new sirens installed at the Ferry Building and on police and fire stations would issue a warbling alarm for two minutes to signal an air raid, and two minutes of unvaried pitch to announce the all clear. As people tried to remember which was which, *San Francisco Chronicle* columnist Herb Caen called the sirens' call the "goldardest noise you ever heard; each one can be heard for at least six miles."

"Who'd have thought," asked Caen in his December 18 column, "That the friendly town crier that marked the hour of our day—the Ferry Building siren—would become the grim announcer of possible disaster.... That we who see would stumble and grope blindly along paths we thought we knew so well—while the blind move about in confidence on our traffic-free streets.... That this or any generation to come would see the Bay Region as dark as the first night a Spanish explorer looked upon this same mountain-ringed spot. That the beam of a tiny flashlight could carry so far or that a shooting star could so easily be interpreted as a flare dropping from an enemy plane.... That the sight of street lights coming on could make a San Franciscan feel that here was a good and precious friend he'd taken for granted too long.... Who ever would have thought it? Well, not me."

EIGHT

A Theater of Woeful Shortages

On December 11, the day the Third Reich declared war on the United States, and the United States responded in kind, General DeWitt became a theater commander in a world war.

As Stetson Conn and his colleagues wrote in *Guarding the United States and its Outposts*, "The most vital installations along this coast were military aircraft factories that had sprung up during the prewar years at Los Angeles and San Diego in the south and at Seattle in the north. In December 1941 nearly half of the American military aircraft production (and almost all of the heavy bomber output) was coming from eight plants in the Los Angeles area. The naval yards and ship terminals in the Puget Sound, Portland, San Francisco Bay, Los Angeles, and San Diego areas, and the California oil industry were of only slightly less importance than the aircraft plants to the future conduct of the war. In the first two weeks of war it seemed more than conceivable that the Japanese could invade the coast in strength...there appeared to be a really serious threat of attack by a Japanese carrier striking force.... This was the outlook that persuaded the War Department to establish the Western Defense Command as a theater of operations."

Conn and his fellow authors pointed out that it was an operational theater in name only, where antiaircraft artillery regiments "lacked two-thirds of their equipment... The Second and Fourth Air Forces had only a fraction of their assigned strength in planes, and they were critically short of bombs and ammunition."

General Stilwell wrote bluntly on December 11 in the wake of the great Los Angeles invasion scare, "had the Japs only known, they could have landed anywhere on the coast, and after our handful of ammunition was gone, they could have shot us like pigs in a pen."

Back on November 27, the War Department had warned DeWitt, along with commanders in Hawaii and the Philippines, that the Japanese probably were preparing for war. Though the specifics of the impending Pearl Harbor strike were not known, intercepted intelligence from "Magic," the top secret project that had broken Japan's diplomatic codes, made it clear that *something* was afoot. The next day, DeWitt had promised the War Department that he was ready for war, ready, that is, "except for a woeful shortage of ammunition and pursuit and bombardment planes."

One can imagine DeWitt and his air commanders watching with some jealousy as a squadron of B-17 bombardment planes passed through Hamilton Field near San Francisco, on December 6, heading toward Hawaii, where, on December 7, Oahu, low on fuel, they were forced to land amid the Japanese attack.

Overseas on December 11, the Japanese armed forces were on the offensive. Bangkok had fallen, and Thailand had officially joined the Axis. The Japanese 25th Army was in Malaya and driving south toward Singapore. Both Guam and Wake Island were under attack, and both Hong Kong and the Philippines had been invaded. The two largest British warships in the Far East, the HMS *Prince of Wales* and HMS *Repulse*, had been sunk by Japanese airpower on December 10—just as Japanese airpower had put the battleships at Pearl Harbor out of commission.

John DeWitt had two Regular U.S. Army divisions, bivouacked 900 miles apart, and two National Guard divisions, also bivouacked 900 miles apart, to guard a 1,300-mile coastline. There was no immediate effort to rush reinforcements to the Coast. Nearly half of the ground troops in the Western Defense Command were occupied with guard duty, harbor defense, or patrolling the coastline and the "Southern Land Frontier," the military euphemism for the Mexican border.

DeWitt's command was not alone in having shortages of men and materiel. Despite a year and a half of rebuilding, the regular Army throughout the continental United States was so short of equipment that it was forced to reclaim the stocks of World War I surplus rifles that it had lent to State Guards.

The Navy was spread as thin, or thinner, on the Pacific Coast as the Army. The backbone of the Pacific Fleet had been at Pearl Harbor—although, luckily, the fleet's three aircraft carriers had not been. The USS *Enterprise* and USS *Lexington* were at sea, and the USS *Saratoga* was in San Diego, having just arrived from Bremerton, Washington, after a major refit. The only battleship on the Pacific Coast was the USS *Colorado*, which was being overhauled at Bremerton. The only cruiser on the West Coast was the USS *Concord*, then being overhauled in San Diego. The Pacific Fleet's only active warships in the theater were fourteen destroyers scattered from Bremerton to San Diego, and a half dozen submarines, of which two were being overhauled at Mare Island.

The U.S. Coast Guard was in worse shape than the Navy. On the afternoon of December 7, Fritz Dickie at Stembridge Gun Rentals in Hollywood had received a phone call from the Coast Guard. Founded in 1920 to supply firearms to the motion picture industry, Stembridge operated what was known in the trade as the "Gun Room" on the Paramount Pictures lot, a facility that was one of the biggest private arsenals anywhere. The Coast Guard needed guns—especially Thompson Submachine Guns—and they knew about the Gun Room.

"We loaded them on trucks and, by night, the guns which had been used mostly in gangster pictures were ready for the feared Japanese invasion," Dickie recalled after the war. "During the next few days, we also loaned rifles to the Coast Guard stationed at Catalina and machine guns, pistols and shotguns to the California State Guard. It was several months before all of the weapons were returned. Subsequently, we received a letter from the Harbor Defenses command which said, in part: 'Due to the critical shortage of such weapons on Dec. 7, 1941, those provided from your stock were a most welcome addition to our defenses.'"

While the Army's leadership was focused on preparing to take on Germany and Japan in a global war, the War Department was being deluged with requests to detach troops to take up guard duties at thousands of locations within the United States. Now that the country was actually at war, even Fiorello La Guardia, President Roosevelt's own director of Civil Defense, was dubious about entrusting the task to civilians. "No city has enough police for [this] emergency," he wired nervously to Roosevelt. "States can't help much. Home Guard not constituted or prepared for such duty day-in and day-out."

The president forwarded La Guardia's comments to Stimson under a handwritten memo that read: "Harry Stimson—How about this?"

Stimson and Marshall resisted, knowing that they did not have the trained manpower to both take up the slack for the Home Guard *and* build an Army to strike back at the Axis overseas. Their protests were to no avail. On December 16, Roosevelt issued Executive Order 8972 "authorizing the Secretary of War and the Secretary of the Navy to establish and maintain military guards and patrols, and to take other appropriate measures, to protect certain national defense material, premises, and utilities from injury or destruction." The War Department announced plans to activate fifty-one new military police battalions for service inside the continental United States, but it would be months before they would be ready for service, and their creation would divert valuable manpower from other activities.

In fact, this manpower situation was at its most critical on the Pacific Coast. DeWitt could ill afford to divert his personnel to static guard duty when he and those around him assumed and expected that the Japanese would be bringing the war to their doorstep at any moment. Adding to their concern was the fact that they had no idea where on their 1,300-mile front line this might happen, and which of their thinly spaced units would be first to respond.

Air defenses were thinly spaced along the Pacific Coast. General Ryan's IV Interceptor Command, and General Wash's II Interceptor Command did have fighters that could intercept Japanese aircraft, as the USAAF pilots had done over Hawaii on December 7, but they had too few to concentrate effectively, and they lacked adequate training for night missions. Radar-equipped night fighters would not be available for a few years.

Nor would Ryan have wanted to send airplanes up into the darkness when he was so short of them. In *The Army Air Forces in World War II*, the official USAAF history, Wesley Frank Craven and James Lea Cate note that "with the extremely limited resources available to the Army Air Forces in December 1941, it was impossible to provide even token defenses for all vital targets in the hemisphere." They add that on the Pacific Coast, USAAF "crews of both fighters and bombers were handicapped by an acute shortage of ammunition." With few exceptions, therefore, the Pacific Coast was essentially naked to air attack.

Addressing the perceived threats that had resulted in the disastrous Los Angeles blackouts, Craven and Cate delved into the "what if" scenario. They wrote that "to reconstruct the problem as it appeared to air officers at the time, let us assume that the report of the presence of thirty-four Japanese ships off the California coast on December 9, 1941, had proved to be true. With what forces could so threatening a surface fleet have been opposed? There is good evidence on this point, for the Fourth Air Force actually issued an order to 'attack and destroy' the enemy task force. By good fortune, fourteen bombers destined for the Southwest Pacific were in the vicinity; but it was found that the machine-gun turrets on the planes would not operate, that there was no adequate supply of oxygen for high-altitude operations, that only a few 300- and 600-lb. bombs were on hand, and that the bombers would have to enter an engagement without fighter support."

USAAF reinforcements were coming, but they were slow in arriving. The first USAAF unit to be relocated to the Pacific Coast was the 1st Pursuit Group from Selfridge Field, Michigan, but all of its P-38s would not reach Southern California until December 22.

The ideal air defense scenario would have been to replicate that with which the Royal Air Force had during the Battle of Britain. However, compared to the situation with the II and IV Interceptor Commands, the RAF had nearly eight times the number of interceptors to cover a quarter of the distance. Radar and a thoroughly integrated command, control, and communications system were the key to detection of the enemy and deployment of RAF fighters to the right places at the right times. There was nothing like this on the Pacific Coast.

As previously mentioned, there were SCR-270 and SCR-271 radar systems at ten sites, but most had proven unreliable. At least DeWitt could have blamed a failure to detect an enemy air attack on "technical difficulties."

And it wasn't just the reliability of the equipment that was hampering the use of radar. "Many of the original [radar] sites having proved unsuitable, extensive resiting work was carried out," recounted Craven and Cate. "The process was difficult, costly, and time-consuming. Rugged terrain often made the work difficult even for experts—and there were few men of experience available. Good radar sites often were relatively inaccessible, far removed from roads, communications, power, and water; it was frequently necessary to build pioneer trails or roads for considerable distances before preliminary tests of radar equipment could be made, and the effort might be wasted then by the discovery of unpredictable operational difficulties."

Meanwhile, "when the Western Defense Command desired an expansion of radar coverage to protect California's southern flank, delicate diplomacy was required to assure Mexico that no infringement of her national sovereignty was contemplated."

Speaking of Mexico, many people in Southern California, both civilian and military, believed strongly that Japanese air attacks, and perhaps even attacks by Japanese paratroopers, would originate from south of the border.

Latin America had long had a large German presence, and many of the major airlines were operated by German interests. Concern for the threat from Latin America intensified after December 18 when the Associated Press reported on a "startling" Congressional investigation spearheaded by John Conover Nichols of Oklahoma that revealed information about "Axis air bases, arms depots and jungle radio stations" in seven countries from Argentina to Guatemala. The majority were German, but "a Japanese colony, located approximately 30 miles from [Cali, Colombia] has become a veritable storehouse for rifles, ammunition, pistols and hand grenades."

A few days later, on December 23, a *New York Times* article datelined Mexico City reported that "the presence of Japanese submarines off the coast of California has led defense experts here to suspect that they may be refueling at small harbors along the remote, almost uninhabited coasts of the Gulf of California or along the Pacific side of the [Baja California] peninsula." The same article reminded readers about "the Japanese smuggling of some $300,000 worth of mercury out of Manzanillo just before the Pacific war began."

During the second week of December, General Stilwell stopped in at Muroc Field (now Edwards Air Force Base) about seventy miles from San Bernardino. He found that Lieutenant Colonel Archibald Smith, commander of the 41st Bombardment Group, had B-17 heavy bombers, but he complained that his men were virtually defenseless on the ground, especially if an attack came from Mexico.

"He was sure the Japs could fly in at any moment and shoot his men down," Stilwell recalled. "The Engineer Battalion was leaving him, and he didn't see how he could get ditches dug for his men to hide in. The only weapons available were pistols, so he was fearful of a parachute attack that would come in off carriers or from a secret base in [Baja] California, and murder them all."

The blizzard of rumors about secret Japanese bases in Baja California that were making the rounds in December 1941 had reached the point where there were discussions between Stilwell's staff and that of Brigadier General E. R. Mittelstadt of the 40th Infantry Division in San Diego over whether or not to send troops into Mexico.

Before anything could happen, however, the Mexican Army sent a seven-man delegation, including General Juan Felipe Rico Islaz, the army's commander in Baja California, across the border to sit down with Stilwell and other American officers. In turn, Major General Charles Price, who succeeded Clayton Vogel as commander of the 2nd Marine Division, traveled to Tijuana in mid-December to meet with Brigadier General Manuel Contreras, Rico's man for northern Baja.

The Mexicans were nervous about their own vulnerable coastline and willing to work with the Americans to protect their country, but with reservations. In *The Framework of Hemisphere Defense*, Stetson Conn and Byron Fairchild note that the "local Mexican commanders either were uncertain of their authority to commit the [Mexican] federal government or were reluctant to accept instructions from Mexico City; the difficulties and delays in obtaining full permission for a reconnaissance in Baja California were inauspicious.... Actually, the Mexican commanders made clear their willingness and desire to cooperate, and if they were reluctant to place their names to a document committing them to joint action, they made it plain by word of mouth that in an emergency they would call on General DeWitt to send American troops into Mexico."

By the end of December, the Mexican Senate was considering legislation to legalize the operations of American ground and naval forces south of the border.

On December 22, Stilwell was suddenly summoned to Washington, D.C., writing in his diary that "I am to shove off at once for work on a war plan, for some expeditionary force." He turned the reins of the Southern Sector over to General Walter Wilson and was in the nation's capital by Christmas Eve. At first, Stilwell was considered for a combat command against the Germans in North Africa, but his previous experience in China meant he would spend the war fighting the Japanese in the Far East. On February 15, General Wilson moved the headquarters of the Southern Sector of the Western Defense Command to Pasadena.

General DeWitt began moving some of his own command as well. On December 20, Lieutenant Colonel W. S. Conrow, DeWitt's "spokesman," announced that the headquarters of the Ninth Corps Area, specifically Major General Jay Benedict and 150 military and civilian personnel from his staff, would be moving from the Presidio of San Francisco to Fort Douglas on the east side of Salt Lake City, Utah, "because it is the center of a railroad network over which supplies can be readily distributed to the entire coastal region."

"Normally," Conrow explained, "a theater of operations consists of a combat zone nearest the enemy and a communications zone to the rear. Until now the communications zone had not existed in the Ninth Corps [Area] and creation of this element in Salt Lake City is a prime purpose of the change."

The new location was around 750 rail miles "to the rear." DeWitt now had his "communications zone."

NINE

The Japanese Next Door

For most Americans, the Japanese were the perpetrators of a heinous surprise attack. For the people on the Pacific Coast, they were *also neighbors*, and in most cases, those Japanese-American neighbors were as much offended by the sneak attacks as anyone else, indeed *doubly* offended, because their country had been attacked by the land of their ancestors.

"The hour is here.... We are Americans," said attorney Saburo Kido of the Japanese-American Citizens League on the afternoon of December 7. "There cannot be any question. There must be no doubt. We, in our hearts, know that we are Americans—loyal to America. We must prove that."

In the wake of the Pearl Harbor attack, there came a questioning of allegiances. The presence of Japanese and Japanese-Americans on the Pacific Coast was suddenly perceived in a much different light than they had been on December 6. The Fujiwaras who ran the corner grocery store, or Mr. Hashimoto who had the tomato farm down the road, were of the same ethnicity as the enemy who had perpetrated the nefarious sneak attack. Was their loyalty to the United States—where many had lived for decades and where *most* had been born—or was it to the land of their ancestors?

The answer was, overwhelmingly, that their allegiance was to the United States, and it remained so despite the cruelty that Japanese-Americans suffered from their own country during World War II.

Nearly three-quarters of the people with Japanese surnames living in the United States were *nisei*, born in the United States and American citizens. Virtually none had ever seen Japan, and only a small fraction could speak more than a few words of Japanese.

"Our duty as American citizens is clear," Kido told Milton Silverman of the *San Francisco Chronicle*. "We shall serve the United States of America, our country, without reservation. The American citizens of Japanese ancestry have been proclaiming their loyalty—the time to prove their true feelings has arrived. To have to prove one's loyalty on the battlefield is what we had least expected, but the Japanese-Americans are not afraid to meet the acid test."

Shortly after the declaration of war on December 8, 1941, James Sakamoto, the blind editor of Seattle's *Japanese-American Courier*, issued a statement which read "no matter what develops involving the United States in the present tragic world situation, we Americans of Japanese ancestry must be prepared and remember that there are certain fundamental truths from which we cannot depart. One of them is that we were born in these United States as American citizens. Now that we have become involved in the Far Eastern conflict that is going to test our worth and mettle as citizens, we cannot fail America. There is a remote possibility of our becoming the victim of public passion and hysteria. If this should occur, we will stand firm in our resolution that even if America may 'disown' us—we will never 'disown' America."

He told the *Seattle Star* that "it is easy for us at this time to shout our patriotism and declare our loyalty. But we must do much more than mere lip service. Our biggest job, and the hardest, will be to go ahead, doing our work as diligently and as efficiently as we can, to contribute to America's defense. This is a time for calm thinking and quick action, in behalf of America."

◗▬

In contrast to the large numbers of Chinese who immigrated to the United States over the preceding century, the numbers of Japanese had been small. In 1890, when the Chinese population was numbered in the tens of thousands, there were only about two thousand Japanese in the United States—excluding Hawaii, which was not annexed until 1898— of whom more than half lived in California.

By the turn of the twentieth century, exclusionary legislation being passed at the national level denied citizenship to the *issei*, people who had been born in Japan, though under the Fourteenth Amendment, their American-born *nisei* children were citizens.

By 1940, there were 157,905 people of Japanese descent in the Territory of Hawaii and 127,210 living in the mainland United States. Of the latter, there were 4,071 living in Oregon, 14,965 in Washington and 93,317 in California. The largest concentration was the 36,866 who made their homes in Los Angeles County. Within each of these figures, more than six in ten were *nisei* rather than *issei*.

As has always been typical of American-born children of immigrants, the *nisei* grew up speaking English and readily embracing American culture. As they reached their teens in the late 1930s, they danced to Benny Goodman and Glenn Miller, they snacked on hamburgers and milk shakes and they followed major league baseball. In short, most young *nisei* were more culturally American than Japanese. Though many parents sent their kids to Japanese language schools, and some of them learned to speak Japanese, they preferred English—and they spoke it with the same accent as their white classmates at school.

The *nisei* were just as likely to be strongly patriotic as were their white neighbors. The Japanese-American Citizens League, which originated as a respected organization of *nisei* professionals, had a strong pro-American outlook. In California and Hawaii, where most Asian Americans lived, schools were integrated, the *nisei* thought of themselves as American, and their classmates thought of them that way.

After Japan brought the war to America on December 7, however, in the climate of fear and panic, the people who had looked at Japanese-American neighbors as just that, neighbors, on Saturday, looked at them differently on Sunday. For some, old racial prejudices bubbled to the surface, justified in the minds of some by fears of a Japanese "fifth column."

▶━

The term "fifth column" had originated in 1936, during the Spanish Civil War, when Nationalist General Emilio Mola captured Madrid from the Spanish Republicans. He had attacked the city with columns of troops from four sides, but later told reporters that the most effective force had been his supporters on the *inside*, operating covertly, whom he described as his *fifth* column. Thus, the term became synonymous with traitorous agents operating from within in support of outside attackers. Throughout the German campaigns in Western Europe, there had been numerous incidents of support from fifth columnists.

Within hours of the Pearl Harbor attack, there were stares and glares all across the West. Stones had been thrown through the windows of Japanese-American-owned retail stores from Tacoma to Los Angeles, but these were isolated incidents.

Public officials across the Pacific Coast initially counseled calm. Oregon's governor Charles Arthur Sprague called for "vigilance against espionage and sabotage" but made an appeal for the rights of Americans of Japanese descent, asking that "these Japanese-Americans who are citizens should not be molested."

Seattle mayor William "Earl" Millikin said that his city "must have tolerance toward American-born Japanese, most of whom are loyal. But I also want to warn the Japanese that they must not congregate or make any utterance that could be used as grounds for reprisals." To this,

Seattle's police chief Herbert Kimsey proclaimed that his men would patrol the "Japanese quarter" and that anti-Japanese riots would be "crushed with force."

Los Angeles county sheriff Eugene Biscailuz sent deputies to the Little Tokyo district of the city, but if he was expecting an uprising by its residents, he was disappointed. He discovered that "people on both sides of the fence there are remaining calm and decent, which is certainly good news." The story was the same in every *nihonmachi*, or Japanese-American neighborhood, up and down the Pacific Coast.

The violence, when it came, did not originate with Japanese-Americans. On the evening of December 19, as he was entering his home in Redondo Beach with a bag of groceries, Hawaii-born Satorii Okada was shot in the back with a 12-gauge shotgun. The assailant escaped into the darkness.

In San Francisco, there was a flurry of discussion on the streets during the third week of December about the schoolyard mistreatment of Chinese-American children under the supposition that they were Japanese-American. *Chronicle* columnist Herb Caen merely mentioned this in passing, but upon reflection, a few days later, he wrote that "I failed to stress the important overtone involved—that the maltreatment of minority children, be they Japanese, Chinese or whatever, is a dangerous little monster that must be ground down into the earth whenever and wherever it lifts its ugly head. Thanks to the several pointed letters in today's contributions. I won't miss that point again."

❿

As for the personnel of the Japanese government, and the assets of Japanese companies, the United States government acted quickly. Japanese diplomats, including Consul General Yoshio Muto in San Francisco, as well as those at the embassy in Washington, D.C., were interned for later exchange for American embassy personnel trapped in Tokyo.

Japanese banks and shipping companies received visits from agents of the U.S. Treasury Department early on Monday, December 8. They seized the assets of the Seattle, San Francisco, and Los Angeles branches of the Yokohama Specie Bank and the Sumitomo Bank, as well as a branch of the latter in Sacramento. George Knox, the California State Superintendent of Banks, took over operations of those within his state.

On a lighter note, when the Nippon Yusen Kaisha (NYK) shipping line closed its San Francisco office during the week preceding Pearl Harbor, executives were each handed substantial bonuses. Instead of cashing his $5,000 bonus check, one man, who was unaware of *why* the bonuses were being issued, decided to show it around to friends over the weekend. On Monday morning he learned, much to his chagrin, that since the bank accounts of Japanese companies had been frozen, the check was now worthless.

Also on that Monday, U.S. Attorney General Francis Biddle sought to draw a distinction, knowing of the complexities that were about to evolve. "There are in the United States many persons of Japanese extraction whose loyalty to this country, even in the present emergency, is unquestioned," he said charitably. "It would therefore be a serious mistake to take any action against these people. State and local authorities are urged to take no direct action against Japanese in their communities, but should consult with representatives of the FBI."

Among the "Japanese next door" on the West Coast in late 1941, was a covert contingent almost literally next door to General DeWitt at the Presidio of San Francisco. Although they went about their business quietly and surreptitiously, they wore the same uniform and saluted the same flag as the other soldiers under the command of General DeWitt.

Early in 1941, a pair of U.S. Army intelligence officers conceived the idea of a Japanese language school, enlisting Japanese-Americans with a basic understanding of the language as students. Lieutenant Colonel John Weckerling and Captain Kai Rasmussen fought an uphill battle against official War Department indifference to get the project off the ground. Finally, they received the official green light, and their facility quietly opened for business on November 1, 1941 in an unused hangar at the Presidio's Crissy Field. Rasmussen—who had been born in Denmark, graduated from the United States Military Academy in 1929, and served four years at the United States embassy in Tokyo—became the school's first commandant. Within weeks, fifty-eight Japanese-Americans and two Caucasians had enrolled.

Although the Japanese Americans understood the Japanese language, the purpose of the school was to instruct them in *heigo*, Imperial Japanese Army and Navy terminology, including instruction about Japan's military organization and weapons systems.

As Rasmussen and his men came together on the morning of Monday, December 8, their work took on a new urgency, and the already clandestine nature of the school became even more closely guarded.

TEN

The Battle of the California Coast

"**F**ive shells were fired at us," Captain Nels Sinnes of the 1,172-ton coastal lumber carrier SS *Samoa* told the Associated Press. "One apparently aimed at our radio antenna burst in the air above the stern. Fragments fell onto the deck. Then we saw the telltale wake of a torpedo coming directly at us amidships. It was too late to do more than just wait for our destiny. The miracle happened. The torpedo went directly beneath us, didn't touch the hull and continued beyond. Evidently it struck some object beneath the water, because while the torpedo was still at a comparatively short distance from the *Samoa* it exploded. There was a huge shower accompanied by smoke and flame."

In the foggy, predawn half light of December 18, 1941, only about fifteen miles off California's Cape Mendocino, Sinnes, and Commander Nishio Kozo, skipper of the submarine *I-17*, stared toward one another from a distance of only about forty feet.

"Hey," shouted someone from aboard the *I-17*.

"What do you want of us?" Sinnes replied.

There was no reply, and the submarine quickly disappeared beneath the waves. Sinnes later speculated that the submarine commander assumed the *Samoa* to have been hit because of a port list that was due to asymmetrically trimmed oil tanks.

This was the first encounter in the Battle of the California Coast, a frightening campaign that took place within sight of the American homeland in the weeks following Pearl Harbor.

Nine Japanese submarines operated within sight of the coastline throughout much of December. They were formidable warships, some of them even carrying aircraft, that were part of the Japanese maritime strategy for dominating the Pacific Ocean.

The Type B1 class of Junsen Otu-gata Sensuikan cruiser submarines were half again larger than U.S. Navy fleet submarines—nearly 360 feet long and displacing nearly four thousand tons while submerged. With a range of sixteen thousand miles while surfaced, the B1 boats could easily reach the Pacific Coast from Japan and operate there for an extended period of time before returning to Japanese bases in the western Pacific to refuel. And, the B1 boats were *new*. Nearly all of the eighteen boats in the class had been commissioned since the beginning of 1941. They were each armed with seventeen Type 95 torpedoes fired from six forward torpedo tubes. During attacks on merchant shipping, the preferred tactic was to surface in order to fire on their prey with their 14 cm (5.5 in) deck guns.

Each of the B1 submarines had a watertight hangar forward of its conning tower that was designed to accommodate a disassembled, two-seat, single-engine observation floatplane. Some carried a Watanabe E9W1 biplane, but most carried the Yokosuka E14Y monoplane, which the Japanese nicknamed "Geta," after the platform sandal with wood blocks on the sole that look like pontoons. For Americans, these aircraft probably are better known by the code names, respectively, "Slim" and "Glen," assigned to them later in the war. The E9W1 had a range of around 450 miles, while the E14Y could travel 550 miles. The submarine's crew could unfold and assemble their floatplane on the submarine's narrow deck in a matter of minutes, then launch it using a compressed air catapult. None of them, as it turned out, were launched during December. The submarines generally used the hangar space to carry extra fuel.

Vice Admiral Mitsumi Shimizu, commander of the 6th Fleet, the Imperial Japanese Navy's submarine force, initially deployed a dozen B1 boats into Hawaiian waters in early December. Their mission was to pick off American shipping around Pearl Harbor. Nine of them were then to proceed to attack shipping on America's West Coast, just as German U-Boats were attacking shipping along America's East and Gulf Coasts.

On December 7, minutes before the first bombs fell on the Pacific Fleet, *I-26* had attacked and sunk the SS *Cynthia Olson*, a civilian transport ship under contract to the U.S. Army. Traveling from Tacoma, she was about one thousand miles northeast of Oahu when she went down. No survivors were found.

Two days later, *I-10* claimed the Danish—but Panamanian flagged— MS *Donerail* about 700 miles southeast of Hawaii. The 4,132-ton vessel was en route from Fiji to British Columbia with sugar and pineapples and a few passengers—hardly a strategic cargo. Many of the forty-three people aboard were killed in the surface attack that sank her, but eight survivors reached Tarawa after thirty-eight days adrift.

On December 11, about seventy miles northeast of Oahu, Captain Hanso Mattiesen watched from the bridge of the SS *Lahaina* as *I-9* surfaced at a range of two thousand yards and opened fire with its deck gun. Closing to 300 yards, *I-9* finished off the 5,646-ton Matson Navigation Company freighter and sent her to the bottom. This time, there were thirty survivors, who watched the submarine slip beneath the waves from their lifeboat. "Gaunt and exhausted," they reached Maui on Christmas Eve. The Associated Press reported that, "sailing by a makeshift sail and compass salvaged from the ship, the seamen lived on potatoes, apples, oranges and lemons, and a keg of drinking water." By the third week of December, the Japanese submarines were taking up their positions along the Pacific Coast. From the north, the boats and their stations were *I-26* guarding the approaches to Puget Sound, *I-25* off the mouth of the Columbia River, *I-9* off Cape Blanco on the central Oregon coast, *I-17* off Cape Mendocino, *I-15* guarding the approaches to the Golden Gate, *I-23* off Monterey Bay, *I-21* off Point Arguello in Santa Barbara County, *I-19* off Los Angeles, and *I-10* off San Diego.

The failed attack on the *Samoa* on December 18 that marked the beginning of the Japanese submarine campaign was followed just a few hours later by a second attempted strike. Lieutenant Commander Meiji Tagami's *I-25* was about ten miles off the Astoria, Oregon when he sighted a light at sea and surfaced to pursue it as a possible target. He lost track of it in the heavy seas and the gathering light of dawn, but at a few minutes past 9:00 a.m., he spotted the silhouette of a ship on the horizon and turned to intercept the 8,066-ton Union Oil Company tanker *L.P. St. Clair.* Tagami fired one torpedo, but believing that he had fatally damaged the tanker, he decided against firing a second. After lobbing a few shells at what incorrectly assumed to be a stricken merchant ship, *I-25* submerged and slipped away.

Two days later, *I-17* struck again. At 3:30 on the afternoon of December 20, the Coast Guard station at Table Bluff near Cape Mendocino picked up a distress call from the SS *Emidio*, operating within twenty miles off the coast, and passed it on to the Navy at Eureka, California. The 6,912-ton tanker belonging to General Petroleum Corporation, a subsidiary of Socony-Vacuum (Standard Oil of New York), reported that it had "sustained a torpedo attack from a submarine." Coast Guardsmen ashore, who could see the ship visually, reported that she was lying "low in the water."

Nishio attacked the tanker with his deck gun, chasing it as Captain Clark Farrow attempted unsuccessfully to outrun *I-17*. Five men were killed, two were seen to have died when the engine room was hit, and the other three disappeared when a shell exploded on board while they were trying to launch a lifeboat.

As Farrow ordered the men to abandon the stricken *Emidio*, two U.S. Navy PBY Catalina patrol bombers arrived on the scene. Assigned to Patrol Squadron VP-44 at NAS Alameda, they happened to be patrolling in the vicinity of the Oregon border when they came across the scene. As *I-17* submerged, one aircraft, piloted by Lieutenant (j.g.) Samuel "Pappy" Cole dropped a depth charge. However, *I-17* survived this attack, and as the planes flew away, Kozo resurfaced in order to finish off the *Emidio* with a torpedo.

The crew endured sixteen hours in the lifeboats, battered by a driving rainstorm, before they were picked up by the Coast Guard. The ship, however, did not sink, but drifted north toward Crescent City, where it broke up on the rocks. Part of the wreckage is visible to this day. On the afternoon of December 20, the same day that *I-17* attacked the *Emidio*, *I-23*, skippered by Commander Genichi Shibata, surfaced twenty miles from Cypress Point, off Pebble Beach, near Carmel and attacked the Richfield Oil Company tanker SS *Agwiworld* with its deck gun.

"The first thing I knew there was the explosion of a shell over our stern," reported the *Agiworld*'s captain, F. B. Concalves. "I put the helm hard to port and headed straight for the sub. When the second shot came, I put the helm hard over to starboard and then presented the stern to the sub. There was a heavy ground swell that kept the sub's gun deck awash. The next six shots missed us, but some of them came awful close. If we had only had a gun that sub would never shoot at another ship. It was a beautiful target for us." Having failed to score a single hit, a chagrinned Shibata took his submarine back beneath the waves.

These attacks in the course of three days certainly caught the attention of the people of the Pacific Coast who now felt themselves to be much closer to the war.

For its part, the Navy issued statements that bordered on the matter-of-fact. "The Navy does not deny, but it cannot confirm these reports," said Vice Admiral John Wills Greenslade of the Twelfth Naval District in San Francisco. "It has been confirmed that there are enemy submarines operating off the California coast destroying American shipping. This shipping will have to be replaced if the United States can prosecute the war successfully." The latter comment was a form of plea to shipyard workers, who were considering a strike, to stay on the job.

From Washington, D.C., Secretary of the Navy Frank Knox was more forthcoming. In remarks to the press that dealt mainly with German submarine attacks along the Eastern Seaboard, he said that "several Japanese submarines" off the Pacific Coast had been "effectively dealt with." What he meant by "dealt with" was unclear, however.

On December 21, the same day that Admiral Greenslade was neither denying nor confirming, Commander Shogo Narahara's *I-19* was off California's central coast, cruising southward toward Los Angeles. Spotting 4,200-ton freighter *Panama Express*, Narahara launched a torpedo, but it missed. He surfaced to give chase, but the Norwegian-registered vessel outran *I-19*. At around 8:30 a.m. the following morning, Narahara tried again, engaging the 10,763-ton SS *H.M. Storey* off Point Arguello. He fired two torpedoes in rapid succession, and was compelled to launch a third when it was armed accidentally, threatening to explode inside *I-19*. None of the torpedoes hit the big Standard Oil Company tanker. The *Storey*'s crew laid down a heavy screen of black smoke, and the ship escaped.

Farther north, *I-21*, commanded by Commander Kenji Matsumura, attacked the 8,272-ton tanker SS *Montebello*, out of Avila Beach and bound for British Columbia, at 5:45 a.m. in the predawn half-light of December 23, four miles from the Piedras Blancas Light Station near Cambria. Matsumura fired two torpedoes at the Union Oil Company tanker, scoring one hit amidships, striking a hold containing oil but missing one containing refined gasoline. Had the latter been hit, the ship would have instantly become a torch. As the *Montebello* began listing heavily, the tanker's captain, Olaf Eckstrom, ordered his thirty-eight crewmen to abandon ship.

The *Montebello* sank in dramatic fashion. "She upended like a giant telephone pole and slowly settled into the sea," wrote M. L. Waltz, editor of the *Cambrian* newspaper. "There was no fire or explosion about the ship that we could see."

Some of the crewmen came ashore in lifeboats at Cambria Pines and Cayucos, between San Simeon and San Luis Obispo, while others were picked up by the Standard Oil Company tugboat *Alma*.

A few hours later, Matsumura brought *I-21* to the surface to use his deck gun to attack the SS *Idaho*, but the 10,000-ton Texaco tanker escaped with minimal damage.

Meanwhile, Kozo Nishio, whose *I-17* had put the *Emidio* out of business was in action again in the early hours of December 23. At 3:10 a.m., he took his boat to the surface about eighty miles southwest of Eureka, and let his gunners set their sights on the 7,038-ton Richfield Oil Company tanker SS *Larry Doheny*.

Having scored four hits at a range of 3,060 yards, Nishio detected the sound of Navy patrol bombers, and immediately took *I-17* down. When the PBYs had gone, Nishio took the submarine back to periscope depth, and fired a single torpedo at the tanker. Having seen a large explosion, he assumed the ship had been hit, so he submerged and left the area. In fact, the torpedo had exploded prematurely, and the *Larry Doheny* survived.

The submarine campaign reached its crescendo on Christmas Eve. The 2,119-ton freighter *Dorothy Phillips* was shelled and damaged by a Japanese submarine, and run aground near Monterey. Most sources, including Robert Cressman in the official U.S. Navy chronology of the war, blame Genichi Shibata's *I-23*, because that submarine was the one assigned to this section of the California coastline. However, Bob Hackett and Sander Kingsepp, in their detailed chronology of Imperial Japanese Navy activities, have *I-23* departing the Pacific Coast for Palmyra Island on December 22, so the submarine in question is a mystery.

Farther south, Shogo Narahara's *I-19* struck twice on December 24. At dawn, he surprised the lumber schooner *Barbara Olson* in the San Pedro Channel off the entrance to the Port of Los Angeles, but, the torpedo he launched passed beneath the ship. The plume of water from the blast was seen at 6:25 a.m. by the USS *Amethyst*, a submarine chaser that was about four miles away guarding the harbor entrance. The *Amethyst* altered its course to attack, but by the time it reached the scene, *I-19* had slipped away.

Narahara headed west, past Point Fermin, where he spotted the SS *Absaroka*, a 5,698-ton lumber ship owned by the McCormick Steamship Company of San Francisco. The *Los Angeles Times* reported that "hundreds on shore," alerted to the presence of the Japanese submarine by the earlier attack "watched the spectacular whish of two torpedoes through the water." At approximately 10:40 a.m., the second of these struck the starboard side of the *Absaroka* below the waterline causing a jolt that knocked three men overboard. As he rushed to help pull them back aboard, San Franciscan Joseph Ryan was killed when a stack of lumber on the deck toppled onto him.

As the ship's radioman, Walter Williams, sent an SOS signal, there were already USAAF aircraft on the scene dropping depth charges, and the *Amethyst* arrived shortly thereafter. The *Absaroka*'s captain, Louie Prindle, ordered his thirty-three-man crew to abandon ship, but when she did not sink, Prindle went back aboard with a skeleton crew. With the aid of a U.S. Navy tug, they succeeded in beaching the ship near Fort MacArthur.

I-19 escaped a second time that day with Narahara reporting that he had sunk the *Absaroka*.

Meanwhile, the USAAF crews claimed that they had sunk a Japanese submarine. An official War Department announcement issued on December 26 claiming that "an American Army bomber from General DeWitt's Western Defense Command successfully attacked an enemy submarine off the California coast. Soon after the submarine was sighted, it made an emergency dive. A bomb was dropped and the submarine emerged and then sank. Two more bombs were dropped, apparently scoring direct hits and filling the air with debris."

The location off Redondo Beach was deemed a "military secret," but residents of that community witnessed the attack and shared their accounts with newspaper reporters. Police who investigated the debris that washed ashore said that it was not from a submarine, but probably from the water-logged fishing barge *Kohala*, which had been floating offshore and probably mistaken for a submarine in foggy weather. The *Los Angeles Times* reported that, when told of this theory, "Army and Navy officials were noncommittal."

The last action of the 1941 submarine campaign came on the night of December 27–28, when a torpedo struck the Texaco tanker SS *Connecticut* about ten miles at sea. Though damaged, the 8,684-ton vessel managed to reach the mouth of the Columbia River and run aground without sinking. To this day, the attack remains mysterious because the identity of the attacking submarine is unknown. Most sources credit *I-25*, as it operated off the entrance to the Columbia. However, on December 22, *I-25* had been one of three boats that had been ordered off station to intercept three U.S. battleships—the USS *Idaho*, USS *Mississippi*, and USS *New Mexico*—that the Imperial Japanese Navy's headquarters had been informed were transiting the Panama Canal and due in the Los Angeles area by Christmas Day. The three ships were indeed being relocated from the Atlantic Fleet, but they did not pass through the Panama Canal until late January. How the IJN learned that they were coming at all remains a mystery.

By the end of December, with their fuel running low, the Japanese submarines all had slipped away from the North American coastline and headed toward home.

During a campaign lasting just ten days, the nine submarines had engaged at least ten merchant ships and had fatally damaged two, the *Emidio* and the *Montebello*. Two others, the *Absaroka* and the *Connecticut*, were seriously damaged. The flotilla did go away with their skippers believing that these two and several others had also been destroyed or sunk.

Four of the nine submarines, however, had failed to engage any targets off North America. In the north, off the Strait of Juan de Fuca, the entrance to Puget Sound, heavy seas prevented *I-26* from engaging in any meaningful action. Having sunk the *Lahaina* in Hawaiian waters before coming to the Pacific Coast, *I-9* also did not engage any Allied warships or merchantmen.

Curiously, the submarines posted offshore two of the U.S. Navy's busiest ports also came away without any engagements. *I-10* had sunk the MS *Donerail* in Hawaiian waters, but found nothing to shoot at while patrolling off San Diego. Though her crew had a chance to see the lights of San Francisco when she surfaced to recharge her batteries, *I-15* also could not find any suitable targets off the Golden Gate.

The first Japanese submarine offensive was over, but only for the time being. Nevertheless, they maintained their presence in the banner headlines telling of enemy attacks within sight of American soil and in the minds of Americans, fearful of further such actions. It was a presence that sharpened the growing anxiety among people up and down the Pacific Coast.

ELEVEN

The Spies Next Door

M any fears gripped the Pacific Coast in late 1941 and early 1942. Fear of sabotage. Of imminent air raids. Of the continuing submarine attacks so close to shore that you could watch helplessly. Of the dreaded invasion. And, the constant nagging dread of a fifth column. Of these, the fear of a fifth column—of an internal threat lurking in nearby shadows—was perhaps the more prominent in both official discussions and private conversations.

On December 8, even as he had urged local authorities to refrain from "direct action against Japanese in their communities," Attorney General Francis Biddle had already ordered the FBI into action against known Axis intelligence agents in the United States.

German spies had already been on the front pages. Earlier in 1941, the FBI had arrested thirty-three German agents, who were part of the notorious spy ring run by Frederick Joubert "Fritz" Duquesne, in what was the largest espionage case in United States history to end in convictions. Indeed, the last fourteen of the Duquesne ring were on trial in Federal District Court in Brooklyn when Pearl Harbor was attacked, and they were convicted on December 13.

German espionage in North America had a long and infamous history. During World War I, the United States had been the target of such intrigues—from the nefarious efforts of German ambassador Johann Heinrich Graf von Bernstorff, working in concert with Franz von Papen, later part of Adolf Hitler's government, to the infamous "Zimmermann Telegram" in which Foreign Secretary Arthur Zimmermann surreptitiously tried to engineer an attack on the United States by Mexico.

German agents also had mounted extensive sabotage operations, including the 1916 destruction of a munitions ship tied up in Jersey City, New Jersey. The resulting explosion broke windows in midtown Manhattan, damaged the Statue of Liberty, and measured 5.5 on the Richter Scale. The severity of these incidents during the Great War loomed large in the institutional memory of American counterintelligence agencies.

When it came to actionable intelligence on Japanese espionage and subversion, though, government officials had not uncovered substantial activity, but it was not for want of trying. Beginning in July 1941, the House of Representatives Special Committee to Investigate Un-American Activities, chaired by Texas Democrat Martin Dies, had investigated Japanese-American civic organizations and Japanese language schools, as well as connections between ethnic Japanese living in the United States and the government of Japan.

The Dies Committee had been particularly suspicious of the language schools, seeing this a potential conduit for Imperial Japanese propaganda. With the onset of Japanese submarine attacks in December 1941, some people paid a great deal of attention to a possible connection between Japanese-American fishermen and the submarines. The Dies Committee had already been looking into this as well.

Victor Hansen would later mention FBI reports that he had seen which indicated that, "for several years prior to Pearl Harbor, Japanese naval officers were placed as crew members on fishing boats that fished the waters from Southern California to Panama. Detailed charting of the West Coast harbors were made by these Japanese naval officers. High-ranking naval officers posing as Japanese businessmen visited coastal areas and communicated and visited with California Japanese, including *nisei*. In many cases when these California Japanese were interviewed by the FBI, they either denied that there were such visitations, or said that they had no knowledge that the visitors were in fact Japanese naval officers." He added that for the FBI, such denials "created immediate suspicion that there must be disloyalty."

Perhaps the most intriguing single line of inquiry, and one which received a great deal of media attention after the Dies Committee report was published in February 1942, was the interest that the Japanese government had in the water supply of the city of Los Angeles, a system which was wholly dependent on an extensive aqueduct system.

In June 1934, K. Kageyama, the chancellor at the Japanese consulate in Los Angeles wrote to Harvey Van Norman, the chief engineer and general manager of the Los Angeles Bureau of Water Works, asking for "information that will explain every point of the system, including reservoirs, quantity of water supply, number of consumers, filtering, purifying, pipe pressure, kind of pipes used, office organization, number of employees, etc." Kageyama did not say *why* he wanted this information, but he did offer to "defray any expenses" in gathering it.

Van Norman promptly forwarded the letter to the Los Angeles office of the Department of Justice's Division of Investigation (the predecessor to the FBI), pointing out that Kageyama's request was quite far-reaching, and asking for advice. When J. E. P. Dunn, the special agent in charge, wrote back to say that he could "be of no help to you in connection with this matter," and suggesting that Van Norman try the Army, Van Norman did so.

On July 17, after sharing Van Norman's letter with the Ninth Corps headquarters at the Presidio of San Francisco, Lieutenant Colonel Homer Oldfield, commander of the 63rd Coastal Artillery replied that the matter "does not pertain to the peace time functions of the regular Army." Oldfield thanked Van Norman for his "interest in this matter," and suggested that he contact the Division of Investigation. The bureaucratic

circle through which Van Norman had been given the runaround illus-
trates the prewar lack of official urgency about potential sabotage, an
attitude that had changed completely in December 1941.

In the 1930s, though, even as the Justice Department and the Army
were ignoring Kageyama's fairly overt efforts, American cryptographers
had made substantial progress in breaking Japanese diplomatic codes
under a program codenamed "Magic."

The information about Japanese espionage in the United States that
was disclosed through Magic included the contents of a January 30, 1941
message from Foreign Minister Yosuke Matsuoka, in which agents working out of consulates under diplomatic cover were instructed to determine
"the total strength of the US . . . political, economic, and military, and
definite course of action shall be mapped out."

Matsuoka called for "Utilization of our 'Second Generations' and
our resident nationals. In view of the fact that if there is any slip in this
phase, our people in the US will be subjected to considerable persecution,
and the utmost caution must be exercised."

As for the use of "second generation" Japanese-Americans in espionage efforts, Kenji Nakauchi, the Japanese consul in Los Angeles,
reported to Tokyo on May 9, 1941, that "with regard to airplane
manufacturing plants and other military establishments in other parts,
we plan to establish very close relations with various organizations and
in strict secrecy have them keep these military establishments under
close surveillance. Through such means, we hope to be able to obtain
accurate and detailed intelligence reports. We have already established
contacts with absolutely reliable Japanese in the San Pedro and San
Diego area, who will keep a close watch on all shipments of airplanes
and other war materials, and report the amounts and destinations of
such shipments. The same steps have been taken with regards to traffic
across the US-Mexico border. We shall maintain connection with our
second generations who are at present in the [US] Army, to keep us
informed of various developments in the Army. We also have connections with our second generations working in airplane plants for intelligence purposes."

Two days later, Yuki Sato, the Japanese consul in Seattle, told Tokyo that "recently we have on two occasions made investigations on the spot of various military establishments and concentration points in various areas. For the future we have made arrangements to collect intelligences from second generation Japanese draftees on matters dealing with the troops, as well as troop speech and behavior."

This type of information, known at the highest level of the United States government, probably helped to drive decisions made later, which seem to us with the luxury of hindsight to have been excessive.

Meanwhile, the FBI had already been gathering information on Japanese-American organizations on the Pacific Coast. In a report dated July 3, 1941, its San Francisco Field Office outlined dossiers that had already been prepared on various entities with ties to the Japanese government and which collected money for the Japanese war effort.

These groups included the Los Angeles-based National Flower Association, as well as the Service Association and Imperial Reservists Association, both centered in Central California. Between them, two other groups, the Shinshu Society in Berkeley and the Isshin (One Spirit) Society in Stockton, had "contributed" more that $19,000 to the "Japanese War Relief." Another group with a sinister sounding name, the San Francisco-based Association of Japanese in America Obligated to Military Duty, seems to have been an organization of men who avoided conscription by living abroad—draft dodgers—rather than men with a special allegiance to Imperial Japan.

This report did not mention the paramilitary Kokuryoki, or Black Dragon Society. Though it was mainly an international criminal gang that supported itself through theft and extortion, the Kokuryoki had been utilized on a contract basis by the Imperial Japanese Army in Manchuria for sabotage and targeted assassination. Although most of its overseas affiliates were in the Far East and Central Asia, Kokuryoki also operated in South America and in California's San Joaquin Valley.

In the immediate aftermath of Pearl Harbor, the FBI, which had already been active against German espionage, undertook an aggressive counterespionage operation against other Axis nationals nationwide.

Since the beginning of his tenure as FBI Director in 1935, J. Edgar Hoover had transformed the bureau into an effective crime fighting organization staffed by agents who had been honed to the standards set by their boss, from meticulous attention to detail to fast and energetic action. Based on the anti-radical efforts that Hoover himself had led in the 1920s, the Bureau had become the lead counterespionage organization in the United States government.

Under Presidential Proclamation 2525 of December 7, Roosevelt had redefined Japanese nationals as "alien enemies" (aka enemy aliens) and had ordered that those "alien enemies deemed dangerous to the public peace or safety of the United States by the Attorney General or the Secretary of War, as the case may be, are subject to summary apprehension."

On December 8, Proclamations 2526 and 2527 extended the same treatment to Germans and Italians, stating that "all natives, citizens, denizens, or subjects of the hostile nation or government, being of the age of fourteen years and upward, who shall be within the United States and not actually naturalized, shall be liable to be apprehended, restrained, secured, and removed as alien enemies." In the field, these documents would give DeWitt's Western Defense Command, as well as Hoover's FBI, unprecedented latitude for action during the coming weeks and months.

Richard Hood, the FBI's Special Agent in Charge (SAC) for Southern California, had been working for years compiling records on aliens using an index-card system. On December 7, he started to put those records to work. On December 8, the *Los Angeles Times* reported that in that city "close to 200 suspicious Japanese were rounded up by police, deputy sheriffs and special officers working under the direction of FBI agents."

Two days later, Attorney General Biddle announced publicly that the roundup of aliens was "nearly over," with 2,303 people in custody nationwide. It was reported that police and FBI agents in San Francisco had "rounded up" sixty Germans, sixteen Italians and ninety Japanese, detaining them at the Immigration Service compound on Silver Avenue. In Los Angeles, the numbers were fifty-two German and Italians, and thirty-two Japanese, while thirty-four aliens had been detained in San Diego, and fourteen in Santa Barbara.

Despite Biddle's assurances, the arrests would continue for months. As directed by the FBI, the information released to the public by other agencies in December was supposed to be limited to the number of persons arrested. Los Angeles police chief Clemence Horrall told the press that "our hands are tied, we are under strict orders to reveal nothing."

However, reporters were to milk other sources for the details. It was reported that those picked up in Los Angeles included Hermann Schwinn, the Pacific Coast leader of the notorious German-American Bund, as well as the archeologist and explorer Dr. Victor Wolfgang von Hagen. Also arrested were Haruo Inai and Toshio Asanuma, who were in possession of a map of San Gabriel Dam. On December 14, Dr. Rikita Honda killed himself while in FBI custody. The *Los Angeles Times* described him as the reputed head of the Japanese Imperial Reservists Association, it cast as a "vast network of Japanese espionage on the Pacific Coast."

FBI agents in Seattle arrested Martin George Dudel, the editor and publisher of the German-language *Staatszeitung* newspaper as an enemy alien. According to Peter Blecha in the *Online Encyclopedia of Washington State History*, he was taken from his home to an undisclosed location, where he penned a note which read: "So here we are like the caged beasts of the jungle in Woodland Park [the Seattle Zoo], walking forth and back, back and forth behind barred doors and windows, thinking, hoping."

Weeks later, when he was finally brought before an internment panel, he told those who were to judge him, "I stand before you accused, of what, I do not know." No matter. In February 1942, Dudel was confined to an internment camp at Fort Lincoln at Bismarck, North Dakota.

In San Francisco, those arrested included August Meurer and Anton Brunner, both building contractors, as well as nursery owner Kotoharu Inouye, and Carl Williams, who had been "the Japanese interpreter at the Hall of Justice for years." The FBI arrested Hans von Bernhard, former attaché to consul general Fritz Wiedemann. Until he was reassigned to China shortly before Pearl Harbor, Wiedemann had been one of the most popular figures on the San Francisco social scene, an A-list party guest, and a member of the exclusive Olympic Club.

If some took comfort in the growing number of arrests, seeing them as evidence that the FBI was on the case and protecting the Pacific Coast, others drew an opposite lesson. If an apparently endless number of spies *were* being picked up on a daily basis, then the espionage threat must be dire, indeed. This served to magnify the level of tension among the public, a level that was only heightened by the alarming pronouncements that DeWitt's Western Defense Command was making.

On Christmas Eve, Lieutenant Colonel S. F. Miller of the IX Corps headquarters at Fort Lewis issued a series of memos warning that the Japanese were likely to strike over the holidays. In his memo to the Oregon Defense Council, preserved in the State Archives, he wrote that "it is the crafty nature of our enemy to choose those periods when the country is least likely to guard, to launch their attacks."

The submarine campaign off the coast had itself boosted concerns and spawned rumors. One particularly widespread and resilient rumor—despite the fact that censorship was keeping it out of the newspapers—concerned reports of "signal lights" flashing between sea and shore from Washington's Olympic Peninsula all the way down to San Diego.

Numerous people reported—in apparent sincerity—that they had seen white lights, red lights and even flares. The widely accepted supposition was that enemy agents were either guiding airplanes or submarines. Added to these reports were ones of unauthorized shortwave radio messages being sent and received. Local authorities demanded action from the FBI, but chasing flashing lights on remote shores in pitch darkness was not a priority for the Bureau. For the record, no one was ever caught in the act of sending these mysterious signals by local, state, or federal authorities.

Attorney General Biddle did, however, take action that seemed appropriate to quelling the concerns about shortwave radios, both household receivers and transmitters capable of reaching Japan. On December 27, the Saturday after Christmas, he ordered enemy aliens—German, Italian and Japanese—to turn in their radios, as well as their cameras, to the nearest police station by 11:00 p.m. on the following Monday. Biddle picked a bad day. Having been issued on the weekend after Christmas, the press did not widely disseminate the order.

In San Francisco, there was a great deal of confusion when the police—except at Northern Station—refused to accept the equipment. Chief Dullea told the press that he knew nothing about the order "except what I read in the newspapers," and the local papers had yet to carry the news of the order. It took a telegram that afternoon from Agent Hood of the Los Angeles FBI office to clear things up.

Over the coming days, the enemy aliens dutifully started showing up at the designated police stations. One of those turning in a camera was Cenkuro Nishioka, who had been the butler for the family of the great San Francisco philanthropist Sigmund Stern for twenty-five years.

Some tried to sidestep the order. Eric Livingston, a German from Cologne who had been in the United States for three years, was taken into custody by the FBI for attempting to sell his radio-phonograph console to an audio equipment dealer.

On the night of January 28, the FBI, led by Special Agent Hood himself, arrested Dr. Hans Helmut Gros and his wife, Frances, both American-born, along with German-born Albrecht Rudolf Curt Reuter, as German spies. The charge was that they had passed coded messages to Berlin through German agents operating in South America. Exhausted after a week of questioning, Gros confessed, and both he and his wife were tried and convicted.

On the last day of the month, Hood's agents, backed by men from the Los Angeles County Sheriff's Department, arrested a number of Japanese truck farmers on the Palos Verdes Peninsula and in Torrance, as well as near Fort MacArthur and the Lomita oil fields. On February 5, the FBI arrested twenty Japanese men between the ages of forty and sixty-two and a forty-nine-year-old woman near the Mare Island Naval Shipyard. They were reportedly in possession of two guns, two cameras, and five radios, along with a set of Navy signal flags.

In a forty-eight-hour period beginning on the night of February 11, Nat J. L. Pieper, the Special Agent in Charge at the FBI's San Francisco office, led a series of raids across northern California. Near the Navy's Moffett Field in Mountain View, thirty-two Japanese-Americans were picked up. A series of operations across the Monterey area resulted in nearly forty arrests. As reported in the newspapers, the haul also included documents, weapons, spotlights, and uniforms—as well as binoculars and radios—all of which were considered potentially useful for spies.

Much was made of the arrest of Shunso Matsuda, the foreman of the Japanese labor camp at the Ellis Spiegel lettuce ranch at Chualar near the Salinas Army Air Field. He was described by agents as the "emperor of Chualar," and the camp was called the Japanese "mystery colony." At a Buddhist temple in Salinas, Pieper put the handcuffs on Koyo Tamanaka, a Buddhist priest and former Japanese policeman—the *San Francisco Examiner* called him a "former Tokyo Police Chief"—who had entered the United States in 1940.

Bunkichi "Ben" Torigoe, a Watsonville sporting goods store owner was arrested with a dozen shotguns and eight rifles. Such an inventory was hardly out of place at a sporting goods store, but it was deemed suspicious by the FBI. Many media reports spoke of the thousands of rounds of ammunition seized, but the *Santa Cruz Sentinel* clarified that it was mostly shotgun shells, clearly not out of place in rural farm country.

On February 13, Pieper arrested three Japanese nationals, Yasoyouki Doi, Haruo Aoki, and Uma Ikeda, who were executives of the Yokohama Specie Bank in San Francisco. The latter two admitted to being Imperial Japanese Army reserve officers. "I would die rather than fight Japan," Aoki told the FBI agent when he suggested that the Japanese banker switch sides.

In Sacramento, after seventeen arrests, the United Press reported that "seized records confirmed that espionage was being carried on near

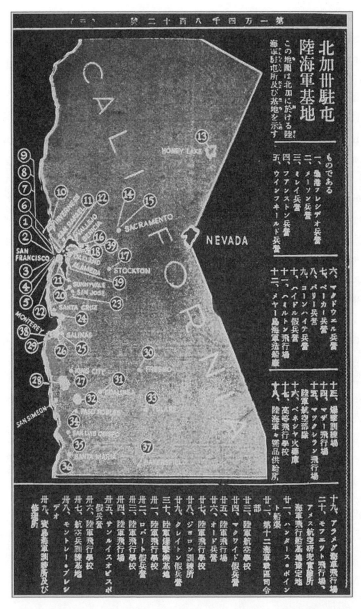

This map of California, with military and transportation facilities highlighted, is from among the exhibits contained within the final report of the Congressional committee into Japanese espionage that was headed by Congressman Martin Dies of Texas. The map was one of a small number of documents that showed serious evidence of espionage in a report that was long on innuendo, but short on proof. *House Un-American Activities Committee, U.S. Congress*

McClellan Field, Mather Field [both USAAF bases] and Sacramento Municipal Airport." Meanwhile, J. D. Swenson, the Special Agent in Charge of the Portland FBI office led a series of raids on February 18 near the Bonneville Dam, Portland Airport, and Oregon shipyards. Strangely, there were no arrests, though dynamite was reported to have been found.

It would not be until March 27 that the FBI finally got around to arresting about a dozen members of the Black Dragon Society, which probably represented the most serious potential threat to the United States by any Japanese organization because of their connection with the violent criminal organization of the same name in Japan. Though their numbers were small and they are not known to have engaged in any sabotage operations, the Black Dragons caused the FBI a great deal of concern and colored the perception by law enforcement of other Japanese groups.

The aggressive—and very public—counterespionage effort by the FBI and local law enforcement might well have closed down Axis intelligence operations on the West Coast. However, it also stoked the already prevalent concerns about a fifth column and through the law of unintended consequences, it contributed to setting the wheels in motion for a sweeping tide of public opinion, and ultimately overt official action, against people based merely on their ethnicity rather than evidence of any espionage or treasonous activity.

TWELVE

Into the Cold Uncertainty of a New Year

General John DeWitt's dire warnings in the immediate aftermath of Pearl Harbor had created an atmosphere of fear and anxiety up and down the Pacific Coast. His Christmas message did little to dispel it. DeWitt promised that "the relaxation which usually characterizes Christmas Eve and Christmas Day in the Army has been superseded by additional restrictions on admission to Army posts and establishments, by the doubling of guards and by other precautions."

On Christmas Day, the first convoy bringing evacuees from Hawaii sailed under the Golden Gate Bridge. It had been a nerve-wracking, six-day voyage, zig-zagging across the Pacific to avoid Japanese submarines.

Those injured in the Japanese attack on Pearl Harbor came off the ships first, on stretchers or as "walking wounded," bound for stateside military and naval hospitals. For the Red Cross workers and volunteers who greeted these men, they were a powerful reminder of what had happened in Hawaii, and what *could* happen in San Francisco.

Next came the wives and widows of military personnel who had fought or died at Pearl Harbor, along with scores of often-frightened children. They scanned the crowds on the pier, looking for someone they knew among the throngs looking back and hoping to see family or friends. Then came the members of the San Jose State and Willamette University football teams who had arrived in Hawaii before Pearl Harbor to play a demonstration game in Honolulu on Christmas Day.

The evacuees not met by friends or relatives were taken under the wing of the American Women's Voluntary Services (AWVS) and given meals and temporary shelter and medical care by various San Francisco organizations and institutions, such as the California School of Fine Arts, the Jewish Community Center, the Western Women's Club, the Women's Athletic Club, and the YWCA.

In the last week of December, a cold front brought chilly temperatures to the coastal cities, and heavy snow to the mountains. In California, nearly five feet of snow fell overnight at Donner Pass, three feet in Yosemite Valley, and even the higher elevations around Los Angeles and the San Francisco Bay Area were white with snow.

As the *San Francisco Chronicle* reported, the city "played New Years Eve as an indoor sport," largely heedful of police admonitions to avoid the large outdoor gatherings which so concerned John DeWitt. The *Los Angeles Times* reported that "along the Sunset Strip...all the nightclubs frequented by filmland's great and not-so-great are sold out for the evening [but] many motion picture stars will greet the New Year from the seclusion of their own homes...Hotels and nightclubs were sold out to capacity merrymakers, some of whom had paid as much as $18.50 plus federal entertainment tax, per person to make whoopee on their premises."

It was good escapism that night, but as the people of the Pacific Coast looked westward across the whitecaps on the old, gray Pacific on the morning after, there wasn't much cause for a celebratory "Whoopee."

The news from the Far East had become increasingly grim. After Secretary of the Navy Frank Knox returned from his inspection tour of Hawaii on December 16, he revealed the true dimensions of the losses at Pearl Harbor in a bombshell press release. *All* of the battleships were out of action, and casualties were not in the hundreds, but in the *thousands.*

A week later, the Marines on Wake Island who had mounted a gallant defense against overwhelming odds surrendered. On Christmas Day, Hong Kong also fell to the Japanese.

Before the war, it had been said that in the worst case scenario, it would take an invader a year and a half to drive south through the entire Malay Peninsula to Singapore. By New Year's Eve, the Japanese 25th Army had already marched two-thirds of that distance in less than three weeks.

On New Year's Day, the news came from the Philippines that Manila had surrendered, and the last American and Filipino defenders had been pushed into the Bataan Peninsula and Corregidor Island in Manila Bay, where they would make their last stand—unaided and unreinforced.

On the Pacific Coast, there was no way of knowing that the last Japanese submarine attack on December 28 was the last one for two months. And the sobering words of Admiral Chester Nimitz, who took up the role of commander of the battered Pacific Fleet from the disgraced Husband Kimmel on New Year's Eve, made them seem imminent. "It is not beyond the bounds of possibility that Japanese submarines operating off the West Coast of the United States may attempt to lay their shells into cities before they leave. The ocean is too big to obviate such possibility...Japanese captains desire to make the utmost use of their weapons when there are no targets for their torpedoes."

On December 27, Attorney General Francis Biddle had ordered enemy aliens to surrender their radios and cameras to local police. On January 2, DeWitt topped him, issuing orders banning the use of cameras by *anyone* to take pictures of military installations and *personnel.* It was a good thing that this had come after Christmas, when people had posed with their family members in the service.

To his list of prohibited subjects, DeWitt added airplanes, ships, and other military equipment. He also forbade photographs of bridges, railroads, reservoirs, seaports, and tunnels as well as any radio, telephone or telegraph facilities.

Another more ominous New Year's greeting came a week later—from Japan. On January 9, *The Japan Times* in Tokyo reported, in an item broadcast over short wave, that when Japanese armies landed on the North American continent, "it will be a simple matter for a well-trained and courageous army to sweep everything before it...the contention that the United States cannot be invaded is as much a myth as that the Maginot Line could not be taken, or that Pearl Harbor or Singapore are impregnable...it will be for us to say when, where and how we will strike."

On New Year's Day, Pasadena was incongruously quiet, with DeWitt having ordered the cancellation of both Tournament of Roses Parade and the Rose Bowl Game—at least at the actual Rose Bowl. In fact, there *was* a Rose Bowl Game that year, but well away from Southern California. Duke University had generously offered to host the game at its stadium in Durham, North Carolina. Although favored by fourteen points, Lon Steiner's Blue Devils lost a close 20–16 game to Wallace Wade's Oregon State Beavers. At least that was *something* which the Pacific Coast—and certainly those in Oregon—could celebrate. This win, by the way, stands as Oregon State's only Rose Bowl victory.

Applying the same fearful thinking that had prompted him to cancel the Rose Bowl, DeWitt decided to shut down California's lucrative horse racing industry. On January 5, he summoned Charles Strub, the general manager of the Los Angeles Turf Club, to the Presidio. There, Strub was told by Colonel D. A. Stroh—DeWitt was otherwise occupied—to scrub the season. Strub objected, explaining that around 4,300 exercise boys, grooms, jockeys, parimutuel clerks, ticket sellers, trainers, and veterinarians would suddenly be out of a job if the season were cancelled.

Stroh was unmoved. He explained that DeWitt had decreed a ban on large public gatherings, like the Rose Bowl, and horse racing drew large numbers of people.

A devastated Strub returned to Santa Anita to break the bad news to owners, jockeys, and others. It was the same story at Bay Meadows and Tanforan, south of San Francisco, and other tracks across California.

Faced with devastating financial losses, horse owners and track officials agreed to attempt an end run around DeWitt and take the matter directly to Governor Culbert Olson, who agreed with them completely. In turn, on January 28, Olson invited DeWitt to Sacramento.

During the closed-door meeting, the governor pointed out that Southern Californians were traveling in droves to watch and wager upon the races at the Agua Caliente Racetrack in Tijuana. Olson argued that if they were clogging California highways to travel to Mexico, they might as well be spending their money in California.

DeWitt angrily replied that they should not be clogging California highways at all, and that it was Olson's duty to obey orders and to assure that the roads remained unclogged. After two hours, Olson at last bowed to the will of the emphatic general. "Attention is called to the serious condition caused by horse racing at Agua Caliente," the beaten Olson conceded sheepishly after his audience with DeWitt. "Thousands upon thousands of Californians are congesting the highways with traffic in going to and from these races—highways in the combat zone, which are needed every day in the movement of military forces and war supplies. I take this occasion to ask Californians during this emergency not to use the highways in going to and from the races in Agua Caliente...if this is not voluntarily discontinued, then steps will be taken by international arrangements to prevent the crossing of the Mexican border for this diversion."

It was an impressive display for DeWitt's power and influence as was how the California Railroad Commission reacted to his imperious demand that it approve—*without* public hearings—the discontinuance of various passenger trains for the purpose of making the railroad equipment available for DeWitt's needs. "We have and do insist that the railroads meet our demands," he told the commissioners. "These demands undoubtedly have and will cause the curtailment of railroad service to the general public."

In response, Commission President C. C. Baker meekly told the general that his request would be granted without delay.

Not all went poorly for horse racing on the rest of the West Coast, however. In Washington, governor Arthur Langlie asked Joseph Gottstein, the owner of the Longacres Race Track, to cancel the 1942 season at his facility in Renton, outside Seattle on Lake Washington. Gottstein flatly refused. Instead, the track owner donated three days' worth of the parimutuel handle to the Army Relief Fund, the Navy Relief Fund, and the Red Cross.

However, horse racing was not the paramount concern on the West Coast at the beginning of 1942. In San Francisco, the Civil Defense system was an apparent state of disarray. The *San Francisco Chronicle* reported that the city "was in an uproar over the status of Civil Defense." There was a pervasive sense that the city fathers were merely fiddling while the Japanese threat was growing.

Within a week of Pearl Harbor, San Francisco had thirty thousand Civil Defense volunteers, and by Christmas, there were forty-four thousand, but there was no program to train them. On December 30, Eric Cullenward, whom San Francisco mayor Angelo Rossi had appointed to serve as his first director of Civil Defense, resigned without warning. The *Chronicle* called it a "bombshell." Cullenward told the mayor that "undoubtedly you realize I have been constantly hampered in my efforts properly to carry out the functions of my office."

"I appointed Mr. Cullenward to represent me and carry out my orders," Rossi told the press. "There could not be any misunderstanding about that...There is nothing to get excited about. Everything will go along as usual."

The following day, as Cullenward's resignation became the talk of the town, Rossi announced that he would look for and appoint a "strong man" as a coordinator of Civil Defense. In the meantime, Rossi himself would be the strong man, and *he* would assume the title of director.

Unfortunately, Cullenward's departure came on the same day that Police Chief Charles Dullea was called to active duty with the Navy. Rossi immediately contacted Admiral Greenslade at the Twelfth Naval District and asked him to defer Dullea's call-up. The admiral granted the mayor's request. The *Chronicle* editorialized that Rossi made this move "despite the fact that inquiries and reports fail to indicate that the chief has done anything toward assisting in preparations for national defense. Training of auxiliary policemen has bogged down."

To get out of *both* conundrums, Rossi appointed Dullea, who also was a personal friend and important political ally as well as twenty-seven-year veteran of the department, to the now-vacant post of Civil Defense Coordinator, and announced that he would hold that position in addition to that of police chief. The *Chronicle* saw politics in this move, tartly observing that the appointment gave Rossi "a member of [the mayor's] political family in the job" rather than someone from the private sector who, if he were successful, might become "a well-publicized opponent at the next [mayoral] election in 1943."

On his first day on the job, January 2, Dullea moved to consolidate the city's numerous Civil Defense organizations—scattered all over town—into a single location near City Hall, and to reinvigorate the long-languishing training program for the city's civilian volunteers. Although there were 50,786 of them, in early January, only 6 percent of the volunteers had yet been trained. The city's emergency communications system was still a work in progress. An auxiliary pumping system for the fire department, recommended in August 1941, had yet to materialize, and the city's ambulance fleet was not equipped with blackout lights. Those lights would have come in handy the following evening, when there *was* a blackout.

DeWitt's headquarters reported unidentified aircraft eighty miles offshore, but thousands of people did not hear the sirens and, therefore, did not turn out their lights. Meanwhile, Civil Defense officials failed to show up at City Hall as they were supposed to, Dullea most conspicuous among them. To make matters worse, no one on his staff had any idea where he was.

When he finally appeared several hours after the all clear had been sounded, Dullea explained his absence. "I was up on Twin Peaks looking at the blackout. It looked good." Twin Peaks is the highest point in the city reachable by car, and thus he was out of reach. "I wish I could have gone up in a plane," the chief continued calmly. "I could have gotten a better look. I hope to take a plane up during the next blackout."

When questioned by reporters about the wisdom of having the city's police chief and civil defense coordinator sitting on a mountain top for several hours at the height of an emergency involving eighty enemy aircraft, Dullea said, "Remember, I've only been in charge for a couple of days. I'll get the wrinkles out as soon as I get things under control. The big job now is to get that central communications center functioning. We've been all right. If bombs had started falling, we would have turned on the lights and gone to work."

It may have been his first day on one job, but Dullea had been a member of the police department since 1914.

The *Chronicle* reported that the citizenry was "shocked and a little frightened by the complete collapse of the Civilian Defense set-up...The mayor may have been satisfied, but the people of San Francisco were not."

Rossi shot back. "The Japanese can withdraw all their spies from San Francisco if they want to. The *Chronicle* will keep them informed of our weak spots."

"What are you worrying about—no bombs fell—did they?" Mayor Rossi asked reporters. "The Civilian Defense program is in good shape. There's no question about that. It always had been in good shape."

Juliette Hauck asked in a letter to the editor, "Do we have to have bombs dropped on us to get some action on our civil defense?"

The *San Francisco Call* rose to the defense of its rival newspaper, issued its own pointed barb: "Mayor Rossi is an astute politician. We just don't happen to need or want a politician at this time. It isn't just the newspapers, Mister Rossi: It's the people who have no confidence in you or your political moves. Who was apathetic about civilian defense before Pearl Harbor, Mister Mayor, the public or YOU? Seattle wasn't asleep at the switch. Los Angeles wasn't dozing in politics corner. No, Mr. Rossi, it was YOU who were asleep and apathetic."

A groundswell of support for a recall election ensued, but the *San Francisco Chronicle* insisted that "a recall is not the answer...Enemy planes or fifth column saboteurs will not wait, while we gather and verify signatures and go through the formalities of a recall election."

In time, the demand for a recall election would dissipate, but the woes of the San Francisco civil defense organization endured. As late as March 5, it was revealed that the only item of equipment that the city had ordered for its air raid wardens and auxiliary police were 30,000 police whistles. A January 14 request by civil defense staff for 27,500 surplus helmets, a like number of "blackout type" flashlights, and 7,500 first aid kits had never been processed by the organization's leaders.

For his part, after his solitary evening atop Twin Peaks had raised questions about his competence, Chief Dullea rolled up his sleeves and got to work. Whether deliberately or not, he reinvented himself somewhat in the image of General DeWitt, complete with lurid warnings of looming disaster and a firm determination to bend others to his will. On January 28, Dullea chose a luncheon of the San Francisco Advertising Club to deliver his first formal Civil Defense report to the people of his city.

"There is no reason to think we are immune," he began. "We are in a combat zone, and you've got to add two and two. I don't want to alarm you unnecessarily, but I am thoroughly confident of this. The danger is grave and it's imminent. We must be conscious all the time that it's confronting us. Use the reasoning power that God gave you. We'll depend on the Army and the Navy to take care of the fighting—but we must protect ourselves."

The following night, as though on cue, a four-alarm fire exploded in a building on San Francisco's Van Ness Avenue that housed an automobile warehouse and showroom, doing several millions of dollars in damage. Sabotage was eventually ruled out, but the conflagration made San Franciscans even more jittery.

THIRTEEN

In a Climate of Fear

General John DeWitt did not create the high anxiety that dominated the Pacific Coast in December and into the New Year, but he nurtured it with his doom-laden pronouncements and predictions of widespread death and damage. And, by doing so, he created a mindset that, in turn, would spawn one of the greatest injustices in American history—the internment of around 120,000 Americans. This, in turn, would define his legacy.

The threat of a Japanese fifth column—which was read on the Pacific Coast as meaning a Japanese-American fifth column—had been discussed fearfully and widely, on editorial pages, in homes, on street corners, and in the offices at the Presidio of San Francisco almost from the moment that the news of the Pearl Harbor attack reached the Coast.

The report of the investigation of the Pearl Harbor disaster by a committee chaired by Supreme Court Justice Owen Roberts, released on

January 24, 1942, proved to be a turning point. It assigned the lion's share of the blame for American unpreparedness to the top commanders in Hawaii, Admiral Husband Kimmel and Lieutenant General Walter Short, declaring them guilty of "dereliction of duty." This seems to have jolted the already anxious DeWitt, who had been dreading a debacle similar to what happened in Hawaii if the Japanese struck at the still woefully unprepared Pacific Coast. One of DeWitt's biggest fears was to share the fate of Walter Short.

The Roberts Commission report also made mention of a network of Japanese spies and fifth columnists in Oahu, which soured public opinion against the Japanese on the Pacific Coast even further. Sacramento governor Culbert Olson said that the people of his state, reacting to the Roberts Commission report, "feel like they're living in the midst of enemies. They don't trust the Japanese, none of them."

Fearful constituents on the West Coast pressed their Congressmen and Senators for federal action, and these legislators soon became the most vocal advocates of the removal of Japanese and Japanese-Americans from their districts and states. In the Senate, for example, recently-appointed first term Washington Democrat Monrad "Mon" Wallgren, asked "that the War Department be given full and immediate power to clear all strategic areas of enemy aliens, 'dual citizens,' their families, and their children—even though the children may be U.S. citizens—and place them in internment camps." Congressman John Costello, a Southern California Democrat, told the House of Representatives that "if we don't move in advance of...sabotage, Pearl Harbor will be insignificant to what will happen here. All of the Japanese should be moved out of the area for their own good as well as ours."

Among the first of those within the top leadership of the Army to take the Japanese fifth column threat seriously was Major General Allen Gullion. Born in Kentucky, he had graduated from West Point in 1905 and from the University of Kentucky Law School in 1914. Thereafter, he had been a military attorney, rising through the ranks of the Judge Advocate General's Corps until 1937, when he became the Judge Advocate

General, the Army's top lawyer. In 1941, as the Army mobilized for possible entry into the war, the office of Provost Marshal was activated, Gullion became Provost Marshal General, the U.S. Army's top law enforcement officer and a man with direct access to the chief of staff, General George Marshall.

Gullion had known DeWitt since they had served together before World War I, and he took notice of his old friend's assessment of the dire tactical situation on the Pacific Coast. When he read of DeWitt's suggestion on December 19 that all citizens of the Axis powers over the age of fourteen ought to be "removed" to locations inland of the Pacific Coast and kept "under restraint," the wheels apparently started turning in Gullion's mind.

A week later, on the day after Christmas, Gullion telephoned his friend. As an attorney, he was in a position to explain to DeWitt that there *was* legal authority for doing as he had suggested. The presidential proclamations of December 7–8 had defined Axis nationals as "alien enemies," and made them subject to "summary apprehension" in the case of the Japanese, and "liable to be apprehended, restrained, secured, and removed," in the case of Germans and Italians. Gullion was most concerned about the Japanese.

While the proclamations did not apply to American-born children of foreign nationals, Gullion drew no distinction between *issei* and *nisei* and he urged DeWitt to consider removing them all.

As nervous as he was about his precarious tactical situation on the Pacific Coast, DeWitt rejected Gullion's idea. "I'm very doubtful that it would be common sense procedure to try and intern 117,000 Japanese in this theater," DeWitt told his old friend, insisting that he wanted to detain only the *issei*. "An American citizen, after all, is an American citizen. And while they all may not be loyal, I think we can weed the disloyal out of the loyal and lock them up if necessary." Then too, there were the practical, logistical concerns related to uprooting, moving, and interning so many people. In addition to around forty-five thousand non-citizen Japanese, there were twenty-two thousand foreign-born Germans and fifty-eight thousand Italians.

If Gullion was dismissive of the legal implications of internment of American citizens, Attorney General Francis Biddle was not. For both political and practical reasons, he was content to have the FBI chasing spies and saboteurs, but he did not want to go too far toward a potential collision with the Fourteenth Amendment.

Sharing Biddle's point of view within the Justice Department were men such as Assistant Attorney General James Rowe and Edward Ennis, both of whom were strong proponents of the civil rights granted by the Fourteenth Amendment. Knowing how Ennis felt, Biddle named him as the director of the newly-formed Alien Enemy Control Program. On New Year's Eve, hoping to head off the more draconian actions that he knew Gullion to be discussing with DeWitt, Biddle ratcheted up the restrictions on enemy aliens himself. He issued a decree drastically restricting travel outside the "municipality" in which aliens lived, worked or attended school, requiring them to obtain written permission from the nearest U.S. Attorney to travel farther, and prohibiting them from traveling by air.

Biddle also decided that it was prudent to assert a strong civilian Justice Department presence to temper the influence of Gullion on DeWitt and others in the Army on the West Coast. So, as the West Coast civilian coordinator of the newly formed Alien Enemy Control Program, which was managed by the Justice Department, Biddle picked Tom Campbell Clark. An antitrust litigator and former special assistant to Biddle, Clark had headed the West Coast office of the Justice Department's antitrust division since 1940, and was ideally placed to be Biddle's man on the ground and keep an eye on DeWitt.

What Biddle apparently did not realize was that the man he had picked to restrain any move toward internment fully shared the concerns of those who were beginning to advocate *for* internment. Clark's daily interactions with local officials had convinced him that the people on the Pacific Coast would demand nothing less than the strong approach being advocated by Governor Culbert Olson and Attorney General Earl Warren—and that this was the right thing to do.

In California, Olson had formally requested federal permission to begin revoking business and professional licenses from enemy alien doctors, dentists, barbers and business owners, while his State Board of Equalization had already suspended liquor licenses of "enemy alien" retailers. Earl Warren had declared "open warfare against subversive Japanese organizations," explaining that "it's impossible to distinguish between dangerous enemy aliens, of which we are sure there are many here, and Japanese-American citizens genuinely loyal to the US." He opened his campaign with a San Francisco conference attended by more than a hundred district attorneys, sheriffs and police chiefs.

Meanwhile, Gullion had put his own man on the ground at the Presidio to further influence DeWitt. A West Coast attorney, Major Karl Bendetsen had attended Stanford University and had joined a San Francisco law firm. An Army reservist, he had been called to active duty in 1940 as a lawyer in Gullion's office, but he quickly became his boss's favorite troubleshooter. When the war began, Bendetsen had just returned to the nation's capital after a trip to Hawaii to consult on a never-implemented plan for the internment of Japanese-Americans there.

One of the first men to whom Bendetsen was introduced when he reached the Presidio was Victor Hansen of DeWitt's G-3 staff, who recalled him as "a very ambitious young man, politically astute, [who quickly] gained favor with General DeWitt."

On January 4, Clark and Bendetsen met in DeWitt's office to map out the measures that would alter the lives of Japanese-Americans across the Pacific Coast. The idea was to compile a list of zones, including "forbidden zones," from which enemy aliens were to be removed completely by February 24, and "restricted zones," in which aliens could live, although they were subject to curfews and other limitations. No exemptions for political or religious refugees—including Jewish exiles from Nazi Germany—were to be allowed.

On January 29, the Justice Department announced the first twenty-nine forbidden zones, ranging from airports to waterfronts, across the Pacific Coast states. According to the announcement, these zones, selected "after a long study conducted by Lieutenant General John L. DeWitt... were only the beginning."

DeWitt initially had seen the Japanese threat to the Pacific Coast as one from without—one that took the form of air raids and submarine attacks—but he had now become obsessed with a fear of the threat from within. The constant reports of unseen enemy agents or fifth columnists signaling to submarines prowling off the coast only heightened those concerns.

Victor Hansen, who was close to DeWitt during this period, recalled the general's persistent preoccupation with sabotage and what he'd be asked by Washington if it occurred. He paraphrased the General's frequent comments in which he asked rhetorically, "Should there be sabotage, what did I do to prevent it?"

DeWitt had secondarily embraced the fear of dangers within, while for General Short in Hawaii, the fear of sabotage had been his first concern. This had pushed him to the point of ordering that the USAAF interceptors on Hickam Field be lined up wingtip-to-wingtip in the open to make them easier to guard against saboteurs, which made them easy targets for Japanese pilots on December 7. The irony was that, while he addressed the threat from within, Short had been oblivious to the threat from outside. His inaction, as perceived by the Roberts Commission, and actions such as running his radar stations only four hours a day, were what resulted in Short's being cited for dereliction of duty.

The disgrace that had befallen Short, and the fear of this happening to him, were among DeWitt's greatest motivators. As illustrated by the anecdote related by Hansen, DeWitt was determined that he would not suffer that form of humiliation, and this concern overwhelmed his initial reluctance to act against Japanese-Americans.

On February 11, DeWitt officially recommended a complete removal of all people of Japanese descent from the areas west of the Cascades and the Sierra Nevada, asserting that "the Japanese race is an enemy race and while many second and third generation Japanese born on United States soil…the racial strains are undiluted…There are indications that these are organized and ready for concerted action at a favorable opportunity. The very fact that no sabotage has taken place to date is a disturbing and confirming indication that such action will be taken."

By that time, the number of forbidden zones on the Justice Department lists had increased to more than 120, including seven in Washington and two dozen in Oregon—such as the areas around the Columbia River dams. The deadline for leaving the newly prescribed zones was February 15, a week earlier than for zones announced in January.

"I am confident that the program…will receive the cooperation of the public, including the aliens involved," Biddle said ominously. "The exclusion of aliens from the prohibited areas will not only aid national defense but also will protect the aliens themselves."

Among the things the *San Francisco Chronicle* predicted the new rules would do was to "rout approximately 1,400 Italians from the 2,000 men employed in San Francisco's $500,000-a-year fishing industry" because it was located on the strategically important waterfront.

Fred Duerr of the *Chronicle* went down to Fisherman's Wharf, where "the shadow of army transports has fallen like a blight across once lively scenes [and] fishing boats stand idle under the grim eye of armed sentries [and] where old men stand in little knots of twos and threes."

Duerr spoke to Luciano Maniscalco, age fifty-eight, who resided in the restricted zone. He had been fishing out of the Wharf since he was eighteen, and who had three sons in uniform. He explained that he never became a citizen because he couldn't write and that he couldn't attend school without papers. Duerr also spoke with Giuseppe DiMaggio, the father of New York Yankees star hitter Joe DiMaggio, who was also an alien—and who was now required to leave the home where his three sons, each now a major league ballplayer, grew up. Stories like this could also be found on waterfronts from Seattle to San Diego.

Widely covered in the press was the eviction of Adelaide "Grandma" Firpo, who immigrated to Alameda, California from Genoa in 1876 at the age of four, and who had spent her life working in vegetable fields and raising her family. Her sons had served in the Army in World War I, and her grandson was now in the Navy. The naval air station in Alameda made it a forbidden zone.

Also forbidden because of its proximity to naval operations was Terminal Island in Los Angeles Harbor, where around 2,200 Japanese-Americans made their homes. On February 2, FBI agents, backed by deputies from Sheriff Eugene Biscailuz's department, descended on the island, taking 336 *issei* men, mainly fishermen, into custody without resistance. "I'm sort of glad this happened," one man observed grimly. "If anything happens here now in the way of sabotage, I know they can't blame me."

Harry Masai, a naturalized United States citizen who had served in the U.S. Army Coast Artillery Corps in World War I, said "that's our contribution to the war. We have no resentment."

With the biggest *nihonmachi* in the country located within his city, Los Angeles mayor Fletcher Bowron was anxious for the other shoe of internment drop. "Los Angeles has the largest Japanese population in the United States," Bowron said publicly. "We're particularly concerned about those near our airplane factories. We're not hysterical, but we have been patiently waiting for some solution. This Japanese problem is critical." On February 12, he hurried up to San Francisco for a closed-door meeting with DeWitt, as well as with Tom Clark and Earl Warren. In it, he formally demanded the internment of the entire Japanese and Japanese-American population of Los Angeles.

Towing Biddle's line, Clark said that the Justice Department was not ready to go as far as to recommend martial law. Though the Pacific Coast was technically a theater of war, President Roosevelt resisted a groundswell of support for declaring martial law as had been imposed in Hawaii after the attacks in December.

Tom Clark did promise, however, that "if at any time the Department of Justice cannot carry out the requests of the Army and Navy, then I will recommend that restricted martial law be inaugurated…The Army and Navy are charged with the protection of the Western war zone and know what they want. I will not recommend any other action unless they feel additional steps are necessary."

"I don't know that there is a necessity for martial law, but something must be done," Warren told reporters. "Since the [federal] government declared [the Pacific Coast] a war zone, the government must believe there is grave danger here. If that is true, in my mind, we ought to do everything we can to make the area secure. But that should be a military problem. The Army should say who's to be admitted and who isn't."

Though the meeting took place a short walk from San Francisco City Hall office, Angelo Rossi was conspicuously absent. Nor was Mayor Earl Riley of Portland at the meeting, but he had already made it quite clear that he wanted to see the federal government take the lead in bold measures to head off sabotage.

"Full responsibility for the situation on the coast rests with the federal government," said Riley. "The Pacific Coast is as wide open to a fifth column attack as Pearl Harbor on December 7.... know a few things that can't go in the press. I believe, on the basis of that knowledge, that the only reason the fifth column haven't struck so far is because their respective governments haven't given them the go ahead."

On February 13, Rear Admiral Ralston Holmes of the 11th Naval District placed Terminal Island under direct Navy control.

By then, Tom Clark had been summoned by Biddle to Washington, D.C., where people were starting to share the concerns that were dominating official circles on the Pacific Coast, and, thus, which could not be ignored. When asked by Kyle Palmer of the *Los Angeles Times* whether he thought that the people on the Pacific Coast were panicky, Biddle replied that "panicky is too strong a term...the people on the Coast have a very strong feeling that the Japanese situation is dangerous."

On February 17, Francis Biddle hosted a meeting at his own home in Washington, D.C. Here, the "Japanese situation" would be debated for one last time by the opposing lawyers from the Justice Department and the U.S. Army, and a final decision would be made.

Challenging internment were Justice Department attorneys James Rowe and Edward Ennis, handpicked by Biddle. Representing the hard line of the Army were Allen Gullion and Karl Bendetsen. With them at the meeting was John McCloy, Assistant Secretary of War, representing his boss, Henry Stimson.

Since January, Bendetsen had been convinced that a massive internment was the only solution, and he had returned to Washington determined to make it happen. Now that DeWitt had spoken, and had spoken of an "enemy race" which was "organized and ready for concerted action," there was nothing to stand in Bendetsen's arguments now had the imprimatur of the theater commander.

Confident in his position, Bendetsen had been drafting an executive order for Roosevelt's signature that would put DeWitt in charge of defining the zones and what would happen to Japanese-Americans within those zones.

Ennis and Rowe presented an argument that hinged on the rights of citizens under the Fourteenth Amendment. So, when Gullion produced the executive order which Bendetsen had drafted, they were incredulous. Rowe even laughed out loud, thinking they were joking.

Finally, Biddle explained that the concerns voiced by so many West Coast politicians—local, state, and federal—were so loud and so insistent that the President could not ignore them. A consummate political operator, Franklin Roosevelt had decided to swim with the tide, and had agreed, earlier that day, to side with the Army rather than with the Justice Department. The President had spoken, and Biddle would support him.

On February 19, Roosevelt signed Bendetsen's document, which became Executive Order 9066. It authorized Secretary of War Henry Stimson and "the Military Commanders whom he may from time to time designate, whenever he or any designated Commander deems such action necessary or desirable, to prescribe military areas in such places and of such extent as he or the appropriate Military Commander may determine, from which any or all persons may be excluded, and with respect to which, the right of any person to enter, remain in, or leave shall be subject to whatever restrictions the Secretary of War or the appropriate Military Commander may impose in his discretion."

Roosevelt had given the people and the politicians of the Pacific Coast that for which they clamored, and had given the men of the War Department what they wanted and the broad authority to go about it. Despite delegating such sweeping powers to a military commander, Roosevelt continued to resist the calls for him to impose martial law on the Pacific Coast.

It is interesting to note that in Hawaii, where martial law *had been* imposed in December, Lieutenant General Delos Emmons, the Army commander who replaced Walter Short, actively *resisted* any call to the round-up and intern Japanese-Americans. In fact, the Army's all-*nisei* 100th Infantry Battalion, which later served with distinction in the Mediterranean Theater, was originally formed out of Hawaii National Guard units. General Marshall authorized the creation of the 100th in May 1942 and, later, the famous 442nd Regimental Combat Team, comprised also of *nisei* men from the mainland who had joined the U.S. Army despite internment.

In approving the creation of the 100th, Marshall wrote succinctly that "I don't think you can permanently proscribe a lot of American citizens because of their racial origin."

One of the most awkward situations involving Japanese-Americans was that of those men who lived and worked close to General DeWitt at the Presidio of San Francisco, specifically, at the Japanese language school that had been created on the eve of Pearl Harbor. With Captain Kai Rasmussen as its commandant, it had grown substantially and was officially designated as the Military Intelligence Service Language School (MISLS). It was busily—and secretly—turning out Japanese-speaking linguists for the Army's Military Intelligence Service (MIS). The MISLS was performing a vital service, but there was a problem. Almost all of its students, and much of its staff, were Japanese-Americans.

When Rasmussen opened the school in 1941, it had made sense logistically to locate a Japanese language school in San Francisco, a major West Coast city with a large Japanese-American population from which recruits could be conveniently drawn. By the spring of 1942, however, maintaining such an institution within California was simply impossible. After the school's first class graduated in May 1942, the school was relocated to a former Civilian Conservation Corps facility at Camp Savage in Minnesota, far from the forbidden Pacific Coast.

Within days of the signing of Executive Order 9066, Karl Bendetsen had been promoted to full colonel and was elevated to become DeWitt's chief of staff for Civil Affairs (or G-5 in Army vernacular). In March, he became director of the newly-created Wartime Civil Control Administration (WCCA), and took over a whole floor of the Hotel Whitcomb on San Francisco's Market Street for his headquarters.

Reflecting upon Bendetsen in this new role, Victor Hansen recalled that "General DeWitt became very fond of him and had him handle his public relations with the Congress and with the civil authorities on the coast on getting support for Japanese evacuation. Bendetsen, I assume, carried out his instructions, but sometimes I think Bendetsen went a little further than he was authorized...[but] DeWitt gave Bendetsen quite a free hand."

Tom Clark, who headed WCCA's civilian staff, effectively became DeWitt's civilian chief of staff, the man who dealt with the civilian organizations that would be involved in the internment process. Clark became the West Coast coordinator of the Justice Department's Alien Enemy Control Program, and the man who would be tasked with running the evacuation of the Japanese-Americans. The actual internment would be handled by yet another bureaucracy, the War Relocation Authority (WRA), which would be directed by Milton Eisenhower, a former New Deal spokesman who had served as Director of Information at the Department of Agriculture and was the younger brother of General Dwight Eisenhower.

On March 3, the *San Francisco News* reported that "the entire California, Washington and Oregon coasts, as well as the Southern sections of California and Arizona along the Mexican border, today were designated Military Area No. 1 by Lieut. Gen. John L. DeWitt...From this vast area, General DeWitt announced 'such persons or classes of

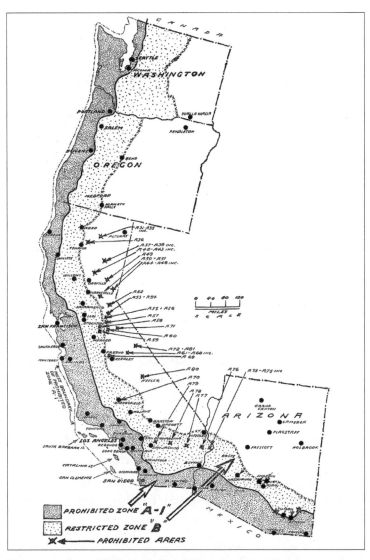

This official map of the Pacific Coast exclusion zones was released by the Western Defense Command in March 1942. The Forbidden, or Prohibited Zone, known alternately as Military Area No. 1 or Zone A-1, was a coastal strip west of U.S. Route 101 in California, south of Eureka and west of U.S. Route 99 in areas to the north. Military Area No. 2, or Zone B, was the Restricted Zone to the east, which was generally west of Route 99 in California. The arrows point to Prohibited sites outside Zone A-1, which included power plants, hydroelectric stations, dams, and water department facilities such as pumping stations. The Prohibited perimeter around each of these was about one mile.

U.S. Army, Western Defense Command

persons as the situation may require will by subsequent proclamation be excluded.'"

Gone now were the dozens of forbidden and restricted zones, replaced by two military areas in which DeWitt was the absolute authority. Military Area No. 1, also seen listed as "Zone A-1," was a forbidden zone generally along a coastal strip west of U.S. Route 101 in California south of Eureka and west of U.S. Route 99 in the areas to the north. Military Area No. 2, or "Zone B," was a restricted zone of similar width that adjoined the eastern side of Area No. 1.

Initially, it was announced that people from Area No. 1 could move to Area No. 2, but soon, Japanese-Americans were ordered out of the Pacific Coast states entirely. With the first zone designations in February came a short period of "voluntary relocation." People were allowed to take with them whatever they wished, to travel on their own, and to go wherever they wished outside the forbidden zones—so long as they *did* move and were gone by the specified deadlines.

On March 24, however, DeWitt signed the first of many targeted mandatory exclusion orders. The voluntary relocation was superseded by enforced relocation of Japanese-Americans—with only whatever possessions they could carry—to WRA "Relocation Centers." The soft touch had ended.

"General DeWitt has warned the Japanese they must immediately settle their affairs," Bendetsen told the media the next day. "Any neglect of crops is sabotage. A chain of 64 services has been opened throughout Military Area No. 1 to help Japanese settle their affairs. If they do not take advantage while there is time, they must suffer any property losses that ensue."

By March 29, with the last of the voluntary evacuees already gone, convoys of army trucks and commandeered buses began arriving in Japanese-American communities to take people away.

Exclusion Order No. 1 ordered the nearly 300 Japanese-Americans on Bainbridge Island in Washington's Puget Sound to be off the island by noon on March 30 or they would be removed. They had this dubious distinction of being the first because of their proximity to the nearby

Navy Yard Puget Sound in Bremerton, and because of the presence on the island of a mysterious "annex" to the Japanese consulate in Seattle that was situated on Rich Passage, which connects the Navy Yard to the Sound. Coincidentally, the so-called annex was only about a mile from the U.S. Navy's top secret Station S at the U.S. Army's Fort Ward, which was one of the key locations for used to intercept Imperial Japanese diplomatic radio traffic.

DeWitt's Exclusion Order No. 2, issued on March 30, affected people in coastal Los Angeles County. Other orders, two dozen within a month, followed in rapid succession until all of the Japanese-Americans, except those in the two internment camps located in California, were gone from the Pacific Coast states.

Although the expulsion of Japanese-Americans had removed the threat of a fifth column from his theater, it did not lessen any of the other concerns DeWitt had about its vulnerability to attack—or invasion.

FOURTEEN

The Cactuses of Goleta

On the evening of Monday February 23, 1942, millions of Americans gathered around their radios to listen to one of President Franklin Roosevelt's familiar and folksy Fireside Chats.

Because George Washington's birthday had fallen on the day before, Roosevelt chose comparisons of America in 1942 to Washington's difficult winter at Valley Forge as his theme. He called it "a most appropriate occasion for us to talk with each other about things as they are today and things as we know they shall be in the future...Washington's conduct in those hard times has provided the model for all Americans ever since—a model of moral stamina. He held to his course, as it had been charted in the Declaration of Independence."

As he was reminding people that "the broad oceans which have been heralded in the past as our protection from attack have become endless battlefields on which we are constantly being challenged by our enemies," on the Pacific Coast, enemy began the first bombardment of the United States by a foreign power since the War of 1812.

ᴰ◖

In the November 21, 1982, issue of *Parade* magazine, a small story appeared in a column edited by screenwriter and novelist Irving Wallace, along with his son and daughter. This story, whose source was not given, has been widely repeated since, and may well have been true, despite its apocryphal tinge. It told of an incident that had occurred in Santa Barbara County, California sometime in the 1930s. Kozo Nishino was the captain of a Japanese oil tanker that came to the United States to load crude oil at the Ellwood oil fields, near the town of Goleta, about eight miles north of Santa Barbara.

As Wallace told it, as Nishio was coming up from the beach to a formal welcoming ceremony for his crew, he "slipped and fell into a prickly-pear cactus. Workers on a nearby oil rig broke into guffaws at the sight of the proud commander having cactus spines plucked from his posterior. Then and there, the humiliated Nishino swore to get even."

Whether this engaging element of local folklore is merely that, or is in fact a true story, Kozo Nishio *did* show up offshore from the fields of Ellwood on the night of on February 23, 1942. This time, however, he commanded the submarine *I-17*. In December 1941, Nishio and *I-17* had attacked two American freighters off Cape Mendocino, and now he was back. Nishio had arrived from Kwajalein on February 19, when he made an audacious covert landing on Point Loma at the entrance to San Diego Bay without being detected to check his position, and had headed north.

"At 7:10 p.m. one large submarine came to the surface about one mile offshore and fired approximately 15 shells from a deck gun," F. W. Borden, the superintendent of the Bankline Oil Company refinery in the Ellwood fields told 11th Naval District investigators. "One direct hit was registered on a well causing minor damage to the pumping unit and the derrick. There were several close misses on a crude oil storage tank and a gasoline plant. Apparently no damage was caused by those shells...

no fires were started as a result of the firing. No tanks were hit. From fragments of shell on the ground it is believed a four or five-inch gun was used. The firing was done quite leisurely, apparently only one gun being used."

In the few homes dotting this sparsely populated stretch of the coast, many people were listening to Roosevelt's speech when the shells began to fall. A California Highway Patrolman stopped traffic on U.S. Route 101, the main coastal highway, which ran through the Ellwood fields, and the Southern Pacific Railroad halted its trains on the parallel tracks.

"The first explosion sounded distant," recalled Lawrence Wheeler, the owner of Wheeler's Inn, a motel on the ocean side of Route 101. "They grew nearer and nearer. Beginning with the third, they shook our building. I rushed out of the house and saw a shell explode against the cliff about three fourths of a mile from our place...Another shell whiled over my head and landed in the canyon on the Staniss place, which is across the road from us."

"I was scared to death," added Mrs. Wheeler. "Great fountains of dirt were shot into the air, just like pictures in the newsreels. The shelling was so heavy it shook the house, just like an earthquake."

Over the course of twenty-five minutes, *I-17* had fired with seventeen rounds, after which Nishio ordered the boat to submerge and leave the area. During the barrage, no one ashore heard any American aircraft coming to attack the attacker, so there was an eerie sense of vulnerability and abandonment as the huge submarine disappeared beneath the waves.

Through the night, there were numerous calls to local authorities from people who thought they had seen flashing signal lights from boats in the Santa Barbara Channel. As with stories of flashing lights that had populated news reports since December, these were attributed to "enemy agents."

Undersecretary of State Sumner Welles observed hopefully that "such stunts are hardly likely to have any effect on this country's war effort." While he may have been correct about the physical effects—damage was estimated at $500—it *did* have a serious effect on the morale of Pacific

Coast residents, and it set the stage for the reaction the following night to what became known as the Battle of Los Angeles.

According to an obscure oral history document in the collection of the El Fornio Historical Society, *I-17* apparently lingered in the vicinity of Goleta overnight. The following morning, Jess Ueda, a *nisei* farmer went out to check his six acres of strawberry fields located along the coast near the tiny town of El Fornio. Probably on his mind more than the attack at Ellwood was the fact that his family had been summoned to turn themselves in for expulsion from the land that he and his father before him had farmed.

When Ueda's dogs began to bark, he noticed that they were reacting to a group of five men standing next to a small boat on the beach below. He assumed that they were fishermen. He followed his dogs as they ran toward the men, and finally he could see that they were wearing Japanese Navy uniforms. As he reached them, he heard them speaking Japanese. Ueda had learned some of the language from his father, but he was not fluent.

Soon, they were joined by Ueda's wife Jane and some of the farm workers whom he employed. One of these men spoke fluent Japanese and engaged the sailors in conversation.

"I think they simply wanted to set foot on American soil and then make a clean getaway," Ueda recalled. "They had come all the way across the Pacific in that submarine. In all of my astonishment, I started thinking—and I could see my wife, who was born here like me, felt the same way—here we are trying to explain to authorities that we are loyal Americans, with no political connection to Japan, and suddenly here I am talking to the Japanese military! I politely asked them to go. And they obliged…One of my colleagues brought them strawberries, which they took on board the boat, although I strictly forbade them from taking any pictures. Can you imagine? We were fortunate the light was bad because one of them had a camera…. The whole encounter lasted about five minutes, really. A long five minutes!"

The Ueda family surrendered for internment on May 7 and spent the duration of the war at the Manzanar Relocation Center, where their second son, John, was born. It was not until 1982 that John, now an attorney, finally won the battle to reclaim the family's strawberry farm.

After the landing, *I-17* headed north, mounting an abortive attack against the 8,298-ton Standard Oil Company tanker *William H. Berg* on March 1, and coasting as far north as Oregon's Cape Blanco before returning to the waters off San Francisco. On March 12, *I-17* departed for Japan.

After failing to attack *I-17* on February 23, the IV Interceptor Command, then in the process of a leadership change from Brigadier General William Ord Ryan to Brigadier General William Ellsworth Kepner, put its units across Southern California on alert. At 7:18 p.m. on February 24, roughly twenty-four hours after the attack at Goleta, Ryan told the AWS to tell the media that his command was at a "state of readiness." This was certainly in reaction to the night before when no aircraft were heard to respond to the shelling. The all-clear signaling an end to this show of force came three hours and five minutes later at 10:23 p.m.

The Battle of Los Angeles would begin less than five hours later.

FIFTEEN

The Battle of Los Angeles

Several times in December, and a few more times in January, uniden-tified aircraft were seen, heard, or probably just imagined over San Francisco, Los Angeles, and other places along the Pacific Coast. Each time, their presence, either real or perceived, went unchallenged by the Army's antiaircraft guns. On the night of February 24–25, 1942, that would change.

As had been the case during the blackout of December 11, there was something that made Angelinos believe that tonight would be different, that tonight was not just another blackout.

A continuous stream of bad news from the Far East had darkened the public mood. Weeks of reports of Allied defeats—Singapore had fallen just a week earlier—and FBI raids on what seemed to be an infinite underworld of Japanese espionage had taken their toll on the public psyche. Then the Japanese had shelled Goleta, which constituted an actual attack against American soil. In the darkness of February 24–25, therefore, many people in the Los Angeles area had ample reason to think the Japanese were coming, and they were coming *soon.*

The yellow alert, warning that attackers were one hundred miles or twenty minutes away, came at 7:18 p.m. Curiously, this was exactly the same moment that the IV Interceptor Command had launched a show of force—probably meant to calm fears and instill confidence—over the Southland. Perhaps, the AWS observers detected the American aircraft, and their reports worked their way through the filter center without being cross-checked.

A blackout was ordered, but the all clear was issued 10:33 p.m. About four hours later, however, things became much more exciting. As Wesley Frank Craven and James Lea Cate note in *The Army Air Forces in World War II*, radar "picked up an unidentified target 120 miles west of Los Angeles." The antiaircraft batteries of the 37th Coastal Artillery Brigade were alerted at 2:15 a.m. and were put on green alert, meaning ready to fire, shortly thereafter. Quoting the daily intelligence summary in the official history of the IV Antiaircraft Command, the radar tracked the approaching targets to within a few miles of the coast, and the regional controller transmitted the blackout order to local authorities at 2:21. Air raid sirens began wailing across the Southland within four minutes. Searchlight batteries sprang into life and soon probed the sky with their stark white light.

Craven and Cate write that "the information center was flooded with reports of 'enemy planes,' even though the mysterious object tracked in from sea seems to have vanished." They go on to say that at 3:06, "a balloon carrying a red flare was seen over Santa Monica and four batteries of antiaircraft artillery opened fire." As the *Los Angeles Times* reported, "the air over Los Angeles erupted like a volcano." The Battle of Los Angeles was on.

The *Times* told of Long Beach police chief Joseph Henry McClelland, atop City Hall beside a Navy observer, watching the passing of "a flight of nine silvery-looking planes from the Redondo Beach area across the land side of Fort MacArthur, and toward Santa Ana and Huntington Beach."

A great many other people claim to have seen aircraft in the sky that night, although the numbers varied greatly. However, after their patrol on the evening of February 24, the American fighters remained on the ground throughout the Battle of Los Angeles. According to the *Fourth Air Force Historical Study III-2* the IV Interceptor Command kept its aircraft out of the action "preferring to await indications of the scale and direction of any attack before committing its limited fighter force."

The balloon mentioned by Craven and Cate and other similar objects were also widely seen, drifting along the coast and inland. Some witnesses thought these might have been escaped barrage balloons, while others insisted they were not. In later years, UFO enthusiasts would, and still do, focus a great deal of attention on this aspect of the night's excitement.

Times reporter Ray Zeman was at his father-in-law's house in Inglewood when the fireworks began, and as the family headed for shelter in the basement, he realized that "this might be the biggest story in years" and that it might center on the huge North American Aviation aircraft factory in the city. He convinced his wife that they ought to try to walk to the Inglewood City Hall. In the dark, they stumbled across two policemen watching the searchlight beams above.

"Have you seen any planes?" Zeman asked.

"Plenty. They must be 25,000 or 30,000 feet high, out of range of the ack-ack guns."

"How many planes?"

"Oh, 150 or 200, I guess. They came in great dark clouds. We haven't heard any bombs dropped, though."

Zeman and his wife continued on their way, and reached the Inglewood Police Station. There, they were met by several officers who had known Mrs. Zeman when she had been a reporter with the *Times*. When they reported what they had heard earlier, the policemen were incredulous.

"Two hundred planes?" one officer replied. "Why those men had hallucinations. There were seven planes, maybe nine."

"Seven," the jail matron interjected. "I counted them."

Suddenly, there was a roar from a nearby antiaircraft gun, and then another.

The policemen told the Zemans where the guns were hidden, but hastened to add that it was a "military secret," admonishing Zeman, "Don't print that."

Suddenly, there was a bright flash, which one man interpreted as a flare dropped by a submarine-hunting airplane. Another insisted that it was just an especially bright antiaircraft shell.

Just as unexpectedly, there was a moment of silence in the immediate area and as cigarettes were extinguished to comply with the blackout, talk turned to the policemen having witnessed some air-to-air combat between American and hostile aircraft. Others, however, insisted that there had been no such thing.

After a few moments, distant searchlights began stabbing the sky in the vicinity of Terminal Island the harbor at the Port of Los Angeles, and there was another round of antiaircraft file in that direction.

Zeman found a phone booth and attempted to phone the *Times* offices to report his story, but the telephone operator insisted that he give her the number from which he was calling.

"It's dark in here," he explained, his tone suggesting the unspoken qualification that they were in the midst of a blackout. There was a nearby explosion as the operator finally relented, and put the call through.

Across Los Angeles, another *Times* reporter, Marvin Miles, looked upward, watching as "objects in the sky slowly moved on, caught in the center of the [search] lights like the hub of a bicycle wheel surrounded by gleaming spokes."

He went out onto the street to join his neighbors who had also been rudely awakened. In the intermittent light from the sky, he took notes of their comments.

"It's a whole squadron."

"No, it's a blimp. It must be because it's moving so slowly."

"I hear planes."

"No you don't; that's a truck up the street."

"Where are the planes then?"

"Dunno. Must be up there, though."

"Wonder why they picked such a clear night for a raid?"

"They're probably from a carrier."

"Naw, I'll bet they're from a secret air base down south [in Mexico] somewhere."

"Maybe it's a test."

"Test, hell! You don't throw that much metal into the air unless you're fixing on knocking something down!"

Gene Sherman of the *Times* reported on the public's reaction that night, writing that "the people you met weren't rattled or scared or particularly nervous. But their eyes were turned unbelievingly southward toward those [searchlights] and bursting shells. They looked up. And they were awake—wide, wide awake."

A Los Angeles Police Department motorcycle officer told Sherman, "Well, this might do the folks around here some good. This ain't no picnic and now they know it."

Later, during a ride-along in a squad car, Sherman and his hosts passed a brightly illuminated store on Wilshire Boulevard. Some bystanders asked what they should do, and the police gave them the green light to do what it took and they went looking for rocks.

In Huntington Park, a dozen store owners were later cited for leaving their display lights on through the blackout. In Santa Ana, twenty-one shopkeepers were fined $50 apiece for similar violations, but Judge Donald Harwood suspended $45 and let them off after a reproachful warning. The long arm of the law reached the other way, too. At First and Broadway in Los Angeles, a man was picked up for breaking out the window of Mandel's Jewelry. He claimed that he was enforcing the blackout, but the arresting officers suspected he had "another motive." Meanwhile, a dozen Japanese and Japanese-Americans—from Gardena to Glendale—were arrested for being associated with "suspicious lights" which witnesses thought might be attempts to signal enemy aircraft.

Area hospitals reported that fourteen babies had been born during the battle, but there had been numerous injuries and five fatalities because of the blackout. In Arcadia, for example, a milk truck driven by Goldie

Wagner collided with the passenger car driven by Harry Klein, whose wife Zeulah was fatally injured.

As the antiaircraft shells were bursting above the Southland, two volunteer civil defense volunteers died of heart attacks in the line of duty. Henry Ayers, age sixty, was driving through Hollywood, his station wagon full of ammunition for his State Guard unit, when he slumped over his steering wheel and died. George Weil, age thirty-six, was on duty as an AWS warden when he was stricken. He later died at home. Several other air raid wardens suffered injuries, some serious, while enforcing the blackout or making their way through the darkness.

Blanche Sedgewick and her fourteen-year-old niece got out of bed to look at the fireworks, and while they watched, an enormous piece of shrapnel plummeted out of the sky and crashed into the bedroom they had just vacated. In Long Beach, the kitchen and home office of Dr. Franklin Stewart were demolished by falling debris—perhaps an unexploded shell. Numerous similar reports came in to police and the news media during the ensuing days.

The gunfire tapered off around 4:15 a.m., and at last daylight replaced the searchlights. All clear signals were sounded between 7:21 and 8:34 a.m.

The next morning, the public transit system was in disarray because more than two dozen streetcars had been stranded during the blackout. Los Angeles deputy police chief Bernard Caldwell reported the "worst transportation tie-up in the history of the city" as people who usually used public transportation attempted to drive to work. Looking at the bright side, Los Angeles deputy police chief Ross McDonald, in charge of the department's "war activities," credited the ten thousand wardens with "helping to prevent countless accidents in traffic during the blackout."

Craven and Cate report that the 37th Coastal Artillery fired 1,440 rounds of antiaircraft artillery ammunition, and many sources recall .50 caliber machine guns also being in action.

In San Francisco, General DeWitt told Major General Fulton Q. C. Gardner, commander of the IV Anti-Aircraft Command, of his "gratification at the readiness of the officers and men to meet possible enemy action, as demonstrated by their alertness and ability to promptly open fire when called upon to do so during the blackout of the Los Angeles area…reports indicate very definitely that the officers and men of the antiaircraft units were prepared when the test came to meet with fire a hostile attack."

But, had there been any "enemy action?" Were there *really* enemy airplanes in the sky to be hit? Bill Henry of the *Los Angeles Times*, and Scripps-Howard columnist Ernie Pyle—later to become a legendary war reporter—both wrote emphatically that they had seen no aircraft at all. For many of those who went through the Battle of Los Angeles, however, there was no doubt. But where did these aircraft come from and where did they go?

The official word from the Western Defense Command in San Francisco via Major General Walter Wilson's Southern Sector headquarters in Pasadena was that "the aircraft which caused the blackout in the Los Angeles area for several hours this a.m. have not been identified…Although reports were conflicting and every effort is being made to ascertain the facts, it is clear that no bombs were dropped and no planes were shot down."

❧

The second phase of the battle would be waged in Washington, D.C. Secretary of War Henry Stimson told the Associated Press that there were "probably" unidentified aircraft over Los Angeles, *but* Navy Secretary Frank Knox announced that it was a "false alarm."

"There were no planes over Los Angeles last night; at least that's our understanding," Knox told a press conference. "None have been found and a very wide reconnaissance has been carried out."

The Associated Press reported that Knox used the opportunity to reiterate his belief that vital industries, specifically aircraft factories, would eventually have to be relocated to "safer inland regions." However, in his comments to the Associated Press, Knox wrote off the Battle of Los Angeles as a case of "jittery nerves."

"Whose nerves, Mr. Knox? The public's or the Army's?" The *Los Angeles Times* indignantly replied in a front-page editorial. "And just where, and the question is a fair one, did Secretary Knox get the information leading him to believe that the air raid was a phony? The official and only official source of such information in this case is the Army. What the Army's information was has been made very clear, both by its own statement and by its vigorous action. It is not for a moment to be believed that the Army did not act in good faith in the matter. It is equally incredible that Secretary Knox would even remotely intimate anything of the sort. Least comprehensible of all is what the Navy head sees in the case to abet the desire of some government officials and some inland communities to transfer coastal industries to the latter."

Los Angeles county sheriff Eugene Biscailuz took Knox to task, scolding him for "the very great damage done to our Civilian Defense morale by the reported statement...It is highly important that we deal in good faith with thousands of air raid wardens, auxiliary policemen and other volunteers in the defense effort."

Stimson, meanwhile, seemed to have the evidence on his side when it came to his assertion that the enemy incursion was real. Referring to an assessment from DeWitt's Western Defense Command headquarters that came to him by way of Chief of Staff General George Marshall, he said that "as many as 15 planes may have been involved, flying at various speeds from what is officially reported as being 'very slow' to as much as 200 miles an hour, and at an elevation of from 9,000 to 18,000 feet."

Stimson even repeated the widely circulated theory, not discounted by DeWitt's command, that the aircraft had been procured by enemy agents from commercial sources and were being flown from secret land bases, perhaps in Mexico.

"It is reasonable to conclude that if unidentified airplanes were involved, they may be some from commercial sources, operated by enemy agents for the purpose of spreading alarm, disclosing location of antiaircraft positions, or the effectiveness of blackouts. Such a conclusion is supported by [the] varying speed of the operation, and the fact that no bombs were dropped."

As for the antiaircraft barrage, Stimson asked that "perhaps it is better to be too alert than not alert enough. In any case, they were very alert there [in Los Angeles]."

When asked whether his information had originated with DeWitt's Western Defense Command on the Pacific Coast, Stimson explained that it had come to him directly from Chief of Staff Marshall, "and it is evidently a report from out there."

United Press reported that Los Angeles city officials had demanded that "Army, Navy and civilian agencies 'beat the brush' throughout the West for possible [clandestine] air bases. Undersheriff [Arthur] C. Jewell [a thirty-year veteran of the department] speculated that the planes possibly may have come from secret land bases in Mexico, adding that the Mexican government was cooperating to the utmost in searching its territory for such possible bases. Civil authorities in Nevada and Arizona quickly denied the possibility that enemy agents might have secret aircraft bases in their states."

Southern California Republican Congressman Leland Ford was furious when he heard the commercial airplane theory. Said he, "If it was thought that these were commercial planes operated by enemy agents, why [did not] our own planes...go after them, bring them down to a landing, or upon refusal to land, shoot them down, or at least find out where they came from and where they went. In this connection, our people [IV Interceptor Command] know, within a reasonable range, where these planes would have to come from and where they would have to land."

Congressman Ford called for Stimson and Knox to provide a "proper explanation" for what had happened. "Our people ought to know whether this was a practice raid, whether it was a political raid, or what kind of a raid it was," Ford told the House of Representatives, raising some worrisome questions. "Why were unidentified planes fired upon? This was either a practice raid, or a raid to throw a scare into 2,000,000 people, or a mistaken identity raid, or a raid to lay a political foundation to take away from Southern California its industries... [the people of California] are not jittery but are beginning to believe the Army and Navy are."

A Congressional investigation was demanded by the Pacific Coast Congressional delegation, and on March 2, Secretary Knox went to Capitol Hill. Grilled about his "false alarm" comment, Knox walked back his previous statement, telling Congress that he had been "misquoted" or at least misunderstood. He added that since air defense was the Army's job, they should have the last word.

However, that last word was muddled and unclear, as both Army and Navy tempered their initial, emphatic statements. Indeed, in the absence of facts, speculation became rampant.

"Attempts to arrive at an explanation of the event quickly became as involved and mysterious as the 'battle' itself," wrote Craven and Cate when reviewing the incident after the war. "The Army had a hard time making up its mind on the cause of the alert. A report to Washington, made by the Western Defense Command shortly after the raid had ended [and received in Washington at 1:15 p.m. on February 25], indicated that the credibility of reports of an attack had begun to be shaken before the blackout was lifted. This message predicted that developments would prove 'that most previous reports had been greatly exaggerated.'"

Nevertheless, after investigating the matter, the Western Defense Command continued to hold fast to the idea that as many as five unidentified aircraft had been over Los Angeles, despite this making the Army seem inept for its inability to shoot them down.

On February 28, the New York Times weighed in, asking that "if the batteries were firing on nothing at all, as Secretary Knox implies, it is a sign of expensive incompetence and jitters. If the batteries were firing on real planes, some of them as low as 9,000 feet, as Secretary Stimson declares, why were they completely ineffective? Why did no American planes go up to engage them, or even to identify them?"

Craven and Cate point out that "these questions were appropriate, but for the War Department to have answered them in full frankness would have involved an even more complete revelation of the weakness of our air defenses."

When the dust settled, most people who had been there continued to believe that there had been aircraft in the sky that night, though there was never any hard evidence to confirm this. Craven and Cate mention that "at the end of the war, the Japanese stated that they did not send planes over the area at the time of this alert."

That said, the only possible Japanese aircraft that could have attacked the Los Angeles area that night were those carried by Japanese submarines. However, each submarine carried just one, and the *I-17*, which had shelled Goleta the night before, was still in the area and *could have* launched its single aircraft, but there was no other Japanese submarine in the area.

The interpretation of the cause of the Battle of Los Angeles that was advanced in the official history of the IV Antiaircraft Command was that the antiaircraft batteries were reacting to the balloon that had been seen by numerous people on the ground. It was later identified as a "weather balloon," an explanation that would be used for numerous other incidents of unexplained aerial phenomena in the coming decades.

The conflicting initial assessments by Stimson and Knox were never really resolved; therefore, many people have assumed through the years that deliberate government obfuscation was in play. To this day, because of the many mysteries associated with that strange night, the Battle of Los Angeles "cover-up" still attracts its own small cadre of true believers whenever conspiracy theorists congregate.

SIXTEEN

The Boss Out Here

"After a face-to-face chat with Gen. John L. DeWitt, the boss general in the Western States, I feel on good authority to tell you—nothing," Tom Treanor of the *Los Angeles Times* wrote in his March 4 column. He had gone north in the nervous "morning-after" mood that possessed his city of the fuss and fracas of February 25.

"Not only do I feel free to tell you nothing, I am ordered to tell you nothing," Treanor reported. "Gen. DeWitt said that when there is something to be told he will tell you himself. He seems accustomed to obedience, so the chances are I will obey him. Even a secrecy-sealed encounter with Gen. DeWitt is worth a trip to San Francisco. In a military way, he holds us all in the palm of his hand. His is the authority to do what the situation calls for in the Western theater. On his skill and judgment rests the efficiency of our defenses. He is the boss out here."

In the uneasy days of December and throughout the Japanese-American evacuation argument in early 1942, DeWitt had made news. Meanwhile, it is important also to recall that the boss also *managed* and tried to control the news. The trouble was that as much as DeWitt tried to project an image of "the boss general" who had everything under control, the news from overseas overwhelmed that image and the attempts he made to manage the news and the news media. As mentioned before, the initial public mood of determination and optimism that the Japanese would be turned back and defeated in short order had been replaced by a growing sense of dread and rising dismay as grim news of Japanese victories and Allied defeats came to America.

The Imperial Japanese Army and Navy seemed unstoppable. Singapore, Britain's mighty "Gibraltar of the East," had fallen in just one week of fighting in February. All of Malaya and was under Japanese occupation, and the final surrender of the Netherlands's great oil-rich empire in the East Indies came within two weeks of the Battle of Los Angeles. The Japanese captured Rangoon and were already sweeping through the rest of Burma—and toward India. In the Philippines, American and Filipino defenders had been crowded into the toe of the Bataan Peninsula and Corregidor where they were holding on desperately, and the Japanese had moved on to other islands in the Philippine archipelago.

As the news from overseas worsened, uncertainty was manifest at home. Attacks from real Japanese submarines and imaginary Japanese aircraft combined with multiple official statements of the inevitability of enemy strikes increased the feeling of vulnerability. The mood became so tense that on March 5, the Twelfth Naval District issued a "shoot to kill" order to its sentries on the San Francisco waterfront.

The only good news was that a procedure called the "dimout" had superseded the blackout. Asked by the Army to study blackout techniques, Samuel Galloway Hibben, the director of applied lighting at Westinghouse, had concluded that blackouts were disruptive and counterproductive—something that people living on the West Coast knew all too well.

Hibben proceeded to design systems by which subdued lighting in vehicle headlights and a reduction of wattage in building lighting could be substituted for no lighting. He described the process in the April 1942 issue of *Illuminating Engineering* magazine, and it was soon widely adopted on both coasts.

General John DeWitt and Admiral John Greenslade of the Twelfth Naval District ordered an indefinite dimout of 600 miles of California coastline on May 11. Among the measures mandated were that no lights, including traffic lights, could shine upward, and that any lights turned toward the ocean should be blacked out entirely.

Lighthouses shielded their lights so that no light would be shining seaward in order to prevent them from silhouetting passing ships and so making them easier targets for enemy submarines and deny those same submarines a handy navigation aid. Unfortunately, the darkened lighthouses also proved problematic for coastal shipping.

Despite, and arguably *because* of, DeWitt's tight-lipped control of the narrative, a feeling of nervous apprehension pervaded his domain. But DeWitt was not alone in his determination not to part with any detailed information. In the morning after the Battle of Los Angeles, the dispute between the two cabinet secretaries inspired public affairs officers within both the War Department and the Navy Department to want to keep things under control.

Compare for example, the reaction after the Battle of Los Angeles to that of the media and public response to the now little known *second* air raid on Pearl Harbor a week later.

On March 4, in a mission designated as Operation K, two large, long-range Kawanishi H8K flying boats, operating from Wotje in the Marshall Islands had actually attacked Honolulu. Made possible with a clandestine stop at French Frigate Shoals, a remote, uninhabited island between Kauai and Midway to meet refueling submarines, the outbound leg of the mission was nearly 2,500 miles. Over Oahu, their reconnaissance and bombing mission, as well as their interception by American fighters (radar had detected them), was hampered by cloud cover, but they did drop their bombs. This made for some angry finger pointing, but there was little damage and no casualties. Thanks to Army public affairs' management of media relations under the martial law that existed in Hawaii, little was reported of the raid in the stateside press, and what did make it was soon buried on back pages by the bigger news of the fall of the Dutch East Indies and what was imagined as an imminent invasion of Australia.

In late March, as Tom Clark and Karl Bendetsen were wrestling with the logistical problems associated with the uprooting and internment of 120,000 residents of his theater, DeWitt was confronted with an American rite of spring: the opening of the baseball season.

It was widely rumored that DeWitt, who had pushed the Rose Bowl out of state and banned horse racing in California, would cancel the 1942 Pacific Coast League baseball season. On March 24, to the surprise of most, he decided to the contrary. The *Los Angeles Times* reported that "the first bright ray of sunshine broke through the war-clouded sports area of the Pacific Coast sector" as league president and former player W. C. Tuttle announced that the season was on, and that even night games would be allowed so long as the league met "certain conditions relative to lighting and policing," such as quickly extinguishable lighting and measures to prevent traffic jams on major streets.

DeWitt retained his nervousness about large gatherings of people, and he stipulated that crowds at games could not exceed the average numbers from the prewar 1941 season. The San Francisco Seals had once drawn a crowd of more than 16,000, but the team's average attendance had been 3,951. This was exceeded only by the average of 5,650 fans who had turned out to watch the Seattle Rainiers win their third straight championship. The other teams all averaged much less than the 5,000 number which DeWitt had earlier decreed as the maximum size of outdoor crowds on the Pacific Coast.

It was somewhat ironic that California's major race tracks, such as Tanforan and Santa Anita, now empty of fans and thoroughbreds because of DeWitt's ban on racing, were among the places used as assembly centers for the thousands of Japanese-Americans being moved to detention camps. Adding to the irony was the fact that by May, the number of Japanese-Americans assembled at the Santa Anita racetrack reached 14,947, well beyond DeWitt's arbitrary limit on public gatherings!

As the 1942 Pacific Coast League season got underway, uprooted Japanese-Americans—many of them baseball fans who would not see a professional game again until the 1946 or 1947 season—were mostly on their way to one of eight WRA "Relocation Centers" in remote, high desert locations across the West. Only two were in a Pacific Coast state: Tule Lake in California's Mono County, and Manzanar in the Owens Valley, 200 miles due north of Los Angeles.

Were any of their former neighbors to have had any pangs of sorrow about their resettlement in Manzanar, Tom Cameron of the *Los Angeles Times* sought to put them at ease. "If Uncle Sam's children trapped in Japan by the outbreak of conflict fare one-half as well as Japanese whom the fortunes of war and the will of the Western Defense Command place in Owens Valley, they will have reason enough to disagree with General Sherman's opinion [that war is hell]," Cameron wrote floridly after a visit in March 1942. "The present and prospective Nipponese of the fast-building Owens Valley Reception Center at Manzanar are lucky. They couldn't be censured for hoping, in their own behalf, that the war lasts for years. Owens Valley, potentially one of the most fertile in California, and that means all the world, has the makings of a garden spot to supplement its natural attractions. They couldn't wish for better scenery or a cleaner, more healthful atmosphere."

A garden spot Manzanar would never be, and many more accurate pictures of life in it and the other WRA camps have been provided in numerous accounts by people who actually spent years living behind the wire and in the shadows of the guard towers.

SEVENTEEN

Hidden in Plane Sight

One of the most enduring elements of World War II folklore along the Pacific Coast concerns with the monumental effort to camouflage aircraft factories. This project was considered so sensitive that it was never mentioned anywhere in the news media or official sources until the war was nearly over. Yet, in a sense, it was never a secret. The tens of thousands of men and women went to work each day in these camouflaged facilities, assuming the deception was necessary to protect their lives and these vitally important factories, and knowing not to discuss the matter outside the factory gates.

When, in the aftermath of Battle of Los Angeles, the *Los Angeles Times* spoke of "the desire of some government officials and some inland communities to transfer coastal industries," it was specifically referring to aircraft manufacturing. The industry had coalesced on the Pacific Coast in the 1920s because of good flying weather, had flourished, and, in the early 1940s, was growing rapidly thanks to the Roosevelt administration's initiatives to increase military aircraft production.

In the spring of 1940, Roosevelt had made the startling and unprecedented proposal that the United States should build fifty thousand military aircraft. Contemplating a map of the American industrial infrastructure, Roosevelt could see the concentration of strategic manufacturing plants within short distances of the Atlantic and Pacific, where they were potentially vulnerable to air and sea attack. To help him solve the problem, he did as he had so often done when confronting a dilemma; he created a bureaucracy and brought in an expert to run it. The Roosevelt administration created the Office of Production Management, and to run it, Roosevelt hired William Signius "Big Bill" Knudsen, an auto industry executive who was an expert on mass production and had been president of General Motors since 1937.

Roosevelt and Knudsen focused their attention on the Pacific Coast, where five of the six leading manufacturers which dominated the American aircraft industry were located. They were Boeing in Seattle, Lockheed in Burbank, North American Aviation in Inglewood, Consolidated Vultee in Downey and San Diego, and Douglas, which had operations in Santa Monica, El Segundo, and Long Beach. The sixth, Curtiss-Wright, manufactured both aircraft and engines in Buffalo, New York.

Between 1940 and 1945, the five West Coast companies would account for 54 percent of all American aircraft production by the numbers, and 61 percent by weight, which is a valid metric given that such companies as Douglas, Consolidated and Boeing produced so many large multiengine aircraft, including the only long-range, four-engine strategic bombers produced in significant numbers, Consolidated's B-24, and Boeing's B-17 and B-29.

By 1941, as concerns about the United States becoming a target of Axis air raids began to increase, so too did "the desire of some government officials and some inland communities to transfer coastal industries" to less vulnerable locations. A complex scheme evolved under which the federal Reconstruction Finance Corporation and its subsidiary Defense Plant Corporation would build inland aircraft factories and lease them to aircraft manufacturers.

The Big Five Pacific Coast manufacturers, and smaller firms such as Northrop, never abandoned their original plants. However, with the volume of orders mushrooming far beyond prewar levels, they desperately needed more production space, and some of them did utilize new inland facilities—such as Boeing's plant in Wichita, Douglas in Chicago, North American in Dallas, Consolidated in Fort Worth, and the Ford Motor Company facility at Willow Run in Michigan that turned out Consolidated B-24s— but the lion's share of their production remained on the West Coast.

D➡

As they went to work on the Monday after Pearl Harbor, the executives and workers at the aircraft plants turned their eyes nervously skyward. The theoretical vulnerability of coastal factories, which had been a topic of discussion for months, seemed no longer theoretical. Like Roosevelt and the military planners in Washington, they realized that if the same carrier battle group that had zeroed in upon Pearl Harbor had attacked their factories, the bulk of the American aviation industry would be out of business for months, perhaps years. Indeed, a USAAF memo sent to the Operations Division of the U.S. Army on April 21, 1942, nearly five months *after* Pearl Harbor admitted that "even a light enemy force should be successful in pressing home an attack on our two big bomber plants [in Seattle and San Diego] if our air defenses were the only security provided."

Until new factories could be built in places like Illinois, Michigan, Missouri, and Texas, most of the industry would be exposed to potential enemy air attacks. Protecting this vital manufacturing base became an even bigger priority than it had been on December 6.

D►

When Roosevelt had needed expert production advice, he had turned to the president of the world's largest manufacturing company. When the Army needed advice on how to tackle this problem, it turned to a *magician*: Major John Francis Ohmer, Jr. Born in Dayton, Ohio in 1891, Ohmer was the son of John Francis Ohmer, Sr., an inventor, manufacturer, and founder of the prosperous Ohmer Fare Register Company. Young John earned his master's degree in engineering from Cornell University in 1913, and served with the U.S. Army's 404th Engineer Battalion in World War I. He later returned to the family business, but retained a commission as a captain in the Engineer Officers Reserve Corps.

Already an amateur magician and keen recreational photographer, Ohmer developed an interest in the art and the science of camouflage. In 1938, he went to work with the Fourth Army and formed the 604th Engineer Battalion as a camouflage unit. Drawing on the success of the Royal Air Force in camouflaging their fighter fields from the Luftwaffe during the Battle of Britain in 1940 for his inspiration, Ohmer proposed doing the same for the facilities of the Army Air Corps (which became the USAAF in the summer of 1941). He carried out demonstrations of suggested camouflage techniques at Fort Eustis in Virginia, and two Air Corps bases, Langley Field, also in Virginia, and Maxwell Field in Alabama. However, budgets were tight, and there were no funds for operational camouflage.

Major Ohmer left active duty, but was ordered back in March 1941 and assigned to the office of the Chief of Engineers, Operations and Training Section in Washington, D.C. That fall, the Army sent him to Hawaii to study its defenses, and he returned with an extensive plan to camouflage Wheeler Field on Oahu. However, the cost of the project, around $50,000, was too much for the USAAF.

By this time, Major Ohmer was assigned to March Field in California's Riverside County. Someone at Fourth Army headquarters who remembered Ohmer's work recommended him to DeWitt, who tracked him down at March and ordered Ohmer to develop a camouflage plan for the West Coast. Having done a lot of thinking about exactly that, Ohmer found himself with a dream assignment. He began with March Field itself, using it as a demonstration project and an operational training exercise to work out specific techniques and technical details.

His proximity to Hollywood and its movie studios gave Ohmer access to an incredible pool of talent in the form of the best set designers and large-scale scenic painters in the world, people who specialized in many forms of "magic." Just as Fritz Dickie at the "Gun Room" on the Paramount Pictures lot had provided weapons to guard Southern California, all the major studios were more than willing to provide their services for the war effort. Ohmer had his pick of the best talent, therefore, at Columbia, Disney, Metro-Goldwyn-Mayer, Paramount, Twentieth Century Fox, Universal Studios, and others.

"In the early weeks of 1942, March Field came alive with creative talent," wrote Dr. Dennis Casey of the Air Intelligence Agency (now Air Force Intelligence, Surveillance, and Reconnaissance Agency). "Indeed, some Army observers remarked that it looked like a Hollywood studio back lot. Depending on where you might walk, you could run into a small farm being created complete with animals, a barn, a silo and other buildings. Pastoral settings were under construction using frames of lumber and large spreads of canvas. When a pastoral setting was used to conceal an ammunition storage area, the whole thing achieved near reality when a neighboring farmer grazed his cows near the phony buildings."

Eventually, Ohmer and his team disguised thirty-four military air fields in Washington, Oregon, and California, as well as Mills Field, the future San Francisco International Airport. However, their most dramatic attention was reserved for the aircraft plants in the Los Angeles area.

Ohmer's idea was to make the factories "disappear" by cloaking them so that, to an aerial observer at an altitude of five thousand feet, it would appear as innocuous suburban neighborhoods. Bombing tactics of the day called for planes to attack at altitudes that were generally higher. (although the attacks on Pearl Harbor had been executed at a much lower altitude.) So, Ohmer's requirement was a sound, albeit more demanding, one.

The disguises consisted of painting what appeared to be streets and greenery on real runways, and erecting entire faux subdivisions on factory rooftops. Standard issue camouflage netting, stretched on massive wooden scaffolding served as the basic canvas, on which the Hollywood teams painted contrasting color detailing to suggest streets and other features. The netting was foliage green to begin with, but areas were sprayed in subtly different shades to give the scene a more realistic look. Some "lawns" in the subdivisions were painted brown to suggest that they had not been watered.

Dozens of fake houses, as well as schools and public buildings, were made of canvas, like tent cabins. Hundreds of artificial shrubs and other ground details were created, using burlap over chicken wire matrices. The movie industry illusionists developed a method of crafting trees using tar and feathers. Chicken wire was lightly coated with tar, and then dipped in chicken feathers. The finished product, which had a soft, leafy appearance, could be formed into a rigid structure of any shape, and sprayed any shade, or even several shades, of green.

Chimneys and vents in the roofs of the factory buildings were allowed to poke through the netting, and were painted to simulate fire plugs.

It was generally assumed that Japanese reconnaissance aircraft were secretly overflying Southern California, so Ohmer's team wanted to give their fantasy world a lived-in look. In Burbank, full-size inflated rubber automobiles were parked on the streets above Lockheed's plant, and workers went up periodically to move them around from place to place to suggest that they were being driven and reparked. In some cases, clothing was taken on and off real clotheslines that were installed behind the houses.

The villages were as accurate as possible in two dimensions, although not in height. The houses and trees were not very tall, indeed most of the buildings were mostly no taller than a person standing. The reason was that the camouflage was designed to be seen from high above, not from ground level, and to be studied in minute detail only in the form of two-dimensional aerial photographs. In practice, a bombardier would have no more than two minutes, if that, to view the target, and he would be looking straight down.

"Ohmer's camouflage works by deceptively combining a technological feature of photography with one of its contingent social meanings," wrote Austin Nelson in a March 2012 blog post on the Camera Club of New York website:

On the one hand, Ohmer's work took advantage of a fundamental technological truth about the camera, namely that it's mono-focal. Photographed objects are rendered in perspective but by a single lens and onto a flat two-dimensional surface. The effect is that the space around and between things looks squashed, especially in cases like aerial shots where the depth of field is very shallow. At the same time for Ohmer's paintings to work as camouflage when photographed, he had to assume that despite the apparent unreal flatness of any aerial photograph with a shallow depth of field, the enemy still believed in the literal truth of such photographs...If Ohmer could count on the Japanese's belief in the literal truth of photography (and the very existence of their aerial reconnaissance program would have given him reason to do so), he could reliably use the flattening effect of photography to his advantage. That is, as long as the Japanese expected aerial photographs of on-the-ground reality to look flat no matter what, that "reality" could be simulated with an equally flat painted canvass. Ohmer added some three-dimensional props to his tarps, like shrubs and rubber cars, but these were accents to a painted picture that had to be convincing in its own right.

The overall terrain of the "landscape" was not flat. In order to compensate for the irregular height of various factory buildings, the subdivisions appeared at ground level to have been built on gently rolling hills.

In a lecture that he delivered to military personnel on September 15, 1943, Ohmer, now a colonel, described his technique as "visual misinformation." But he was not the only one practitioner of it in town. Donald Douglas of the Douglas Aircraft Company decided not to wait for the Army. In 1941, he had asked engineer Frank Collbaum to find him someone who could design a plan to camouflage the company's flagship plant at Clover Field in Santa Monica. Collbaum, whose work at Douglas included being the flight engineer on the debut flight of the immortal DC-3, suggested the noted architect, H. Roy Kelley.

"Kelley was renowned for his exceptional renditions of period revival homes built from Palos Verdes to Pasadena throughout the 1920s and 1930s, which earned for him a heap of honors from both the architectural press and his fellow practitioners," wrote Steve Vaught of *Architectural Digest*. "His design for the [elegant English County estate, with whitewashed brick exterior, commissioned by businessman Robert J. Pringle] was no exception, taking the 1938 'House Beautiful' prize from the Architectural League of New York, the fourth time he was so honored."

Kelley is also credited with having been an originator of mid-century California "ranch-style" homes, some of which were represented in faux form in the enormous rooftop commission that he undertook for Douglas in 1942. On this project, Kelley teamed up with an equally popular and well-known California landscape architect, Edward Huntsman-Trout, whose credits included the campus of Scripps College in Claremont.

Like Ohmer, Kelley and Huntsman-Trout utilized Hollywood set designers, specifically from Warner Brothers, in their project. According to Cecilia Rasmussen of the *Los Angeles Times*, their creation was made of "burlap supported by a tension compression structure of more than five million square feet of chicken wire and 400 poles." It covered the terminal and hangars, as well as the parking lot.

As Ohmer's Hollywood experts had done, they filled their "village" with houses, fences and clotheslines. In turn, they designed their "street grid" so that it blended into the adjacent Sunset Park neighborhood. They even matched the scale of their "ranch" homes to match those in Sunset Park. Warner Brothers executives later insisted that their own lot receive the "Kelley Treatment." They decided that their sound stages looked too much like aircraft hangers from the air, and feared that Japanese bombardiers, fooled by the Clover Field camouflage—or by that of Lockheed, only three miles to the north—would bomb their studio instead!

The Santa Monica camouflage was so effective that USAAF and U.S. Navy pilots who were supposed to land at Clover Field occasionally got lost, could not find the place, and had to divert to alternate airports. For a while, Douglas had to assign men waving red flags to the ends of the runways so that incoming aircraft knew where to land.

EIGHTEEN

Illusion in the Emerald City

Boeing in Seattle, like its counterparts in Southern California, commissioned an imaginary landscape to protect its factory from Japanese bombers. The first step had been to fully black out the factory. Boeing President, Philip Johnson, put his men to work immediately after Pearl Harbor, and within four days, the company was able to issue a press release tersely reporting that Plant 2, Boeing's primary assembly facility, had been "entirely transformed from a daylight plant to a blackout plant, enabling all night operations during blackouts. This plant is believed to be one of the first, if not the first, major defense plant in the country to complete this transformation."

More details were finally forthcoming four months later as the Boeing News Bureau reported with a bit more colorful detail that "the suddenness of the Pearl Harbor attack and the urgency it created prevented wasting of any time in laying groundwork for the work of blacking out. Painters, janitors, maintenance men—all available non-production workmen who had painting experience—were quickly rounded up and added to a crew furnished by Austin Construction Company. Brushes, spray guns, all necessary equipment was rounded up too. All equipment, including pressure tanks and hoses, was hauled to the roof by hand...War-time censorship rules do not permit revealing of the plant's size or the number of windows painted in those two days and nights, but the number of windows was tremendous, and approximately four miles of air hose were used for operating spray guns."

The project had actually proved harder than the breezy release makes it seem. The crews had to experiment with five types of paint before they found a mixture that would stick to the windows. When they were done, the black windows created a reflection problem and had to be painted over with flat gray to match the rest of the building. Finally, Austin Construction installed three layers of plywood inside the windows to protect workers from shards of glass that might be shattered by bomb blasts.

Unlike Don Douglas in Santa Monica, Phil Johnson *did* wait for the Corps of Engineers to camouflage his blacked out factory. To design the job, John Francis Ohmer sent John Stewart Detlie, an art director whom he had recruited off the Metro-Goldwyn-Mayer lot.

Having earned his degree in architecture from the University of Pennsylvania in 1933, Detlie followed the setting sun to California, determined on a career in Hollywood set design. He had two dozen films under his belt by 1942, including *A Christmas Carol* and the "Thin Man" franchise. In 1940, he was nominated for an Academy Award for his work on Metro-Goldwyn-Mayer's "Bitter Sweet," with Jeanette MacDonald and Nelson Eddy.

Meanwhile, the thirty-two-year-old Detlie had married an eighteen-year-old starlet named Constance Ockelman. Within a year, Constance had become one of the hottest talents in Hollywood, and had changed her name to Veronica Lake. As she was on her way to becoming one of the favorite GI pinup girls of World War II, the Oscar-nominated Detlie was living the Hollywood dream—until Ohmer came calling.

In Seattle, Detlie's team created a large-scale, twenty-six-acre neighborhood atop Plant 2 that came to be known locally as "Wonderland." During construction, crews supervised by the Seattle District of the Army Corps of Engineers, were presented the challenge of a "sawtooth," rather than flat, roof. This uneven surface, stepping up and down with a variation of as much as thirty-five feet, necessitated scaffolding, platforms and framing that consumed an estimated million board feet of lumber—as well as an elaborate sprinkler system to protect it from fire, accidental or caused by enemy incendiary bombs. The variation in height of structures below meant that there were several fairly steep "hills" in Detlie's Wonderland.

The imaginary town had at least three major streets, as well as alleys and driveways. The streets even had street signs and names. Although there was no way that a bomber pilot could read street signs from ten thousand feet, in naming these streets, the people who built Wonderland couldn't resist a little humor. For example, Synthetic Street intersected Burlap Boulevard.

Using the "tar and feathers" method to create fake vegetation being used in Southern California, the Engineers created around 300 artificial trees, some of them as tall as twelve feet. There is an often repeated urban legend that, in order to add a finishing touch of visual veracity to the set-up, a cow was let loose to roam Wonderland. Alas, this charming, but improbable, story is untrue.

Wonderland had fifty-three homes, two dozen garages, three greenhouses, a small store, and even a gas station. All of them were built of wood and canvas like those which John Ohmer had designed in California. Many were only about four feet high at the eves, although some were taller, and there were even a few which represented two-story houses. Inside, most of the homes were furnished only with fire protection sprinklers, though at least two were built to be occupied by non-imaginary people, specifically, soldiers who manned antiaircraft guns on the Plant 2 rooftop during 1942 and 1943.

In Southern California, the imaginary citizens of the imaginary rooftop towns "drove" rubber cars, while the automobiles parked on

Wonderland's streets were made of wood, and were just a couple of feet high. Their angular design made them look more like 1970s AMC Gremlins, than the streamlined Fords and Chevies of the late 1930s and 1940s.

Detlie also worked with Washington State Camouflage Director William James Bain and the Seattle architectural firm of Young and Richardson to design an additional elaborate plan, that included fake streets and foliage detail that would camouflage, across Boeing Field. The "streets" that began on the roof of Plant 2, continued across the runway, crossed U.S. Route 99 and climbed up the slopes of Beacon Hill on the opposite side of the field. The latter was accomplished by cutting the paths through the brush on the hillsides that looked like streets.

Different techniques were used for the sections of the village that were laid out across Boeing Field. As described by the Seattle District Engineers, the "problem was to obtain a texture to which camouflage paint would adhere and yet which would offer no interference to air traffic. After much experimenting, a crushed rock surface from one-eighth to three-eighths of an inch was rolled with an adhesive material for paved areas. For non-traffic areas, wood chips or hogged fuel with cement was used."

In the areas between and beyond the runways, the "houses" were merely concrete slabs six inches thick, because anything higher was deemed to constitute too much clutter for ramp and runway operations.

However, in these areas, "lawns" and vacant lots could be comprised of real grass and real weeds, carefully designed and tended by agronomists from the Agronomy Section of the Passive Defense Division of the Corps of Engineers, headed by LeRoy Robert Hansen, the author of the obscure monograph, *The Use of Grasses and Legumes for Camouflage and Dust Control on Airfields.*

While Detlie and the Engineers managed the passive defense for Boeing, active defense, such as the planning and execution of fire and air raid drills and air raid shelters, was handled by company personnel, such as Glenn Dierst, the company's plant protection manager, and his team of white-helmeted wardens. A 1943 Boeing News Bureau release states that all the plant personnel could reach the shelters in less than twelve minutes.

Seattle presented a unique problem for the passive defense planners. As anyone who has gazed at the ground from an airplane has noted, it is much easier to identify a familiar location through the contrasting color and contours of land and water. New York and San Francisco, for example, are easier to recognize than Des Moines or Topeka, because their shapes are strictly defined by rivers and bays. Such was the case with Seattle, which is sandwiched between the distinctively shaped Puget Sound and Lake Washington.

For this reason, Detlie planned additional phases for the Boeing project. His master plan involved overhead camouflaging of the large Boeing employee parking lots, as had been done at the Lockheed and Douglas employee lots in California and continuing the camouflage cover across sections of East Marginal Way.

Because the Boeing campus is defined geographically by the Duwamish River, which flowed behind Plant 2, Detlie conceived of covering it as well, and painting a faux river which had a different course in the vicinity of the Boeing facility.

A further phase that was also seriously considered by the Corps of Engineers, but never built, involved the construction of an entire dummy aircraft factory at a different location, complete with fake airplanes.

As had been the case in Southern California, some American pilots who had used the prewar Boeing Field were now so confused by the camouflage, and the absence of familiar landmarks meant that when the field was covered by scattered clouds, it was very difficult to make it out from the air.

❯━

The Hollywood marriages in which one party suddenly erupts as a superstar and the other leaves town, typically head for trouble. Such was the case for Detlie's. After the death of their premature son, Lake and

Detlie divorced. Lake went on to become a huge star. For his part, Detlie never returned to Hollywood, choosing to remain in Seattle, where he became a prominent architect.

The existence of all those rooftop villages and other deceptions in Seattle and Southern California was widely known, but remained unheralded in the media until the summer of 1945. Then, no longer needed, the camouflage began to disappear. These amazing villages disappeared virtually overnight, vanishing like mirages, but they continue to live on in the American memory of World War II.

NINETEEN

The Great Japanese Offensive

n the middle of the night on June 2–3, 1942, my father, W. J. Yenne, was awakened at his boarding house in Seattle and ordered to report immediately to his workplace. A Japanese radio transmission had been intercepted, he was informed, and enemy bombers were headed for Seattle's Harbor Island!

At the time, my father was a welding foreman at Seattle-Tacoma Shipbuilding (later Todd Pacific) on Seattle's Harbor Island. There, five Fletcher-class destroyers were in varying states of completion, and two more were to be laid down that month. Crews were needed to be on hand to deal with the aftermath of the coming air raid. When the "all-clear" had finally sounded, well after sunrise, the men at the shipyard learned that an intelligence intercept had been misinterpreted, and Dutch Harbor, Alaska, was the target of the Japanese that morning.

Given that Dutch Harbor is nearly 800 miles closer to Seattle than Pearl Harbor is to San Francisco, the phrase "too close for comfort" came up often in conversation that morning. So too did the overwhelming sense that an attack on the Pacific Coast, the fear of which had faded in the past month or so, was, as Secretary of War Stimson had warned a week before the attack, "inevitable."

There was a pervasive fear that the Japanese would follow-up their Alaska action with attacks on the cities of the Pacific Coast on the evening of June 3. Rear Admiral Charles Freeman of the Thirteenth Naval District in Seattle put the entire city on "full war footing." With the exception of the ferry piers, Freeman banned the general public from the entire Elliot Bay waterfront adjacent to downtown. Blackouts were ordered. The Western Defense Command ordered radio stations from San Diego to Seattle off the air at 9:00 p.m. Authorities in British Columbia ordered all radio stations in the province to close down forty-five minutes later. All the way down in Southern California, Sheriff Eugene Biscailuz, chairman of the Los Angeles County Defense Council, ordered a "heightening of the existing alert."

In this case—unlike in so many others prior to it—those who speculated and those who acted both were correct to be concerned because a great Japanese offensive had just begun across the eastern Pacific.

At 3:07 a.m. that morning, it was just getting light at Dutch Harbor on the Aleutian island of Amaknak when twenty-two enemy bombers from the carriers *Junyo* and *Ryujo*, supported by ten fighters, began to attack. Some of the most northern units of the Western Defense Command were under fire. As had been the case at Pearl Harbor, the raid came as a surprise to the defenders, though Admiral Freeman later insisted to the Associated Press that it was *not* a surprise.

The half dozen antiaircraft batteries of the 206th Coastal Artillery Regiment of the Arkansas National Guard had actually been based at Fort Mears on Amaknak since before Pearl Harbor. The gunners had nearly expired from boredom for nearly a year. Now, they were abruptly awakened to the real thing. The men of the 37th Infantry Regiment added rifle fire to the three-inch antiaircraft rounds. One man even hurled a wrench at a low-flying Japanese aircraft. A well-placed bomb on a barracks at Fort Mears killed seventeen men of the 37th Infantry. The P-40s that were scrambled managed to down one of the attacking bombers and a fighter, and to take out two reconnaissance aircraft launched from Japanese cruisers.

The defenders expected the Japanese to attempt an invasion such they had performed in December at Wake Island and Guam. On the night of June 3–4, therefore, they repositioned equipment and making other preparations to meet such a challenge. A second air attack came in the early afternoon of June 4. Nineteen bombers attacked in waves, supported by ten A6M Zero fighters. This time, the antiaircraft artillerymen managed to destroy a bomber, and the American interceptors downed three bombers and a fighter, while losing four of their own.

The first Japanese attacks on the Territory of Alaska had left seventy-eight dead, caused considerable damage, and destroyed what the Japanese assumed to be a warship. In fact, it was a beached transport that was serving as a dormitory for civilian workers.

Japanese bombers never returned to the skies over Dutch Harbor nor did the Japanese attempt to invade it. But, three days later, Japanese troops occupied two of the Aleutian Islands — Kiska and Attu, 686 and 858 miles, respectively, to its west. IJN Special Landing Forces were used to capture Kiska, which was undefended, except by the ten men assigned to a weather station, while the Imperial Japanese Army took Kiska, which was home to fewer than fifty civilians, most of them Aleut people.

The strategic importance to the Japanese of capturing these two remote and inhospitable islands was that doing so pushed the perimeter of their empire roughly thirty degrees of longitude closer to the Continental United States.

This operation also was part of one of the most ambitious Japanese offensive operations of World War II. Admiral Isoroku Yamamoto, the Commander in Chief of the IJN Combined Fleet had planned the remarkably audacious strike on Pearl Harbor, halfway across the Pacific from Japan, with some trepidation. However, it had succeeded beautifully. In turn, the extraordinary success of the IJA and the IJN in Southeast

Asia—capturing Singapore nine weeks into the war, and the Dutch East Indies in barely seven weeks of operations and eradicating the Allied naval presence there—gave rise to great optimism in Tokyo.

It was both this optimism and an insoluble desire to check the Americans in the eastern Pacific and deal them a major, perhaps war-winning, psychological blow that led Yamamoto to plan and launch his great June 1942 offensive. On a vast ocean chessboard larger than the continental United States, Yamamoto planned to capture Midway Island in the central Pacific, 1,330 miles northeast of Pearl Harbor, *and* secure a foothold in the Aleutian. He also hoped for a decisive naval battle in which his powerful carrier fleet would destroy the American aircraft carriers that not been in Pearl Harbor on December 7.

Although the plan for the offensive against Midway, Operation MI, and in the Aleutians, Operation AL, had been in the works since early in 1942, that plan was not finalized until early April. This was just before the unexpected April 18 raid on major Japanese cities by sixteen B-25 bombers led by Lieutenant Colonel Jimmy Doolittle. While the raid did minimal physical damage, the Japanese considered it a serious affront to their self-esteem that deserved a measure of revenge as well as an indication that the American will to fight had to be broken.

Within the Western Defense Command's theater of operations, DeWitt's defenders may have been scarcely better equipped to fend off Japanese attacks than they had been in December, but at least they knew *approximately* when the Japanese attack was coming. By the middle of May, thanks to the cryptographers of the Magic project who had cracked Japanese codes more thoroughly, the Navy knew about Japanese plans for a major operation targeting the Midway and the Aleutians, and that it would take place around the end of May. Assuming that some form of this information had been passed to Pacific commanders, it is not surprising that Freeman said that he was not surprised by the Dutch Harbor attack.

As Stetson Conn and his colleagues wrote in *Guarding the United States and its Outposts*, an April 19 memo issued by Brigadier General

Lieutenant General John Lesesne DeWitt, commander of the U.S. Army's Fourth Army as well as of the Western Defense Command, which became a theater of war on December 11, 1941. As the theater commander, DeWitt was the de facto military governor of the Pacific Coast in 1941–1943, issuing orders and directives by which the civilian governors abided. *U.S. Army*

California governor Culbert Levy Olson sought to maintain control of his state by taking charge of his State Council of Defense, but when DeWitt made demands, such as in the cancellation of the 1942 Rose Bowl game or the whole 1942 thoroughbred season, Olson dutifully complied. *Courtesy of the Bancroft Library Portrait Collection, the Bancroft Library, University of California, Berkeley*

Washington governor Arthur Langlie was a former mayor of Seattle, where he had created a Home Defense Committee before the war. Like the governors of Oregon and California, he was voted out of office during the war, but unlike them, he made a postwar comeback. *Washington State Archives*

Oregon governor Charles Arthur Sprague was also the longtime editor and publisher of the *Oregon Statesman* in Salem. He reactivated the Oregon Defense Council, and like California's Olson, he retained the title of director himself. *Works Progress Administration*

Dignitaries speak on the record over the Mutual Broadcasting System at an Army-Navy-Marine Banquet held at the National Guard Armory in Los Angeles. On the left is Fourth Army commander Lieutenant General John DeWitt. In the middle is Lieutenant Colonel Rupert Hughes of the California State Guard, who was also a novelist, film director, and composer based in Hollywood, as well as the uncle of Howard Hughes. On the right is Captain Claude Mayo of the U.S. Navy, who commanded the battleship USS *Nevada* and had gone on to serve as superintendent of the California Maritime Academy. *U.S. Army*

On December 7, 1941, the San Francisco Fire Department was called to the Japanese consulate on Jackson Street. Consul General Yoshio Muto and his secretary, Kazuyoshi Inagaki, had been busily shoveling sensitive documents into the fireplaces, and the fires got out of control. The 11,450-square-foot residence, designed in 1895 for George W. Gibbs by renowned architect Willis Polk, survived the fire and many years later it was the home of filmmaker Chris Columbus. *Bill Yenne photo*

Lieutenant General John DeWitt's residence in San Francisco was McDowell Hall at Fort Mason, which had served in that capacity for the senior U.S. Army commanders on the Pacific Coast since 1877 when Major General Irvin McDowell lived there. DeWitt was the last commanding general to live at McDowell Hall. *Bill Yenne photo*

Major General Joseph Warren Stilwell at Fort Ord as commander of the Southern Sector of the Western Defense Command in 1942. Had the Japanese invaded California, Stilwell would have led the defense. Previously the commander of the 7th Infantry Division, Stilwell later achieved fame as American commander in the China Burma India Theater. *U.S. Army*

A six-inch disappearing rifle overlooking the Pacific at Battery Chamberlin inside the Presidio of San Francisco. Manned by Battery D of the 6th Coastal Artillery, it guarded the entrance to the Golden Gate throughout World War II. Installed in 1920, it is today the last gun of its type on the Pacific Coast. *Bill Yenne photo*

NOTICE

Headquarters
Western Defense Command
and Fourth Army

Presidio of San Francisco, California
March 24, 1942

Civilian Exclusion Order No. 1

1. Pursuant to the provisions of Public Proclamations Nos. 1 and 2, this headquarters, dated March 2, 1942, and March 16, 1942, respectively, it is hereby ordered that all persons of Japanese ancestry, including alien and non-aliens, be excluded from that portion of Military Area No. 1, described as "Bainbridge Island," in the State of Washington, on or before 12 o'clock noon, P. W. T., of the 30th day of March, 1942.

2. Such exclusion will be accomplished in the following manner:

(a) Such persons may, with permission, on or prior to March 29, 1942, proceed to any approved place of their choosing beyond the limits of Military Area No. 1 and the prohibited zones established by said proclamations, or hereafter similarly established, subject only to such regulations as to travel and change of residence as are now or may hereafter be prescribed by this headquarters and by the United States Attorney General. Persons affected hereby will not be permitted to take up residence or remain within the region designated as Military Area No. 1 or the prohibited zones heretofore or hereafter established. Persons affected hereby are required on leaving or entering Bainbridge Island to register and obtain a permit at the Civil Control Office to be established on said Island at or near the ferryboat landing.

(b) On March 30, 1942, all such persons who have not removed themselves from Bainbridge Island in accordance with Paragraph 1 hereof, shall, in accordance with instructions of the Commanding General, Northwestern Sector, report to the Civil Control Office referred to above on Bainbridge Island for evacuation in such manner and to such place or places as shall then be prescribed.

(c) A responsible member of each family affected by this order and each individual living alone or affected will report to the Civil Control Office described above between 8 a. m. and 5 p. m., Wednesday, March 25, 1942.

3. Any person affected by this order who fails to comply with any of its provisions or who is found on Bainbridge Island after 12 o'clock noon, P. W. T., of March 30, 1942, will be subject to the criminal penalties provided by Public Law No. 503, 77th Congress, approved March 21, 1942, entitled "An Act to Provide a Penalty for Violation of Restrictions or Orders with Respect to Persons Entering, Remaining in, Leaving or Committing Any Act in Military Areas or Zone", and alien Japanese will be subject to immediate apprehension and internment.

J. L. DeWITT
Lieutenant General, U. S. Army
Commanding

On General DeWitt's authority, the Western Defense Command issued civilian exclusion orders compelling Japanese-Americans to register at designated civil control stations for removal. Exclusion Order No. 1 was issued for Bainbridge Island in Washington on March 24, 1942. Others followed in short order. *War Relocation Authority*

Tagged and ready to go, the members of the Mochida family of Hayward, California, await the bus that will take them into internment. The family operated a nursery and five greenhouses on a two-acre site, raising snapdragons and sweet peas. *War Relocation Authority*

Dorothea Lange took this picture of the Wanto Grocery in Oakland, California, in March 1942, shortly before the owner surrendered for internment when persons of Japanese descent were ordered to leave restricted zones within the state. *War Relocation Authority*

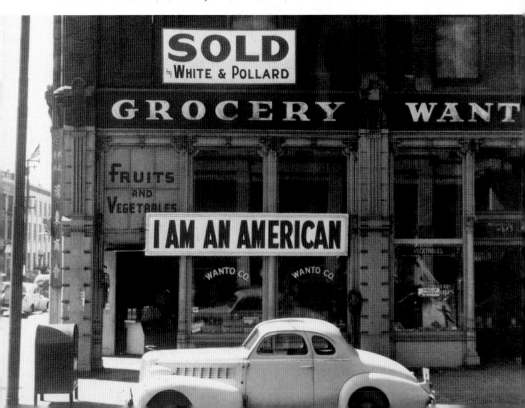

U.S. Army Coastal Artillery Corps personnel inspecting a shell crater at Fort Stevens, Oregon, in June 1942 after the installation at the mouth of the Columbia River was shelled by the Japanese submarine I-25. *U.S. Army*

This excellent overview of the Douglas Aircraft Company factory in Santa Monica and its wartime camouflage shows how detailed the false neighborhoods on the factory rooftops were. In addition to tree-lined streets and ranch homes of varying shapes and sizes, there were sidewalks, detached garages, and empty lots. Note the sizable, but unplanned, "pothole"—actually a rip in the camouflage netting, in the center. The Clover Field flightline is visible in the background. *The Boeing Company*

Boeing Airplane Company employees Joyce Howe and Susan Heidrich ascend a "hill" on a wooden walkway for a better view of "Wonderland," the elaborate artificial neighborhood that was constructed to camouflage the company's Plant 2 manufacturing facility. Note the "cars" on the street. Their angular shape makes them look more like AMC Gremlins from the 1970s than the smoothly rounded Fords and Chevies of the 1940s. *The Boeing Company*

California Attorney General Earl Warren represented law enforcement agencies from across all of the Pacific Coast states on the Ninth Regional Defense Board. An outspoken advocate of the removal of Japanese-Americans from the coastal states, he used the fear of subversion and sabotage in his successful 1942 bid for the governorship of California. Said he in 1942, "the Japanese situation as it exists in this state today may well be the Achilles heel of the entire civilian defense effort." *Library of Congress*

St. Clair Streett in the Operations Division of the Chief of Staff's office suggested that after the Doolittle raid "a more ambitious Japanese attack on the west coast appeared much more probable to authorities in Washington. G-2 pointed out that eight Japanese carriers had returned from their operations around southeastern Asia and that the Japanese could release at least three of the eight for a retaliatory attack on the west coast without jeopardizing successes already achieved."

Secretary of War Henry Stimson noted in his diary on April 21 that he had "called in [U.S. Army Chief of Staff General George] Marshall and had a few earnest words with him about the danger of a Jap attack on the West Coast [and confessed that he was] very much impressed with the danger that the Japanese, having terribly lost face by this recent attack on them...will make a counterattack on us with carriers."

According to Conn, the U.S. Army's Intelligence Division agreed with the Navy assessment that a strong Japanese attack was coming before the end of May, but they predicted that the "first priority" target of the attack would be "hit and run raids on West Coast cities of the continental United States supported by heavy naval forces."

In turn, Marshall told Streett to warn DeWitt to be on his guard against a carrier attack at any time after May 10. With this in mind, the Chief of Staff promised DeWitt that two additional antiaircraft regiments were being sent to strengthen the air defense of Los Angeles and San Francisco.

In a May 16 memo, as reports came to light of the extensive use of poison gas by the Imperial Japanese Army in China, Marshall warned DeWitt that the Japanese attack "in the Eastern Pacific" might involve the use of chemical agents. Marshall also directed that, Conn writes, "during the next two days 350,000 gas masks (all that were available), protective clothing, and decontamination supplies were hurriedly shipped to the West Coast."

Despite a shakeup in the command structure, very little progress had been made in the USAAF's preparations for air defense. In February, General Ryan had been replaced as commander of the IV Interceptor

Command by Brigadier General William Ellsworth Kepner. Redesignated as the IV Fighter Command, Kepner's organization had assumed responsibility for the air defense of the entire Pacific Coast. In early April, Ord's boss, Jacob Fickel, had been replaced as commander of the Fourth Air Force by Major General George Kenney, who was later to achieve fame as commander of the Fifth Air Force in the South West Pacific Theater. Both Ord and Fickel were moved to less demanding training assignments.

Despite the best of intentions, the new commanders were still faced with having to do much with little. In a May 24 memo to Kenney, Kepner admitted that nearly half of pilots assigned to the IV Fighter Command were unqualified to fly the aircraft with which it was equipped. He concluded with the sly comment that "considering the handicaps imposed by lack of sufficient suitable airdromes, inadequate housing facilities, unsuitable aircraft radio equipment, [and] mass replacement of fighter units by new units with less than two weeks training, the efficiency of the Command is excellent."

In fact, it was hardly in better shape than it had been when Ord had kept the interceptors on the ground during the air raid scares in December or during the Battle of Los Angeles in February. Fortunately, by May, the massive camouflage project at the Los Angeles area and Seattle aircraft plants was nearly completed, so at least *passive* defense seemed to be working.

When it came to intercepting and defeating a Japanese attacking force at sea, the Army believed that because of the relatively weak state of the Navy's capabilities along the West Coast, any attack or invasion could be countered only by USAAF airpower, and recommended a maximum effort of all bomber units available in the continental United States to meet the threat.

As Stetson Conn reminds us,

One of the most puzzling problems in air defense along the West Coast was how to provide enough forces to detect an enemy carrier force many hundred miles from the coast and to attack it before it could launch its planes. The problem on the Pacific Coast was complicated by much fog, and by the prospect of a Japanese carrier force sailing in behind one of the normal succession of storm fronts that moved from the northern Pacific toward the west coast. The best defense against carriers was to find and strike at them within a belt 700 to 1,100 miles offshore. The only planes that could do this were Army heavy bombers and Navy patrol bombers. The Fourth Air Force in January estimated that it would require 162 Army and 180 Navy planes of these types to perform this mission, but usually in the first five months of 1942 neither service had more than a tenth of these strengths available.

In May, however, the USAAF's operational heavy bomber strength on the Pacific Coast was less than two dozen, despite the fact that all of them were being manufactured either in Seattle or San Diego. To meet the pressing need for more bombers, the USAAF undertook a broad emergency restructuring of its priorities. Even the flow of aircraft being sent overseas to England to the Eighth Air Force, which was destined to be the air force to conduct the strategic air campaign against the Third Reich—the USAAF's highest operational priority—was interrupted and aircraft were diverted to the Pacific Coast. Major General Carl "Tooey" Spaatz, the commander of Eighth, was at Presque Isle, Maine, en route himself to England when he heard from Brigadier General Larry Kuter, the deputy chief of the air staff, informing him that Marshall had ordered a halt to all further shipments and troop movements to England. As it turned out, the halted troops included Spaatz himself!

"Kuter's relayed order threw Eighth Air Force into turmoil," wrote David Mets, Spaatz's biographer. "The C-47 [transports] of the 60th

Group were fueled and loaded with cargo for the Atlantic crossing. But on the evening of [June 1], they were ordered to off-load their cargo.... Spaatz spent the next day at Presque Isle and flew back [to Washington, D.C.]."

Such was the scale of the impending crisis.

Marshall himself flew to the Pacific Coast on Saturday, May 23 to make a personal inspection tour of defensive preparations in Los Angeles and San Diego. Having visited several aircraft factories, he ordered that finished aircraft lined up in rows should be moved inland or scattered so that each bomb would damage no more than one. At 8:41 p.m. on Sunday night, Marshall was still in Southern California as the detection of "an unidentified flight of planes" spurred DeWitt's Fourth Army to order Los Angeles area radio stations off the air. One minute later, a blue alert was sounded, indicating that the unidentified flight was only twelve minutes from reaching the Pacific Coast. A fifty-one-minute blackout began at 8:46, but the enemy planes never materialized.

On Monday morning, Marshall ordered that the Army Ground Forces, which controlled training units located within the Western Defense Command's theater, as well as combat units passing through the area en route to the Western Pacific, should make all of its troops available to DeWitt for emergency use.

According to Conn, this added four additional regimental combat teams to the three that the Western Defense command already possessed, increasing the total number of personnel from around 172,000 to 192,000, of which about 70 percent were ground combat troops. Between them, the Navy, Marine Corps, and Coast Guard added about 75,000 men to the total armed forces personnel strength on the Pacific Coast. Marshall also ordered the mass deployment of barrage balloons at all the major Pacific Coast ports, which was referred to by the *San Francisco Chronicle* as "the greatest installation of its kind ever attempted."

A confidential wire from the U.S. Army Operations Division, dated May 27, notified the jittery DeWitt of the "War Department conviction that surprise attacks on the West Coast are a possibility from now on."

The next day, Secretary Stimson went public. "Pacific Coast cities are considered the most likely target of the attack," the Associated Press reported the Secretary saying. He added that "a raid on the national capitol was not inconceivable, despite the distance involved." He spoke of Japanese retaliation for the Doolittle Raid, and of the need "to set our house in order for what seems inevitable."

Alerted to the concern about potential chemical weapons attacks, Pacific Coast newspapers started running public service articles written by Ward Mould, the Medical Gas Officer for the Office of Civilian Defense. "Gas might be used in an attack upon a city either alone or in conjunction with other weapons," wrote Mould. "Quick acting gases may be used against a community to produce immediate casualties, throw the population into a state of panic and disrupt protective services. Slow acting types, which may remain effective for several days in liquid form, may be used to 'contaminate' important factories, railroads, highways, etc. to prevent their use." He did add, however, that "a gas attack on a large enough scale to cause injury to a substantial portion of a large city is not regarded in authoritative quarters as feasible."

In San Francisco, it was announced that air raid wardens, otherwise unprepared, would be instructed to "beat pans" to warn of a gas attack. When this story was carried nationwide by the Associated Press, the low technology approach gave an impression of desperation. Meanwhile, the general public was far from reassured when the U.S. Army's entire stock of gas masks, which had been rushed to DeWitt's Fourth Army in May, would have been enough for only about one-fifth of the people living in San Francisco alone—after all of his troops had been issued one. Of course, if it involved chemical weapons, it would not take *substantial* injury to "throw the population into a state of panic."

◗▬

The invasions of Attu and Kiska, which seized the headlines on June 3, had caused great consternation and no small measure of embarrassment, not only at the Presidio of San Francisco, but in Washington, D.C. It was not quite a humiliation on the level experienced by the Japanese over the Doolittle raid, but official Washington decided to downplay it.

On June 7, Admiral Ernest King, the Chief of Naval Operations, told a Sunday morning gathering of reporters of the Aleutian situation that "we had none too clear a picture of what is going on, but it is going on." He quickly changed the subject to speak of another battle—one upon which the headlines and the attention of the American people and the press was rightly fixated: Midway.

Overshadowing the Aleutians campaign, and indeed every other bulletin of war news that week, was the immense naval battle that was taking place off Midway. Isoroku Yamamoto had yearned for this—the centerpiece of his great offensive operation—to be a decisive battle, and it *was*. The Battle of Midway, which took place between June 3 and June 7 simultaneous with the Aleutians operations, turned out to be a disaster for the Imperial Japanese Navy. It lost the four largest aircraft carriers involved in the Pearl Harbor operation—the *Akagi*, the *Hiryu*, the *Kaga*, and the *Soryu*—along with hundreds of aircraft and experienced pilots, as well as two cruisers.

This major U.S. Navy victory shifted the balance of power in the Pacific from Japan to the United States—from Japanese dominance to an equilibrium which the United States would gradually tilt toward an unquestionable superiority.

Despite the victory, the concern that the Japanese still might attack the Pacific Coast remained strong. As Conn and his colleagues wrote, "the Japanese occupation of outer Aleutian islands [sic] nevertheless introduced apprehensions of a renewed Japanese offensive toward the Alaskan mainland and continental west coast, and Japanese submarine operations helped to keep these apprehensions alive."

The submarines that had terrorized the Pacific Coast in December had indeed returned.

TWENTY

The Submarines Return

The initial Japanese submarine campaign against the Pacific Coast had ended in late December 1941, notwithstanding Kozo Nishio's return visit with *I-17* in February. In June 1942, as part of Admiral Yamamoto's great offensive, two of the nine that had visited in December, *I-25* and *I-26*, returned for a second round of mischief.

I-25, commanded by Lieutenant Commander Meiji Tagami, had made her second wartime patrol in the waters off Australia and New Zealand. This cruise is memorable not so much for undersea operations, but for operations *above* the water. As previously noted, B1 class submarines were each equipped with a hangar that accommodated one single-engine floatplane, though not all of the boats had carried an aircraft in December 1941, and none are known to have been used operationally that month.

At the time, *I-25* did have a floatplane aboard, but it had been damaged in high seas as it was being prepared for operations prior to its

intended use during the Pearl Harbor operation. Its pilot, Warrant Officer Nobuo Fujita, therefore, sat out that cruise without flying a mission.
He would make up for lost time during *I-25*'s second war cruise.

On February 17, Fujita and his navigator-bombardier, Petty Officer
Shoji Okuda, making a reconnaissance flight over Botany Bay and Syd-
ney Harbor in their Yokosuka E14Y, met no interference from Australian
forces during their mission. Nine days later, however, on a sortie over
Melbourne, the Royal Australian Air Force sent two interceptors up after
the Japanese intruder, but they failed to locate the Japanese aircraft. An
antiaircraft artillery battery at Williamstown had tracked the aircraft,
but the gunners did not receive permission to fire. During March, Fujita
and Okuda conducted more flights over Wellington and Auckland, New
Zealand.

Both *I-25* and *I-26*, which had been one of the refueling submarines for Operation K, along with two other boats that had made
Pacific Coast cruises, *I-15* and *I-19*, had returned to Japan after their
second wartime patrols. By coincidence, all four were in drydock at
the Yokosuka Naval Arsenal shipyard on Tokyo Bay on April 18 when
the facility was attacked by B-25s of Jimmy Doolittle's strike force,
though none were hit.

In May, *I-25* and *I-26*, under the command of Commander Minoru
Yokota, were assigned, as part of Rear Admiral Shigeaki Yamazaki's
Submarine Squadron 1, to Operation AL for operations in the Aleutians
and Alaskan waters. Leaving Yokosuka separately, *I-26* arrived off
Kodiak Island on May 20 before diverting westward toward Dutch
Harbor to rendezvous with *I-25* on May 26. Here, their primary mission
was aerial reconnaissance in advance of the June 3 air raids.

On May 27, having narrowly missed being spotted by a U.S. Navy
cruiser sailing a mile off the island, *I-25* launched her floatplane, and
Fujita conducted an extensive and undetected overflight of Dutch Harbor. Because his boat was not carrying a floatplane, Yokota surfaced to
serve as a backup recovery location, but Fujita was able to return to *I-25*
as planned.

Having finished their mission, and having successfully dodged U.S. Navy ships that detected them, *I-25* and *I-26* left the area a week ahead of the impending air raid, bound for the waters off the Pacific Coast.

Yokota's submarine reached its new station off the Washington coast on the last day of the month, but Tagami's did not arrive until June 2, having paused to pursue a destroyer and the freighter that it was escorting. Even with the use of Fujita's eyes in the sky, the American ships managed to elude the Japanese submarine. On June 5, Tagami attempted an attack on another freighter off the Washington coast, but both his torpedoes missed.

Yokota was luckier. On June 7, he was at the mouth of the Strait of Juan de Fuca off the small town of Neah Bay, Washington, when a westbound freighter came into view. She was the 3,286-ton SS *Coast Trader*, built in New Jersey in 1920 as the SS *Point Reyes*. Owned by the Coastwise Shipping Company, she was homeported in Portland, and under contract to the U.S. Army. The freighter had departed that morning from Port Angeles at the north end of Puget Sound, bound for San Francisco with 1,250 one-ton rolls of newsprint.

With *I-26* following, the *Coast Trader* had just rounded Cape Flattery at the northwest tip of Washington, when Yokota fired a single torpedo at 2:10 p.m. *I-26*'s crewmen later recalled that as the torpedo struck the ship's starboard side near the stern, rolls of newsprint flew fifty feet into the air, and the radio mast toppled, which would prevent their SOS call from being received ashore. As the freighter's engine quit and the ship began taking on water, Captain Lyle Havens gave the order to abandon ship.

Forty minutes after being hit, the *Coast Trader* sank stern first. The crew of fifty-six managed to get away safely, watching the periscope and the conning tower of *I-26* in the distance as their ship went down.

A severe storm blew in, scattering the lifeboats as the men attempted to row toward shore, and it was late on the afternoon of the following day when the first survivors were finally picked up by the San Francisco-based fishing boat *Virginia I*. The Coast Guard was alerted, but the remaining survivors were not finally rescued until the morning of the second day, when they were spotted by the Canadian corvette HMCS *Edmundston*. By then, one man had died of hypothermia.

By the end of the day on June 9, the wire services were carrying the story, with United Press revealing "the first reported sinking of the war in the North Pacific." On June 10, the stories told by the survivors of the *Coast Trader* plucked from the frigid waters had reached Seattle. The headline in the *Seattle Post-Intelligencer* shouted "Sub Sinks Ship Off Neah Bay" and the *Seattle Times* reported "Sailors, Torpedoed Off Neah Bay, Saved Gun Hoping to Fire on Japs."

However, Freeman's Thirteenth Naval District moved quickly to tamp down the news coverage. According to the *Online Encyclopedia of Washington State History*, "the Navy's public information officer in Seattle was told to downplay the incident in the press." The subsequent Navy Board of Inquiry found that the *Coast Trader* "was sunk by an internal explosion and not by torpedo or mine." Oddly, this improbable determination, crafted for contemporary consumption, has never been officially modified.

A little past midnight on June 20, nearly two weeks after Yokota's *I-26* sent the *Coast Trader* to the bottom, Meiji Tagami's *I-25* was prowling the waters about seventy miles south by southwest from Cape Flattery when he detected a target in the darkness. It was the 7,126-ton Canadian freighter SS *Fort Camosun* which had departed on her maiden voyage from Victoria, British Columbia the previous day. She was southbound, heading toward the Panama Canal with a load of plywood bound for Great Britain. *I-25* sent a torpedo into her port side, flooding two of her cargo holds.

Tagami surfaced, ordered several rounds fired from the *I-25*'s deck gun, and submerged. Later, he would report the *Fort Camosun* as sunk. She was not, though in the darkness, even her crew assumed her to be a goner and took to lifeboats.

The Canadian corvette HMCS *Quesnel*, on patrol off Cape Flattery, arrived on the scene at dawn and began an unsuccessful search for the *I-25*. After the HMCS *Edmundston*, a veteran of the *Coast Trader* incident, arrived to cover the *Quesnel*, the corvette finally moved in to begin her recovery of the crew who had abandoned ship. When the *Fort Camosun* continued to refuse to sink, the *Edmundston* took her under tow. With the help of the civilian tugs *Henry Foss* and *Salvage Queen*, along with the U.S. Navy tug USS *Tatnuck*, the damaged freighter was taken to Esquimalt, British Columbia, and ultimately to Seattle, for repairs. In December 1943, the *Fort Camosun* would survive Japanese torpedoes a *second* time in the Indian Ocean, off Somalia.

Scant mention was made, even in the Canadian media, of the *Fort Camosun*'s near miss off Cape Flattery. In fact, the Canadian Press wire service did not release mention of it for a week, and the name of the ship was not given "for security reasons."

Even as the crippled ship was being towed and nudged to port, the Imperial Japanese navy was escalating its war against the American Pacific Northwest and British Columbia.

TWENTY-ONE

Bringing the War Ashore

O ther than those fired in *I-17*'s attack on the Goleta oilfields on February 23, no Japanese shells had fallen on Western North America during the first six months of the war. On June 18, however, Rear Admiral Shigeaki Yamazaki of Submarine Squadron 1 dusted off a plan originally drafted for the December campaign and ordered *I-25* and *I-26* to begin attacking military installations ashore.

After sinking the SS *Coast Trader* on June 7, Commander Minoru Yokota had taken *I-26* north, and was operating off the coast of Vancouver Island when he received these orders. At approximately 10:30 p.m. on June 20, *I-26* surfaced five miles off of the village of Hesquiat, located approximately 160 miles north of Victoria. The gunners then proceeded to open fire on the Canadian government's radio telegraph, weather, and direction-finding station there, and on the 100-foot Estevan Point Lighthouse about four miles to the west. The submarine fired at least seventeen rounds, possibly as many as thirty, over a period of thirty to forty minutes. However, rough seas spoiled the gunners' aim and, none of them struck either the lighthouse or the radio station, and there were no casualties. According to Lieutenant General Kenneth Stuart, the acting commander in chief of Canada's West Coast Defenses, the damage was limited to "[a] few windows...broken by concussion."

The Royal Canadian Navy reacted quickly, sending five warships to search for *I-25*, while the Royal Canadian Air Force sent a patrol bomber. By then, Minoru Yokota already was far away and preparing to return to Yokosuka.

As the shells were falling on Estevan Point, Meiji Tagami's *I-25* was slipping away from its attack on the *Fort Camosun* and running south. Having been ordered to shell targets ashore, Tagami had decided to attack Naval Base Tongue Point, Oregon, a minor facility that had been built in the 1920s on the south side of the Columbia River, about twelve miles upstream from the Pacific. The Navy had intended for it be a major port for both submarines and destroyers, but never developed it as initially planned.

Guarding the mouth of the Columbia—and complicating Tagami's mission—was Fort Stevens, bristling with the guns of the Army's Coast Artillery Command's 18th Coastal Artillery Regiment and the 249th Coastal Artillery Regiment of the Oregon National Guard.

On June 21, Tagami approached to within a few miles of the mouth of the river, closely following a fleet of returning fishing boats in order to avoid a minefield. For some reason, however, he did not proceed the dozen relatively unobstructed miles upriver to Tongue Point. Perhaps Tagami was afraid that he would never escape if he went upriver, or, as some sources contend, he mistook Fort Stevens for the naval base.

Whatever the cause for his decision, he surfaced, and ordered his deck gun crew to open fire on Fort Stevens at approximately 11:30 p.m. Witnesses ashore said that the barrage lasted fifteen minutes, though estimates of the number of shots that were fired vary. Herman Edwards of the Portland *Oregonian*, who visited the scene in the light of day, reported nine, based on the craters that he saw, though some witnesses had counted as many as fourteen shots. In his log, Tagami stated that his gunners fired seventeen rounds. Some of them almost certainly fell short, and some probably were duds.

"Astoria was dimmed out, although nobody really had expected a submarine to bob up here," Robert Lucas of the *Astorian Budget* newspaper told Lawrence E. Davies, a San Francisco-based West Coast correspondent for the *New York Times*. "The first explosion of a shell lit the sky outside my Westview home, in a section of Astoria. As the firing continued we could see the dullish orange-colored glow, then a whistle, then a thud and a boom. These glows spread across the sky at irregular intervals, probably for fifteen minutes."

In his book, *Retaliation*, Bert Webber quotes First Sergeant Lawrence Rude, a Coast Artillery Corps gunner at Fort Stevens, who "opened the door of my room and stood there in my drawers cussing at the guys to shut up. Some nut yells back that the Japs are shooting at us and then tore out of the barracks. It was a real madhouse."

"I was scared to death," Jean Heffling told the Associated Press the next day, referring to shells that had fallen 500 yards from the nearby farmhouse she shared with her husband and two children. Her three-year-old daughter "fell out of bed in fright," but her eleven-year-old son slept through the attack.

Also not bothered was Clatsop County Defense Council Coordinator D. J. Lewis, who explained: "I personally heard every shell that was fired and recognized it for shellfire, but it certainly was not sufficiently alarming to cause me to get out of bed. What assurances have we that it wasn't practice at any of the Army or Navy posts around here, inasmuch as this has been known to happen?"

Colonel Carl Doney, the commander of harbor defenses at Fort Stevens, assured him that the attack had indeed come from a Japanese submarine offshore, adding that the shells had fallen "too damned close."

The American artillerymen quickly manned their batteries, illuminated *I-25* with their searchlights, and trained their guns on the submarine. At the time, the armament at Fort Stevens fortifications, included twelve-inch mortars, and ten-inch disappearing rifles, most of them dating back to the Endicott Era around the turn of the century, as well as two batteries of more modern six-inch rifles.

For Doney, the shells may have been falling "too damned close," but he perceived the enemy warship as being out of range. He ordered his gunners to stand down and *not* to return fire against a submarine that they could see—and which was obviously shooting at them.

Doney would later claim that *I-25* was out of range. But *I-25*'s deck gun had a range of seventeen thousand yards. Furthermore, Tagami estimated being eleven thousand yards offshore. The ten-inch guns at Fort Stevens had a range of 14,700 yards, and the six-inch rifles had a range of fifteen miles or more than twenty-six thousand yards. Also, Doney's estimation that *I-25* was out of range becomes even more odd considering that American coast artillery forts had visual rangefinders—and that the fort's searchlights had illuminated the submarine. When pressed, Coney later said that he did not want to give away the positions of his fortifications—although the searchlights had certainly revealed their general locations. What little damage was done by Tagami's gunners was reportedly limited to a baseball backstop and a bundle of telephone cables. A number of craters were found in the vicinity of the fort's Battery Russell. There were no casualties.

The public reaction to the attack was that it could have been so much worse, and that it could and probably would happen again. The sense of vulnerability to Japanese attacks gave rise to demands for action from many, especially Oregon's junior Senator Rufus Cecil Holman. By coincidence, he was in the state at the time on a fact-finding trip as part of his work on the Military Affairs Committee.

Speaking to reporters in Salem, Holman asserted that the Western Defense Command's coastal defense systems were "criminally obsolete, woefully inadequate and poorly distributed," all of which was true. He also pointed out that no aircraft, Army or Navy, responded to the mouth of the Columbia until many hours after the attack.

"Obviously fully informed of the limitations of the guns at the forts, which are of an obsolete vintage of 1898, the Japs cruised leisurely along the coast," he complained. Again, he was right. Information about the aging fortifications was widely accessible from published sources.

As to the quality of information being provided by military public affairs, Holman griped that "what information we get from the [War and Navy] departments in Washington is the same sandpapered reports they hand out to you newspaper men."

In San Francisco, General DeWitt reacted to the attacks with his customary nervousness. In this case, he demanded that the three Pacific Coast governors ban fireworks over the upcoming Fourth of July weekend. In August, he went even further, expanding his indefinite dim-out to Oregon and Washington, and extending it inland 150 miles to include Portland, Sacramento, and Fresno.

Although Japanese-Americans had been removed from Military Area No. 1 and from most of the rest of his theater, he still spoke with trepidation of sabotage and a fifth column. DeWitt was certainly not alone in his continued fretting about the specter of a fifth column, a worry, like many others, that had been given new life after the attacks in the Aleutians. It was alive in the day-to-day concerns of average people on the Pacific Coast, and it permeated the thinking of people in high places.

In a speech to the Commercial Club in San Francisco on June 7, Attorney General Earl Warren had articulated this fear, as well the continuing apprehension of air attacks. He also brought up the nagging concern of chemical and biological warfare as part of the enemy's probable, and overdue, strike on the Pacific Coast.

"The use of sabotage and fifth column activities as a technique of Axis warfare, the air raid, the need for special handling of our alien enemy population and even the nagging possibility of gas and bacteriological warfare all bring problems that can hardly be solved through the processes of civil government," said Warren. "Enemy planes have no nice regard for State and county lines or neat questions of jurisdiction. The solution of these problems may have to be found in martial rule."

❧

I-25 left the Pacific Coast not long after her one-sided fight with Fort Stevens. Traveling by way of Dutch Harbor, she reached Japan in mid-July. *I-25* would be the only Japanese submarine to again cruise leisurely off the Pacific Coast, but no one in the American defense establishment, nor among the general public, could know that.

Unlike Germany's Operation Drumbeat in late 1941 and early 1942, in which U-Boats had wrought havoc on shipping along the East and Gulf Coasts, the Japanese submarine campaign had shown negligible results. Nine of the advanced B-1 submarines had operated off the North American coast, two of them twice (one of them would be back a third time). Yet, they had sunk only two merchant ships, though they had damaged another two beyond repair. No American warships had been attacked successfully. None of the three deck-gun attacks against installations on shore had caused anything but minor damage.

What the submarine attacks *had done*, however, was to ratchet fears of more and more damaging attacks. They gave the people of the Pacific Coast the sense of being under siege and forced DeWitt and the naval district commanders to dim-out the entire coastline—and prompted them to expel tens of thousands of U.S. citizens from their homes.

The campaign also exposed glaring deficiencies in American defenses. American air and naval forces had rarely, if at all, responded to attacks in a timely manner. The response to the SS *Emidio* attack was the most prompt, but that was only because Pappy Cole's PBY was in the right place at the right time. In most cases, it took hours for an American aircraft to respond. Of course, the bottom line is that no Japanese submarines were ever sunk in Pacific Coast waters. Admittedly, in these early months of the war, American anti-submarine warfare was in its infancy in terms of resources and tactical ability. It would take years before it matured.

In the end, the Americans did have the final word. None of the nine Japanese submarines that had cruised off the Pacific Coast in 1941 and 1942 survived the war, and most were either lost, or presumed to have been lost, to American action.

TWENTY-TWO

The Final Blows Came from the Sky

The Japanese air raids upon the Pacific Coast which General DeWitt consistently feared—and which he believed for months would happen at any moment—eventually *did* materialize. But, their shape and substance and the effects of them would be a far cry from what he and many others on the Pacific Coast had imagined.

By the time *I-25* reached Yokosuka on July 17, 1942 and began to prepare for her next cruise, Nobuo Fujita had probably given up on a proposal that he had sent up the chain of command after the submarine's visit Down Under in February.

His idea—or, at least he would claim it was—was to use the E14Y Geta reconnaissance aircraft as a bomber to attack a high value target such as the Panama Canal, or the aircraft factories of Southern California, which were vulnerably located few minutes flying time from the coast. The repurposing of observation aircraft to deadlier uses has occurred often throughout the history of military aviation. The first time occurred during the 1911 war between Italy and the Ottoman Empire when Giulio Gavotti of the Italian Air Force became the first airman to fly a bombing mission. After the *I-25* reached port in July, Fujita was summoned to Imperial Japanese Navy headquarters for an audience with top naval officers Prince Takamatsu, the younger brother of Emperor Hirohito.

To his amazement, Fujita learned that the Navy had approved his scheme, but to his disappointment, they informed him that rather than flying the delicate and vulnerable Geta against a heavily defended target, like the California aircraft factories, Fujita would attack the vast, but virtually undefended forests of western Oregon.

The top brass went on to explain what the Navy had in mind. The Japanese leaders were inspired by a major forest fire that had devastated the town of Bandon and the surrounding area on the southern Oregon coast in 1936. Incendiary bombs, they reasoned, could spark similar conflagrations. The forests of the Pacific Northwest were an important strategic resource and major forest fires were known to consume hundreds of square miles and tie up thousands of firefighters before they were brought under control. Then too, there was the psychological aspect. Like the earlier submarine attacks, the air attacks would frighten the Americans and demonstrate their vulnerability.

On August 15, 1942, with orders to take the war to Oregon's cedar and ponderosa forests in hand, Tagami and the crew of *I-25*, including Fujita and Petty Officer Shoji Okuda, departed from Japan and headed east to strike the United States.

When they surfaced off Port Orford, Oregon on September 7, the waters were too rough for the launch and recovery of the Geta. Two days later, the seas had quelled to moderate swells from which Fujita was sure were safe for flight operations. The crew assembled the E14Y in the predawn half-light, and mounted a 170-pound bomb filled with hundreds of incendiary magnesium pellets under each wing.

With Okuda in the rear seat, Fujita took off from about twenty miles offshore. The E14Y crossed the foggy Oregon coastline near the town of Brookings in Curry County, not far from the California border.

"I saw the sun rising from the mountains," Fujita later recalled. "It was so huge, so wonderfully gorgeous. I was knocked down by the sight."

Using 2,925-foot Mount Emily as his landmark, Fujita flew about five miles inland, turned northeastward and circled the mountain. He then dropped his bombs in succession. Both Fujita and Okuda later reported that the magnesium pellets ignited like fireworks. Mission accomplished, they turned back to the shoreline and to the submarine, where they landed without incident and the crew stowed E14Y in its hanger.

As *I-25* was submerging, though, a Lockheed A-29 Hudson patrol bomber from the USAAF 42nd Bombardment Group appeared overhead on a routine patrol out of McChord Field near Tacoma, Washington. After two successful cruises off the Pacific Coast, *I-25* was attacked for the first time. Two 300-pound bombs hit the water, and their explosions rolled the sub. Tagami ordered a crash dive, and the *I-25* escaped with only minor damage.

It took some time before Americans ashore realized that they had been attacked, though several observers on the ground had heard an airplane. At 6:42 a.m., Howard Gardner, a U.S. Forest Service observer on duty at the Mount Emily fire lookout, spotted the plane, and heard its nine-cylinder Hitachi Tempus engine sputtering like "a Model T backfiring." When Gardner reported the aircraft to the local center of the civilian Aircraft Warning Service, they shrugged it off.

Later in the day, fires were discovered, Gardner and others went to investigate and contain them. They initially thought a lightning strike had touched off the flames, but when they discovered a crater and shrapnel fragments, they assumed that it was a bomb that had been dropped accidentally by an American aircraft while on a training mission. It was not until the following day when the searchers found a casing fragment and the nose cone of a bomb with Japanese markings, that the reality of situation became obvious.

According to a later memo from James D. Olson, Assistant Coordinator of the Oregon State Defense Council to his boss, Jerrold Owen, "the bomb in falling had struck a fir tree about six inches in diameter, much as though lightning had struck it, and the fin of the bomb had sheared off a tan oak tree five inches in diameter as cleanly as though it had been done with a heavy and sharp axe. Fragments of the bomb had been scattered over a radius of about 100 feet, one of the blazing pieces lodging in a decayed stub, setting it afire."

About sixty pounds of fragments were bagged and taken to the U.S. Army post at Gold Beach, about twenty-five miles north of Brookings. Alarms now sounded up and down the coast. Infantry units were dispatched to prepare for the invasion that was sure to come. Concerned that the Japanese had somehow hidden a squadron of floatplanes on lakes in remote areas, the FBI sent agents on horseback deep into the wilderness to look for them.

The FBI initially attempted to keep the story out of the press, but it was to no avail. Rumors and reasonably accurate versions of the real story soon were flying up and down the Oregon coast and into the welcoming arms of the news media. Even Oregon State Defense Council Coordinator Owen abandoned his attempts to keep the incident confidential when he came to the strange perception that it was *good* for the mood of his people.

"Morale among civilian defense workers was getting low," he told the Associated Press on September 15, "because many believed 'it can't happen here.' Well, it did happen last Wednesday, so the workers can see now just what they are working for. We have been praying for just such an attack to shake people out of their lethargy. We believe this incident will do it. Of course the bombing was ideal, because there was no loss of life and no property damage. The bombing was a perfect answer to the many persons who claimed the Pacific Coast couldn't be bombed."

Foreseeing this attack as the harbinger of a larger Japanese air campaign against the United States, Owen went on to say that "Undoubtedly this small foray is but the forerunner of what may be expected in the future. Similar phosphorus bombs dropped on inflammable wooden buildings in our population centers might be expected to cause extensive fires—but for this possibility thousands of our citizens have been training for more than a year and may be expected to meet the situation promptly and effectively when it develops."

The IV Fighter Command, meanwhile, told the Associated Press that "it is impossible for a plane to fly over the coast without being detected." This was untrue, but when Gardner had reported Fujita's aircraft, the authorities ignored him.

◗━

On September 29, at dawn, the crew of *I-25* unpacked, assembled, and launched the Geta—again with Fujita and Okuda as crew. The plane crossed the Oregon Coast, again undetected, near Cape Blanco and about five miles north of Port Orford. The Cape Blanco Lighthouse had been blacked out, but Okuda could see it in the early morning light and use it as a navigation landmark.

The E14Y made a wide loop over the mountains, passing near the Coos County Fire Patrol Lookout at Edson Butte. Ruby Purdin, on duty at the lookout, recorded in her log that she saw an "unidentified plane" near Elephant Rock at 5:19 a.m. She later told her daughter that she had seen a bomb dropped.

Fujita also steered close to the U.S. Forest Service Grassy Knob Lookout, seven miles east of Port Orford. At 5:22, AWS observer Laurence Giebner was one of nine people in that area who heard the sound of the aircraft as it passed. They did not see the Geta in the overcast, but they did see the orange flash of a bomb hitting the forest.

The Forest Service personnel at Grassy Knob went in search of a forest fire that might have been caused by the attack, but it had apparently burned itself out. This time, the Army and the FBI were able to keep the lid on the story, and no information was released publicly until June 1943.

Fujita had made history with the first air attacks on the contiguous United States, but his mission had failed. The planners who had picked the targets did not take into account the misty dampness of the Oregon coast, which had just experienced a wet summer. These conditions, combined with light winds and the quick response of Forest Service crews, prevented the fires from spreading.

Fujita's career as a bomber pilot ended with the second mission, but *I-25* was not yet through with her patrol.

In the predawn darkness of October 4, she surfaced off Coos Bay, Oregon to charge batteries. As it grew light, sailors on watch spotted a ship in the distance. It was the 6,653-ton Shell Oil Company armed tanker SS *Camden.* Tagami submerged and fired two torpedoes, the second of which hit the tanker on its starboard bow, punching a hole in the hull and starting a huge fire. The captain ordered his crew to abandon ship at 7:05 a.m.

Almost as soon as he submerged after this successful sinking, Tagami was alerted to the propeller noise from another ship. Raising his periscope, he saw the 8,168-ton tanker *Victory H. Kelly* seven miles away and taking evasive action. Tagami did not attack. The crew of the *Camden*, except for one man lost overboard in the fire, was rescued around 11:00 by the Swedish-flagged MS *Kookaburra.*

Two days later, at about 9:20 p.m., the *I-25* was off Cape Sebastian, about eighty miles south of Coos Bay, when Tagami spotted the Richfield Oil Company tanker SS *Larry Doheny*, which was coming north from Long Beach to Portland with 66,000 barrels of oil. The 7,038-ton tanker was the same ship that had survived a December 23 attack by *I-17.*

Tagami decided to surface and shadow the *Larry Doheny*, but briefly lost the big ship in the darkness before nearly stumbling into it. The *I-25* was only around 400 yards from its target when Tagami ordered a torpedo fired, near point-blank range for such a torpedo attack, and the explosion rocked the surfaced *I-25* and showered it with debris. The hit knocked out the *Larry Doheny*'s engines and rudder, killed five of her crewmen, and ignited her cargo.

The following day, October 6, Tagami observed, but did not attack the U.S. Navy Q-Ship USS *Anacapa*, which was headed out to rescue the survivors from the *Larry Doheny.* Q-Ships, also called "Mystery Ships," were heavily armed converted merchant vessels that acted as decoys to lure enemy submarines into making surface attacks. Their use by the Navy in World War II began in March 1942—the *Anacapa* was not converted until August—and lasted about a year. Tagami had apparently deduced that the *Anacapa* was a Q-Ship and did not engage.

I-25 remained in American waters for four days before departing for Japan. On October 11, while running on the surface, Tagami spotted what he initially thought were two American battleships, but as he closed on them he realized they were submarines. He thought they were American, but in fact they were two Soviet *Leninets*-class minelaying subs, the *L-15* and *L-16*, en route from Petropavlovsk to San Francisco.

Tagami fired his last torpedo at a range of about 675 yards, hitting Commander Dmitri Gussarov's *L-16*, which sank with all hands. The *L-15* fired on the *I-25* with its deck gun, trying to avenge its sister, but the Japanese submarine slipped away.

Though Fujita's were the only two submarine-launched Japanese air attacks on the United States, there was a widely circulated story about a Japanese aircraft having overflown Seattle in June 1942. The story originated during a postwar interrogation of Commander Masatake Okumiya of the 26th Naval Air Squadron by U.S. Navy Captain J. S. Russell. In the transcript, Okumiya is recorded to have said that a submarine-launched aircraft "scouted Seattle Harbor and reported no heavy men-of-war, particularly [aircraft carriers], there." When this claim was brought to his attention in 1974, Okumiya, by then a respected military historian, insisted that he never said that, and blamed it all on a faulty translation.

◗▬

I-25's cruise, which was the most destructive Japanese submarine sortie against the Pacific Coast, marked the end of the whole ten-month campaign and of Japanese naval operations off the Pacific Coast.

It might not have ended that way, however. Inspired by Fujita's daring initial idea, the Imperial Japanese Navy had decided to develop what could be described as "submersible aircraft carriers" for offensive operations against such high priority targets as the Panama Canal, New York, and Washington, D.C.

Three of a planned eighteen *I-400* class Sen Toku boats were commissioned in 1944. Four hundred feet long and displacing 6,500 tons, they were the largest submarines built until the development of ballistic missile subs a quarter of a century later. They were large enough to accommodate three Aichi M6A floatplanes, appropriately named "Seiran," which means "Storm on a Clear Day," which had a range of up to 750 miles and could carry a 1,875-pound bomb or multiple smaller bombs.

Some Japanese planner envisioned using the *I-400*s and Seirans to conduct chemical or biological weapons attacks against the Pacific Coast. The Imperial Japanese Army's Noborito Laboratory had produced substantial stocks of tactical biological toxins, and had made extensive use of poison gas against the Chinese. Had this operation gone forward, it would have been a fulfillment of the wildest nightmares of General DeWitt.

In July 1945, *I-400* and *I-401* departed Japan and headed for the Panama Canal, their mission being to take out the Gatun Locks and render the canal unusable. This would have greatly hindered American operations in the western Pacific by adding more than a month to the transit time for supplies coming westward from Eastern and Gulf Coast ports. This mission was later changed to a kamikaze attack on American ships—including fifteen carriers—that were mustering at Ulithi Atoll for the invasion of Japan.

On August 15, two days before this planned strike, Emperor Hirohito broadcast his order for all Japanese forces to lay down their arms. Thus, Warrant Officer Fujita and Petty Office Okuda were the only Japanese airmen to strike the mainland United States.

While Japan made no further *manned* air strikes against the Pacific Coast, there were further incendiary attacks from the sky in the form of Project Fu-Go. This was a low-tech scheme that evolved into the most extensive bombing operation against the United States during World War II, and the world's first intercontinental bombing campaign.

After the Doolittle Raid, Japanese military planners cast about for a means of retaliation. Japanese meteorologists had discovered the jet stream and had calculated that balloons launched from Japan could reach the continental United States in less than three days. From this sprang the basic concept of balloons, laden with incendiary and high-explosive bombs, that would be released in Japan, travel to the United States, and drop their payloads. Realizing that the Jet Stream would carry most of the Fu-Go bombs over the heavily forested Pacific Northwest, the Japanese set using incendiaries to start forest fires the Project Fu-Go's primary goal. There were later plans to deploy biological and chemical weapons using the balloons, but nothing seems to have come of them. Under the program, over 9,300 balloons would be launched from Japan over a five-month period. Developed at the Noborito Laboratory and made of laminated mulberry parchment paper or rubberized silk, the balloons were about thirty-two feet in diameter, weighed about 150 pounds, and were filled with hydrogen. Each was designed to carry up to 1,000 pounds of gear, including varying combinations of incendiary and high explosive devices.

Each balloon was outfitted with approximately 30 six-pound sand-bags that were released one at a time by an aneroid barometer trigger each time that the balloon dipped below thirty thousand feet. Japanese scientists estimated that after the last sandbag was detached, the balloon would be over the United States. As it descended, onboard battery would ignite fuses to drop the payload.

The first attempt to launch the Fu-Go operation came in June 1944, but the first balloons did not have sufficient range and had to be redesigned.

Later efforts were more successful, and, in December 1944, news reports of people finding balloon bombs began to appear in the press. The following month, *Newsweek* magazine reported in a small article that "in a snow-covered, heavily forested area southwest of [Kalispell, Montana], two woodchoppers found a balloon with Japanese markings on it. Made of processed paper, the 33 1/2-foot bag bore on its side a small incendiary bomb, apparently designed to explode and prevent seizure of the balloon intact."

The Office of Censorship quickly asked editors across the United States to desist making any further mention of the mysterious "balloon bombs," and the story faded away. Few people in North America were aware of them until after the war.

There was only one fatal incident involving Fu-Go. On May 5, 1945, two days before the end of World War II in Europe, Reverend Archie Mitchell, of the Bly Christian & Missionary Alliance Church in Bly, Oregon, took his pregnant wife, Elsie, and five Sunday school students on a fishing and picnic trip near Gearhart Mountain in the Fremont National Forest, seventy miles northeast of Klamath Falls.

As he was unloading picnic gear from his car, Reverend Mitchell heard thirteen-year-old Joan Patzke remark that she had found a huge object lodged in a tree. As the others moved in to take a closer look, there was a huge explosion. Everyone in the party, including the four other students, ages eleven to fourteen, were killed, except Reverend Mitchell, who was farther away than the others. He survived, only to be kidnapped by the Viet Cong in 1962. He was taken from a leper hospital where he worked, in the highlands north of Saigon, and never seen again.

Around 350 Fu-Go bombs are known to have reached North America. As expected, most landed in the Pacific Northwest—most of them in Washington—but they landed as far away as Texas, Kansas, North Dakota, and even Michigan. Some are reported to have reached Mexico. In early 1945, one Fu-Go bomb knocked out power to the Hanford Engineering Works in eastern Washington where uranium was being processed for the Manhattan Project. Around 230 of them were discovered before the war ended, but they continued to turn up in later years. In fact, one was found in 2014 in British Columbia.

TWENTY-THREE

The Waning Power of the Boss

T he autonomous balloon bombs notwithstanding, the threat of a Japanese attack on the Pacific Coast ended when Meiji Tagami's *I-25* passed, unseen and undetected, over the western horizon and headed back to Japan. Of course, no one on the Pacific Coast could have known this, and, therefore, the perception was that further Japanese attacks were probable. Some also continued to believe that, despite the internment of tens of thousands of Japanese-Americans, an enemy fifth column was coiled and ready to attack.

For his part, General DeWitt remained vigilant and concerned about the effects of seemingly innocuous activities on the security of his theater. In July 1942, with the Aleutian debacle still playing out and, therefore, still prominent in the minds of the Pacific Coast population, DeWitt had bypassed Governor Culbert Olson and called the California State Fish and Game Commission—and ordered that the August deer hunting season, scheduled to begin on August 10, be cancelled in coastal counties from San Diego to Monterey.

On August 5, DeWitt went one step further, calling Olson this time with a "request" that hunting be banned elsewhere in the state because, he claimed, of the risk of fire. Olson told the Fish and Game Commission that "military necessities in the present serious emergency must be given immediate consideration," and that a request from the Western Defense Command was equivalent to an order. The *Los Angeles Times* editorial page supported DeWitt's edict, insisting that "the public must accept and cooperate with it with no grumbling."

"The boss," apparently, was still the boss.

◗▬

As much as he might have wanted to do so, DeWitt could not suspend the law of unintended consequences. This shortcoming manifested itself in the summer of 1942. Because one-third of the vegetables that were produced in California were from Japanese-American farms, and a good portion of the production on other farms involved Japanese-American labor, there was suddenly a crisis in food production in California. California produced 70 percent of the nation's vegetables, so, in fact, a crisis now loomed regarding the *nation's* food supply.

In June, non-Japanese fruit and vegetable growers across the rich San Joaquin Valley had approached Governor Culbert Olson to ask for a suspension in further evacuations of Japanese-Americans. On June 30, at a meeting with the governor, as well as W. J. Cecil, the State Director of Agriculture; B. C. Moore of the Western Growers and Shippers Association; A. Setrakian, president of the California Grape Growers, and Kenneth Moyer, secretary of the Los Angeles County Agricultural Commission, Frank Palomares, manager of the San Joaquin Valley Agricultural Labor Bureau, put the matter into perspective. He said "some 35,000 to 40,000 workers will be urgently needed in this part of the valley as the harvest season progresses. Some youngsters of school age may prove satisfactory, but in general they are not suited [to the work]."

Olson approached Frank Buckner of the Federal Employment Service, who told him that there would be little chance of "obtaining a fundamental change" in Western Defense Command policies.

Olson's support of the growers might have seemed to be a smart political move in an election year, but it only served to give fodder to his opponent. At a campaign rally in Ventura on August 9, Attorney General Earl Warren, the Republican gubernatorial candidate, addressed the farm labor crisis, telling his supporters that when Olson "realized he hadn't done anything the only thing he could suggest was that he bring the Japs back from the internment camps to help with the harvests."

The *Los Angeles Times* editorial page was less nuanced, writing on August 16 that "since the governor well knew that Gen. DeWitt would never grant [his plea for the return of Japanese farmers] isn't it a fair inference that the Governor was seeking, by an empty gesture, to line up the Jap vote in his favor?" Registered voters inside the internment camps had been promised absentee ballots.

Warren made Olson's failure to prepare an adequate defense against "fifth column as resourceful and as any which helped defeat the little nations of Europe" a key element of his platform. Warren also lambasted Olson for having formed a State Council of Civilian Defense, but "not calling them [sic] into action" for half a year.

Until August, it had been assumed that Olson would skate comfortably to reelection, but Warren's message about the ineffectiveness of the governor in a time of crisis resonated with voters. In the August 25 primary election, Warren secured the Republican nomination by a nine-to-one margin, but there was an even bigger surprise on the Democratic side. As California had an "open primary" system, voters were allowed to cross over party lines. Earl Warren discovered that he had won 45 percent of the votes cast by the members of Olson's own party. An optimistic Warren now decided to package himself, not as the Republican candidate, but as a nonpartisan one. The November 3 election was an anticlimax. Culbert Olson, the man who had once called for a total Japanese-American exclusion, but then backpedaled, lost to Earl Warren, by 57 percent to 42 percent.

In Oregon, Governor Charles Sprague did not even get to run in the general election. He lost the Republican primary to Secretary of State Earl Snell, who leveled the same charges of civil defense bungling at Sprague that Warren used so successfully against Olson in California. In Portland on November 14, Federal District Court Judge James Alger Fee ruled on the appeal of Oregon-born *nisei* attorney Minoru Yasui, who had been arrested in March for a curfew violation. Though he ruled against Yasui, Fee said that without martial law, "the orders of Gen. DeWitt are void as respects citizens, but are valid with respect to aliens." However, Fee decided that because Yasui had worked for the Japanese Consulate in Chicago, he had forfeited his citizenship, so the curfew did apply to him.

The ruling sent a ripple of discussion across the Pacific Coast, but DeWitt's edicts remained the law of the land pending appeal. The case was referred to the Supreme Court, where the justices overturned Fee's decision in a June 1943 decision. They stated that Yasui had not renounced his citizenship, but DeWitt's orders were valid under threat of invasion even in the absence of martial law. This was to be used as a precedent in future cases, but DeWitt had suffered the first serious internal challenge to his omnipotence.

Other attitudes were changing. By 1943, on the West Coast, it was no longer uncommon in everyday conversation—or tantamount to political suicide—to speak of allowing "loyal" Japanese-Americans to return to their homes.

Back east, a more thorough thaw in public and official opinion had taken place. In Washington, D.C., Secretary of War Henry Stimson still favored continued internment, as did Dillon Myer, who had succeeded Milton Eisenhower as head of the War Relocation Administration. However, the U.S. Army's Chief of Staff, General George Marshall, had come to favor an end to internment.

The thaw had reached the White House, too. Less than three weeks short of the first anniversary of his signing Executive Order 9066, President Franklin Roosevelt finally admitted that "Americanism is not and never was, a matter of race and ancestry...Every loyal American should be given the opportunity to serve this country wherever his skills will make the greatest contribution—whether it be in the ranks of our armed forces, war production, agriculture, government service, or other work essential to the war effort."

On February 1, 1943, Roosevelt's action matched his rhetoric when he officially authorized the creation of the U.S. Army's 442nd Infantry Regiment, a unit which, like the smaller 100th Infantry Battalion, would be composed entirely of *nisei* enlisted men and non-coms and in which many of the junior officers would also be Japanese-Americans.

Out on the Coast, if there was anyone who still had the will to defy the winds of change, it was DeWitt. On February 25, the first anniversary of the Battle of Los Angeles, DeWitt's Western Defense Command ordered a blackout in Los Angeles. The enemy of vigilance, DeWitt decided, was complacency, and he wanted to remind Angelinos that the enemy was still out there in the Pacific.

"Enemy inaction along the Pacific Coast during the past several months may well give rise to a relaxation of public interest in civil defense measures," DeWitt wrote in a March 1, 1943 memo to James Sheppard, director of the Ninth Regional Office of Civilian Defense in San Francisco. "A shrewd enemy takes advantage of a public state of lethargy, and may even attempt to cause a civilian population to be lulled into a sense of security, thereby creating a favorable opportunity for attack. The mere fact that enemy raids have not taken place along this coast should be a challenge to civilian defense to renew its vigilance...It is requested that you take the necessary action to bring to the attention of the general public the need for constant vigilance and attention to civilian defense training and preparedness."

On April 13, 1943, the House Committee on Naval Affairs, chaired by California Congressman Edouard Izac, arrived in San Francisco for a series of hearings. A 1915 Annapolis graduate, Izac had served in the U.S. Navy during the Great War. Captured in 1918 when his ship was sunk by a U-Boat in the Atlantic, Izac was taken to Germany. He eventually escaped with valuable intelligence and, for his valor, he received the Medal of Honor. Having made his home in San Diego, he was elected to Congress in 1936.

Naturally, no hearing of such importance on defense matters on the Pacific Coast could possibly be complete without an appearance from the boss, and Izac extended him an invitation. However, DeWitt was unaccustomed to being questioned, especially by civilians he could not intimidate.

Victor Hansen tells the story about the time when California's junior U.S. Senator, Sheridan Downey, had come to San Francisco in 1942 to speak to DeWitt about coast defense matters.

"General DeWitt refused to see him," Hansen recounted to Amelia Fry of the Bancroft Library oral history office, going on to add that DeWitt did agree to send a delegation, including both Hansen and DeWitt's Fourth Army chief of staff, Brigadier General James Barnett, to meet Downey at his suite at the Palace Hotel.

"He was quite angry, and he told us to go back and tell General DeWitt that he was a United States Senator, and he was being offended," Hansen said of the meeting with Downey.

"I'm sure that the General will reply that he recognizes that you're the Senator from the great state of California, and as such you're entitled to much respect," Hansen told the senator. "Also the General would tell you that he's the general in charge of the western states, and that there are probably eight or ten Senators that would like to see him. But if he devotes all of his time talking to Senators, he wouldn't have time for his job."

When Hansen reported back to the boss, DeWitt asked with a chuckle "How'd you know what I wanted to tell the Senator?"

▶━

Fast forward to April 1943, and DeWitt found himself facing Edouard Izac at the aforementioned hearings. As the questions began, the man who, since December 1941, had been accustomed to deference from politicians at every level, lost his composure. DeWitt irritably expressed a sentiment, once shared by most, and still shared by some, that would summarize his legacy in four simple words.

"A Jap's a Jap," DeWitt insisted when Izac asked him about the evolving public opinion on the matter of fifth column activities, and the relaxation of the internment of Japanese-Americans. "It makes no difference whether he is an American citizen or not.... don't want any of them. We got them out. They were a dangerous element. The West Coast is too vital and too vulnerable to take any chances."

DeWitt pointedly told Izac that he would oppose "by every means I can [the] sentiment that Japanese-Americans should return...there are constant requests concerning individuals... You can't change [a Japanese-American] by giving him a piece of paper."

However, less than a week later, DeWitt bowed to pressure from Washington, D.C., and reluctantly issued "a piece of paper" of his own. In it, he proclaimed that "all terms and conditions of public proclamations, civilian exclusion orders and civilian restrictive orders this headquarters heretofore issued, governing the presence, entry and movement of persons of Japanese ancestry within said military areas of Western Defense Command, are suspended [for] persons of Japanese ancestry who are members of the army of the United States on active duty or who have been inducted and are in uniform while on furlough or leave."

Of this announcement, the *San Francisco Chronicle* took pains to note that only "a week ago General DeWitt publicly opposed the return of persons of Japanese descent to the West Coast."

Some in the news media, however, stuck with him. The *Los Angeles Times* editorialized on April 22 that "by a peculiar and perhaps useful coincidence, the current soft-headed agitation for the return of 'loyal'

Japanese civilians to the West Coast areas from which the Army evacuated them as dangerous potential enemies comes just as long-silent Tokyo is issuing almost daily threats of devastating raids on this same West Coast and when our own defense commands are warning us to prepare for them."

Three days later, at 8:19 p.m. on Easter Sunday 1943, DeWitt's Western Defense Command issued a yellow alert, plunging Los Angeles into the darkness. "The boss" apparently determined that the public needed another one of his reminders of "the need for constant vigilance." The "unidentified targets" were soon revealed to have been identified and the all clear sounded at 9:26 p.m.

The alerts and the widely reported "Jap's a Jap" tirade made DeWitt seem to his superiors in Washington as a man who was increasingly out of touch with the evolving nature of the strategic situation. Even the Secretary of War, who had once been a stalwart advocate of DeWitt and his policies, was coming around to the notion that the general had been on the job too long.

As there are no secrets in Washington, the rumors began to circulate that a change of command was in the works. However, his superiors in the Army decided to allow DeWitt to redeem himself by reversing his most serious military embarrassment: the Japanese invasion of Attu and Kiska.

Even as he maintained an iron grip upon the affairs of the Pacific Coast states, DeWitt was nagged by the continuing Japanese occupation of 452 square miles of his theater in the Aleutians. On the American island of Attu, the Japanese had established a garrison of 2,400 men. On Kiska, the ten-man American weather station had been replaced by an even larger garrison of around 5,200 troops and civilians.

In the summer of 1942, the recapture of the islands was hardly a strategic necessity. Besides, retaking them would have stretched American capabilities. A year later, however, a *failure* to recapture them would have stretched American credibility—and public and political credulity.

The operation to recapture the islands initially called for Kiska to be retaken first because it was the largest and relatively more important, but it was decided to invade Attu first because it was smaller and more lightly defended. In either case, the effort was postponed until the summer of 1943 in order to avoid the horrible weather that torments the Aleutians during the winter.

George Marshall made DeWitt the head of the operation because he was the theater commander. In reality, he would be little more than a figurehead. The operation was planned by Rear Admiral Thomas Kinkaid of the Navy's North Pacific Force and Major General Simon Bolivar Buckner of the Army's Alaska Defense Command, with Kinkaid in overall command. The majority of the troops did come from within DeWitt's command, specifically the 7th Infantry Division—still training at Fort Ord, but for operations in North Africa, not Arctic warfare—under the direct command of Major General Albert Egar Brown.

An even more telling indication of DeWitt's declining status was that, when the official news releases were issued, beginning on May 14, 1943, three days after the invasion, their dateline was Washington, *not* DeWitt's headquarters in San Francisco. DeWitt did go up to the Aleutians, but he remained at a command post at Adak, 400 miles away, figuratively looking over the shoulder of Admiral Kinkaid as he ran the show.

The campaign did not go nearly as smoothly as had been hoped. American troops landed in the fog and bitter cold, and battled ice and snow, as well as Japanese air attacks. The fog had prevented an adequate preliminary naval bombardment, and Japanese resistance was much stiffer than anticipated. On May 16, with the American forces bogged down, Kinkaid and DeWitt agreed to relieve Brown—who had purposely left heavy coats and other cold weather gear on the dock in San Francisco—as commander of the 7th Infantry Division and replace him with Major General Eugene Landrum.

It was mere wishful thinking when Secretary of the Navy Frank Knox told a press conference on May 21 that American forces had completed the conquest of Attu Island, and that "the mopping up process is all that's left." In fact, "the mopping up process" consisted of another eight days of bitter fighting. As reported by George MacGarrigle in the U.S. Army Center of Military History's account of the campaign, "out of a US Force that totaled more than 15,000 men, 549 had been killed, another 1,148 wounded, and about 2,100 men taken out of action by disease and nonbattle injuries…Most of the nonbattle casualties were exposure cases, victims of the weather and inadequate clothing." This means that more than a quarter of the U.S. force became some form of casualty. American forces captured twenty-eight Japanese and found another 2,351 dead.

On May 26, as optimistic news releases masked the grim Aleutian reality, Congressman Richard J. Welch blabbed to the press about DeWitt's future. The *San Francisco Chronicle* reported that Welch revealed that it was "generally understood in Washington that a War Department argument over treatment of Pacific Coast Japanese would result in Lieutenant General John L. DeWitt being relieved of his duties as Pacific Coast military commander within a short time."

The California Republican, who had represented San Francisco in the United States Congress since 1926, and who was a DeWitt supporter, added that "we have no right to criticize any personnel orders issued by the commander in chief or the War Department…. but we may demand that policies we think for the best interests of our districts be maintained."

Pressed to comment on reports that DeWitt was being sacked for his policies toward Japanese-Americans from the Coast, Secretary of War Stimson told the Associated Press that "such a story, in that respect is nonsense. General DeWitt has made a fine and successful record as commander of the Fourth Army, particularly in the handling of a very difficult problem." He did *not* deny, however, that relieving DeWitt from his post on the Pacific Coast was under consideration.

A May 28 editorial in the *Los Angeles Times* loyally observed that "if General DeWitt were to receive a genuine promotion to a post of greater usefulness, this area would lose him with regret but would not stand in the way of his advancement. But if he is to be shelved because

Washington conceives it knows more about the situation on the Pacific Coast that he does the public here will tell Washington in no uncertain terms that it is misinformed."

In Washington, D.C., however, the Army was making moves that indicated that General DeWitt's tenure in the Presidio was coming to a close.

When news came that Lieutenant General Delos Emmons, the commander of the Army's Hawaiian Department would be turning his command over to Brigadier General Robert C. Richardson on June 1, rumors of DeWitt's departure intensified. When an Associated Press reporter pressed Emmons for information, the general replied that he couldn't comment on his next assignment, but added, "There wouldn't be a more pleasant place to serve than San Francisco."

PART THREE

What Might Have Been

TWENTY-FOUR

Pacific Vision

The Japanese strategic vision of the Far East and of the events leading to World War II had its roots in ancient times. According to legend, roughly 2,500 years ago, Japan was ruled by an emperor named Jimmu, who in present memory is as mythical as he is real, and who may or may not have existed as more than just an heroic ideal. From Jimmu came the doctrine of *Hakko ichiu*, which is understood as meaning "eight corners of the world under one roof." By the 1930s in a Japan bent on regional dominance, it was understood that the "eight corners of the world" were the Far East and the "one roof" was that of Japan.

From this flowed the idea of the Greater East Asia Co-Prosperity Sphere, a clearly enunciated plan in which, politically and economically, the nations and peoples of the region would be in orbit around Japan like planets rotate around the sun. Japan's 19th and 20th century wars in China, and its forcible acquisitions of Taiwan, Korea, and Manchuria were all manifestations of this grand strategic vision. Complicating this vision was the presence of outside forces—the Russian Empire (later the Soviet Union) in the north and European colonial powers, especially Britain, France and the Netherlands, in Southeast Asia as well as the United States in the Philippines. The establishment of the Greater East Asia Co-Prosperity Sphere demanded that Western powers be ousted from their colonies.

As late as 1941, however, the Europeans to the south, especially the British, assumed that they could stave off any Japanese attempt at conquest. Though the Netherlands had been conquered by the Germans, the Dutch East Indies remained defiant and were planning to resist a Japanese invasion. The Americans in the Philippines were also mindful of Japanese ambitions and guardedly optimistic that they, too, could foil any Japanese attempt to take the islands.

In the summer of 1941, General Hideki Tojo was consolidating his power within the Japanese government. As Minister of War, Tojo was already one of the most powerful men in Japan and would succeed Fumimaro Konoe as prime minister in October.

In 1940, Roosevelt had used authority granted to him by Congress to prohibit the export of aviation fuel and some other petroleum products and scrap steel and certain kinds of iron to Japan. In July 1941, the Roosevelt administration, reacting to the Japanese occupation of French Indochina (albeit with the acquiescence of the pliant Vichy regime), had ramped up economic sanctions on the Japanese. The United States had long been the principal source of petroleum for Japan. On July 26, Roosevelt ordered Japanese assets in the United States to be frozen. Britain and Dutch East Indies almost immediately followed suit. These moves effectively cut Japan off from critical raw materials from the United States and Southeast Asia—and almost 90 percent of its oil imports. Japanese planners estimated that the nation's oil reserves would last about three years at peacetime consumption levels and approximately half that time at wartime consumption levels.

For Japan, the conquest of the British and Dutch colonies in Southeast Asia as well as the Philippines took on a new urgency. And, thus, the overall direction of the initial Japanese offensive in 1941 was set: the striking power of the U.S. Navy—its battleships and aircraft carriers— would be destroyed at Pearl Harbor. Free from concerns about a response from the Americans, Japan would move into Southeast Asia and seize the resource-rich Dutch and British colonies. It would conquer the Philippines and other U.S. possessions in the Pacific, such as Guam, thus, pushing the boundaries of American power and influence out of the Western Pacific. With the influx of raw materials, food, and oil from these areas, Japan then would be able to prepare itself to repel any Western attempts to retake their former colonies.

Without a doubt, Japanese strategy in 1941 and 1942 was audacious in planning and execution. That audacity, coupled with the fighting spirit and skill of Japanese soldiers and sailors and the bold leadership and action of many Japanese commanders, was what made its lightning advance possible and what utterly bewildered Japan's Dutch, British, and American opponents.

But, what if Japan had been even more audacious? What if it had seized a chance to dominate the Western Pacific, but the Eastern Pacific as well? What if it took a chance on seizing complete mastery of the entire Pacific Rim by invading the United States?

In all likelihood, the man who might have been able to persuade Japan's military and naval leaders to adopt such a strategy would have been Admiral Isoroku Yamamoto, the commander of the Imperial Japanese Navy's Combined Fleet. Yamamoto had long advocated a more aggressive naval strategy in the Pacific. For decades, the IJN had subscribed to the idea of a decisive battle (*Kantai kessen*) with the U.S. Navy that would take place in the Western Pacific, after the IJN had lured the U.S. Navy across the ocean (both navies foresaw a Japanese move on the Philippines as the probable *causis belli*). Yamamoto instead proposed that Japan strike deep inside the American sphere of influence and take the battle to the Americans, closer to the United States rather than closer to home. This was the thinking behind the Pearl Harbor operation and the thrust against the Aleutians and Midway in June 1942.

It is intriguing, therefore, to think what might have happened had Yamamoto been able to overcome the chronically dysfunctional relationship between Japan's generals and admirals—and persuade Tojo and the Japanese Army (and many of his fellow naval officers) to truncate the Southeast Asian operation and, along with the strike against Pearl Harbor, launch a full-blown assault on the Pacific Coast.

Tojo probably would have insisted that on assurances that the IJN could protect the forces invading Southeast Asia as well as Japanese home waters. Considering what the balance of naval power was in the Pacific at the time, Yamamoto could have issued those assurances (albeit on the condition that the Pearl Harbor operation was a success). Apart from the battleships and aircraft carriers in Pearl Harbor, the Americans had only the Asiatic Fleet, based in the Philippines, in the Far East. It had but one heavy cruiser (the USS *Houston*, which would earn eternal fame in 1941 and 1942), two light cruisers, and thirteen destroyers as well as a number of submarines, many of which were older and less effective. Between them, the British and the Dutch had eleven cruisers and a dozen destroyers. As we know from historic hindsight, this Allied naval strength in Southeast Asia—to include two British capital ships sent to Singapore as a deterrent to Japanese aggression—was virtually erased in a series of battles in January and February 1942.

After the success at Pearl Harbor, the striking power of the American navy was limited to three aircraft carriers. Thus, the naval dominance that would have allowed Japan an immense freedom of action across the Pacific would have been in place.

As it had proven in China and Southeast Asia, the Imperial Japanese Army was a formidable fighting force. Between December 1941 and May 1942, it conquered Hong Kong, the Philippines, the Dutch East Indies, Malaya, most of Burma; forced the surrender of Singapore Britain's strategic linchpin in Southeast Asia; and turned Thailand into an ally.

As had occurred in the Russo-Japanese War, the world was stunned by the unanticipated prowess of Japan's Army.

Five field armies out of the roughly two dozen in the IJA were devoted to these operations. The 14th Army, under Lieutenant General Masaharu Homma, was used in the Philippine operations. The 15th Army, commanded by Lieutenant General Shojiro Iida, went into Thailand and, later, Burma. Lieutenant General Hitoshi Imamura's 16th Army attacked the Dutch East Indies, and the 23rd Army, under Lieutenant General Takashi Sakai, took Hong Kong. Under the brilliant command of Lieutenant General Tomoyuki Yamashita, the 25th Army rolled through Malaya and captured Singapore, earning Yamashita the enduring *nom de guerre*, "Tiger of Malaya."

Organized into the Southern Expeditionary Army Group, the umbrella organization for all Southeast Asia operations, these armies came under the command of a former minister of war, General Count Hisaichi Terauchi, who had his headquarters at Saigon in French Indochina.

If parts of the massive Southeast Asian offensive had been delayed or postponed, some of these troops (probably most of them) and the supplies that supported them and ships that moved them could have been used for operations in North America. With unquestioned air and naval superiority in Southeast Asia, the Imperial Japanese Army could have contained Allied land forces in Southeast Asia and the Philippines, bottling them up and effectively neutralizing them.

Certain operations still might have been conducted in Southeast Asia without seriously eroding the strength of a Pacific Coast invasion force. For example, it took only a brief show of force by the 15th Army to force Thailand's surrender and conversion to a Japanese ally. So this operation could easily have been carried out. In the Philippines, Japanese airpower shredded the USAAF within days, and the invasion achieved most of its goals within a month. A residual force, therefore, might have been left to contain the Americans and Filipinos, while the majority of the 14th Army redeployed to the American operation or operations in Southeast Asia. Alternatively, with American airpower destroyed and naval forces routed, the Philippines could have been contained by Japanese seapower, and the 14th Army could have gone directly to the United States.

Containment might also have worked in Malaya, where a smaller force based in Thailand could have kept British forces on the defensive. The Hong Kong invasion, too, could have been postponed given that the British garrison, isolated by Japanese naval superiority, posed little threat to Japanese operations in China.

Borneo, the center of petroleum resources in the Dutch East Indies, was captured in early February 1942 by the IJA's 35th Infantry Brigade and 56th Infantry Group of the IJA 56th Division, and IJN Special Naval Landing Forces. Thus, Japan could well have taken control of the oil it needed without detracting from force that was necessary for the Pacific Coast operations. Likewise, the assaults on Wake Island and Guam, which took place simultaneously with the Pearl Harbor operation, also could have gone forward as they did.

Moving eastward, American strategy continued to rely on the Pacific Fleet acting as the sole line of defense for the Pacific Coast, especially since USAAF land-based bombers were few and far between. After Pearl Harbor, however, the Pacific Fleet's battleship was neutralized, leaving three aircraft carriers and about twenty cruisers, but they were widely spread and would have posed little threat to a Japanese invasion fleet.

The carrier force later provided the nucleus of the American victory at Midway, but, in December 1941 or January 1942, they might have been picked off one by one by Japanese submarines and aircraft. Alternatively, the U.S. Navy might not have wanted to risk the destruction of what would have been its strategic reserve and so moved the carriers out of harm's way, perhaps as far away as the Canal Zone.

And when would the blow have fallen? Again, a major attack on the Pacific Coast would have been possible if—and only if—the attack on Pearl Harbor had been a success. Considering the Japanese penchant for strategic surprise (e.g., the attack on Port Arthur to open the Russo-Japanese War and the Pearl Harbor raid) and their apparent appreciation of how rapid, unexpected, and decisive action gave them the initiative and a profound psychological advantage over their enemies, the best time for the operation would have been soon after Pearl Harbor.

Yamamoto could have solidified his case for invasion by appealing to the conviction then common among many Japanese political and military leaders that the Japanese people—and more to the point, the Japanese fighting man—had an innate spiritual superiority which could make up for many material disadvantages. He also could have made a practical argument. In late 1941, American industry had yet to hit its stride in terms of military production. Every day that Japan waited to launch an invasion against the United States, therefore was a day in which the Americans would come closer to realizing their undeniable industrial potential and to producing the ships, aircraft, and other means of war that could overwhelm Japan.

The Japanese invasion forces would have had ample time to move into positions off the Pacific Coast. It had taken the Pearl Harbor strike force, which included tankers as well as warships, nine days to steam 3,200 miles from northern Japan, taking a circuitous route so as to avoid commercial shipping lanes and to approach Hawaii undetected. Departing under tight security, maintaining radio silence, and traveling by routes meant to avoid detection, the invasion fleets could have covered most of the distance to the United States before the war began. After the war began, the ships could take a more direct route to their targets, and their escorts could have engaged any ships or aircraft encountered on the last few days.

The six aircraft carriers of the Pearl Harbor force could have made the trip to the Pacific Coast in short order. In fact, given their high speeds, these ships and a fast escort could have refueled and then made a sprint to the Pacific Coast in order to provide air cover for the invasion. With American airpower on Hawaii eradicated and American seapower there severely crippled, the Japanese had no reason to invade the islands, especially Oahu. They could have sealed off the entrance with mines or blockships, bottling up the undamaged part of the Pacific Fleet, let Hawaii wither on the vine. This approach would have been similar to the "island hopping" strategy later used against the Japanese by the Americans in the western Pacific.

Therefore, a Japanese invasion of the United States would probably have taken place in mid-December. But before that battle could have taken place, it would have been necessary for another to have been fought in the interior of the Western United States, a battle waged by spy and saboteur.

TWENTY-FIVE

Invasion Day

An invasion of the continental United States would have required detailed planning and meticulous preparation prior to the invasion force being delivered to the battlefield. The first step would have involved isolating the Pacific Coast battlefield from the rest of the United States.

The fact that the Coast was connected to the rest of the country by a finite number of narrow and fragile corridors was a golden opportunity. As described in detail in Chapter Five, the rail and highways in these narrow corridors passed through remote, rugged and lightly populated areas. Here, there were numerous tunnels, highway bridges, and railroad trestles that were in isolated locations. In most cases, they were hundreds of miles from an alternate route. Likewise, telephone and telegraph lines, which generally paralleled highways and railroads, were extremely vulnerable and would be difficult to repair without road access. The prior insertion of a small number of covert sabotage teams in the weeks ahead of the actual invasion would have had the goal of cutting most, if not all of these lines of communication.

Turning to the invasion itself, Japanese planners would have considered timing and settled on the scenario of "as soon as possible after Pearl Harbor." Next, they would have considered the forces available and the invasion locations.

In Chapter Twenty-Four, I noted that five field armies out of a total of about two dozen in the Imperial Japanese Army were earmarked for the December 1941 Southeast Asia and Hong Kong campaigns. If these operations were cancelled or greatly truncated, those five armies could have been reassigned to an invasion of the Pacific Coast.

For the sake of this hypothetical exercise, let's assume that the forces used in the Pacific Coast Theater were those that, in 1941, had been assigned to the Southeast Asia Theater. Instead of a *Southern* Expeditionary Army Group, General Count Hisaichi Terauchi would have commanded an *America* Expeditionary Army Group. Instead of headquarters in Saigon, Terauchi would have first exercised command at sea. Once ashore, he certainly would have been tempted to establish his headquarters in what was then the greatest city on the West Coast—San Francisco—and probably in the former offices of General John DeWitt at the Presidio of San Francisco.

≈

Insofar as strategic objectives were concerned, Japanese planners probably would have drawn on the Japanese experience in China to guide them. There, where it must be noted the Japanese had successfully taken a country with an area nearly twenty times greater and a population nearly five times greater than Japan's, the first objectives had been the major coastal cities of China, such as Shanghai and Canton, and then a concerted move to seize almost all of China's coastline.

The objectives of the Japanese, therefore, would have been Seattle and the naval base at Bremerton across Puget Sound, then Portland with, perhaps, a tertiary mission of securing at least some of the Columbia

River dams. In California, San Francisco and Los Angeles would have been essential strategic goals as would have been San Diego, with its great naval facility.

Another essential strategic goal, of course, would have been the destruction of the four U.S. Army divisions stationed along the West Coast, especially those commanded by General Joe Stilwell and concentrated between Monterey and San Luis Obispo.

Japanese naval assets would have been divided into three task forces, each centered on a carrier division of the 1st Air Fleet, which included *Akagi* and *Kaga* in the 1st Division, *Soryu* and *Hiryu* in the 2nd Division, and *Shokaku* and *Zuikaku* in the 5th Division. A task force would have been allotted to support the landings in the Pacific Northwest, and the other two would have divided between the landings in Northern California and Southern California. To its usual escort, each division would have been supported by additional destroyers, as well as several cruisers and perhaps two battleships each.

To face this formidable array of naval power, the U.S. Navy had only fourteen destroyers, half of them in San Diego and four in San Francisco Bay. The only battleship, the USS *Colorado*, was being overhauled at Bremerton, and the only cruiser, the USS *Concord*, was being overhauled in San Diego. The Pacific Fleet's three aircraft carriers would have been at sea. The USS *Enterprise* and USS *Lexington* were west of Hawaii, having luckily missed the Pearl Harbor attack, while the USS *Saratoga*, which had been in San Diego on December 7, departed for Pearl Harbor the following day.

The IJN, therefore, could have matched the U.S. Navy's entire available Pacific Coast force with any of its three task forces whether or not the USS *Saratoga* returned to respond to a Japanese attack on the West Coast. Prior to the commencement of hostilities, the locations of American ships were well-known. Yamamoto, therefore, would have had an additional advantage when he planned naval operations on the Pacific Coast.

In all likelihood, the IJN's actions would have commenced with a carrier strike against naval facilities and any ships in port. If any of the destroyers had emerged to fight, Japanese surface forces would have given them battle, and it probably would have turned out to be like those fought in Southeast Asia in late 1941 and early 1942 especially as with the Battle of the Java Sea at the end of February 1942. It would have been a lop-sided Japanese victory.

If the *Saratoga* had returned to defend the Pacific Coast, chances are that she would have been overwhelmed by Japanese aircraft and suffered the same fate as HMS *Hermes* off Ceylon in April 1942.

When we think of amphibious landings in World War II, we probably think of operations like Tarawa and Iwo Jima in the Pacific or Salerno and Normandy in Europe, in which soldiers or Marines assaulted well-fortified, heavily defended positions, often under intense artillery and machine gun fire. In mid-December 1941, virtually the entire Pacific Coast was *undefended*. There were no troops stationed at probable invasion beaches. The only fortifications were the Coast Artillery forts that guarded the entrances to California ports, the mouth of the Columbia River, the entrance to Puget Sound, and these could be bypassed by invading troops.

In terms of airpower, the Japanese had a roughly two-to-one advantage over the Americans in number of aircraft, and, more precisely, in the number of fighter aircraft available for air-to-air combat. Qualitatively, the Japanese Mitsubishi A6M Zero was superior to most of the American types, and the Japanese fighter pilots had extensive training and substantial combat experience—including their recent actions over Pearl Harbor.

As at Pearl Harbor, the first strike by Japanese carrier aircraft would have been aimed at American airfields, especially those at which fighters were based. In the north, USAAF interceptor bases at Portland Airport and Paine Field, north of Seattle along with U.S. Navy airfields in the Puget Sound area, would have topped the target list. In California, Hamilton Field, north of San Francisco, and March Field in Riverside County would be the first to be attacked. Putting these bases out of action would have essentially given the Japanese control of the skies.

With their fighter protection eliminated, the bomber bases at Spokane, Washington and Pendleton, Oregon, as well as in California's Central Valley, would have been vulnerable to attack from the air as well.

They also would have been forced to make any attacks against the invaders without the benefit of fighter escort.

The Japanese would have depended on carrier air power at the beginning. But to conduct sustained air operations against targets inland, the Japanese would have needed longer range bombers such as were used to support operations in Southeast Asia. Just as the IJN Air Force possessed Japan's most formidable fighter plane in the Zero, it also operated the most effective Japanese medium bomber of World War II, the twin-engined Mitsubishi G4M (later known to the Allies as the "Betty"). This aircraft, however, did not have the range to reach the Pacific Coast from Japanese bases, nor could it operate from a carrier.

This conundrum could have been resolved by delivering crated bombers to the Pacific Coast by ship and assembling them at bases established ashore. The Betty was a rugged plane that did not need huge concrete runways in order to operate. Small coastal airports or simple grass strips would have sufficed. Other options to bolster Japanese air-power would have been to use the smaller, slower carriers to act as ferries for aircraft of the Imperial Japanese Army Force. Also, flying boats, such as the Kawanishi H8K, which was used for the *second* raid on Pearl Harbor, and floatplanes, such as the Aichi E13A, both supported by seaplane tenders or ad hoc shore bases, could have provided a stop-gap while land-based air power was established.

It is tantalizing to think that the Japanese might have fulfilled one of the more popular conspiracy theories of December 1941 by capturing airfields in Baja California and using them to mount attacks on southern California.

When considering the locations for the three main landings, Japanese planners would have been looking for lightly defended areas, relatively close to the major cities and set in relatively flat and open terrain in order to allow troops to move swiftly off the beach and toward their objectives. Although the Pacific Coast may have been connected tenuously to the rest of the United States by few highways, the road network *on* the Pacific Coast, especially within one hundred miles or so of the coastline, was excellent. Just as the modern highway built in Malaya by the British greatly aided the Japanese drive to Singapore, American roads would have given an advantage to the invaders as much as they did to the defenders. Access to this road network, therefore, also would have been an attractive feature that Japanese planners would have been pleased to exploit.

In 1909, shortly after the Russo-Japanese War changed the role and standing of the Japanese Empire on the world stage, a man named Homer Lea wrote an insightful book entitled *The Valor of Ignorance*. A Stanford-educated self-styled adventurer, Lea was a co-founder of Roswell, New Mexico and spent several years in China at the turn of the twentieth century, where he served as a confidant of future Chinese leader Sun Yat-sen and as a lieutenant general in the Baohuanghui army. In his book, he laid out a detailed criticism of the unpreparedness of the United States military establishment, and presented a scenario for a Japanese invasion of the Philippines and the United States. His description of the Philippines campaign, including the amphibious landing sites, is exactly as it actually occurred thirty-two years after he wrote about it.

In the Pacific Northwest, Lea suggested Willapa Bay and Grays Harbor, twenty-five miles apart on the Washington coast, as landing sites. Both are deep inlets that would shelter an invading force from often rough seas and inhospitable mid-winter weather of the North Pacific. They also are less than 200 miles from Seattle and Portland.

Once the invading force was ashore, it probably would have moved to capture Aberdeen, which is on Grays Harbor and which had an airport. The invaders could have reached Olympia on the second day, capturing a state capital and, more important, putting the Japanese astride U.S. Route 99, then the only major highway between Seattle and Portland.

Meanwhile, to attack Portland from the south without having to cross the Columbia River, a Japanese force might have landed at Newport,

Oregon, the western terminus of U.S. Route 20. They would have gained access to good roads as well as a small facility adequate for unloading troops and a small airfield. They would have been only around 130 miles from Portland and could have attacked from the south through the level, open terrain of the Willamette Valley.

In central California, with an eye toward taking San Francisco, perhaps the best place to land amphibious troops was by way of the relatively calm waters and open beaches of Monterey Bay, about 120 level miles south of the Golden Gate. There are good beaches farther north, but landing at those locations would require crossing the steep and rugged coastal mountains.

Lea suggested that U.S. Army troop concentrations should be in the Santa Clara Valley, forty-five miles south of San Francisco, and seventy-five miles north of Monterey Bay. In fact, in 1917 during World War I and five years after Lea's death, the U.S. Army did him one better, establishing the gunnery range *on* Monterey Bay that evolved into Fort Ord, the home of the 7th Infantry Division, one of only two Regular Army divisions in the Western Defense Command.

Terauchi would have wanted to engage and defeat the 7th Infantry Division eventually, but his first task would have been to get at least one of his divisions safely ashore. Therefore, a feint either north or south to draw off some of the defending force might have been necessary before conducting the actual landing.

Terauchi might have decided to make an exceptionally bold move: to attack San Francisco directly. The unimaginatively named Ocean Beach, a straight, four-mile stretch of sandy shoreline defines the western edge of the city. Rocky Point Lobos at the north end juts into the Pacific and would prevent the coastal artillery arrayed around the Golden Gate from targeting invaders coming across Ocean Beach.

Once ashore, an invader would have a choice of nearly two dozen perfectly straight streets leading directly toward the heart of the city. City

Hall is but five level miles away, with the city's financial district, then still considered the "Wall Street of the West," less than two miles beyond. General DeWitt's office at the Presidio was only five miles from Ocean Beach.

Immediately south of Monterey, the steep terrain of the Big Sur coast presents its own difficulties. Farther south, however, near San Simeon and Cambria, nearly one hundred miles south of Monterey, there are good beaches suited to amphibious operations, with a relatively level passage on California Route 1 to the U.S. Route 101 corridor at San Luis Obispo. Indeed, this area had been used by the U.S. Army for prewar amphibious exercises.

However, these beaches are only about thirty miles north of the California National Guard base at Camp San Luis Obispo, which was then home to the 40th Infantry Division. Meanwhile, the beaches near Santa Maria, about fifty miles south of Camp San Luis Obispo present an opportunity for a second landing, but again with the drawback of being close to the base of a defending division. Alternatively, either site might be used either for an actual landing and the other for a deception operation.

Once ashore successfully in this area, a Japanese force could occupy the central coast and be positioned roughly 200 highway miles from both San Francisco and Los Angeles so as to be available to move either direction to support other landings.

As San Francisco was the objective in Northern California, Los Angeles and San Diego were those in Southern California. One option would have been a landing between the two, perhaps north of Oceanside in the lightly populated area that would eventually become the U.S. Marine Corps' Camp Pendleton. This would put the invading force ashore seventy-five miles south of downtown Los Angeles, sixty-five miles from the Ports of Los Angeles and Long Beach, and fifty miles north of San Diego, all via the broad and well-maintained U.S. Route

101. The same naval force that conducted any action against Naval Base San Diego could have easily supported operations here without even moving the aircraft carriers.

North of Los Angeles, a landing in rural Ventura County near the city of Oxnard, would have placed the invader about sixty miles west of downtown, again via Route 101. About forty miles to the northwest of Oxnard, Terauchi could have made a regimental-sized landing aimed at capturing the petroleum refining complex around Santa Barbara that was later to be the target of Kozo Nishio's *I-17*.

As in a direct assault across Ocean Beach in San Francisco, Terauchi might also have considered the same for Los Angeles. Landing his troops on the picturesque sandy beaches of Santa Monica Bay south of Malibu, would put them less than twenty miles from downtown Los Angeles or Hollywood, and less than ten miles from the Inglewood oil fields or Beverly Hills. They would also be outside the radius of fire from the big guns of Fort MacArthur, which were situated to protect the entrances to the harbors of Los Angeles and Long Beach.

As in San Francisco, the invaders *might* have made rapid progress on city streets, such as Santa Monica Boulevard, and raced deep into the county, perhaps as far as Pasadena, via the Arroyo Seco Parkway on the first day or two of the invasion. Then again, the volume of traffic present on Los Angeles streets—infuriatingly heavy then, as now—might well have impossibly snarled both the advance of the Japanese, as well as the evacuation of frightened refugees, for many days.

As was the case with the operations of the five field armies of his actual Southern Expeditionary Army Group, Hisaichi Terauchi's hypothetical America Expeditionary Army Group would have been prepared to move quickly, a *blitzkrieg*–style operation aimed at covering great distances, capturing key points, and keeping the Americans off-guard. Also, as in Southeast Asia, there would be an emphasis on simultaneous action across the entire Pacific Coast Theater. Whether it was on December 12 or December 14, Invasion Day would have been Invasion Day at locations from San Diego to Willapa Bay.

TWENTY-SIX

The Battle Is Joined

At full strength, Terauchi's five field armies each had around fifty thousand men, mostly combat troops organized into two or three infantry divisions plus tanks and extra field artillery. Roughly, therefore, 250,000 Japanese troops would have been involved in the invasion. DeWitt had around 172,000 troops under his command, though many were staff personnel at the various posts, or assigned to the especially labor-intensive Coastal Artillery Corps positions.

As previously noted, the only Regular Army Divisions were the 3rd Infantry at Fort Lewis, Washington and the 7th Infantry at Fort Ord, California, and there were two National Guard divisions stationed on the West Coast. There were also about seventy-five thousand Navy, Marine Corps, and Coast Guard personnel within the Western Defense Command area, but the only combat troops among them were fewer than fifteen thousand men in the newly reactivated 2nd Marine Division in San Diego.

It is important to underscore how isolated the units in California were from those in the Pacific Northwest. As I was reminded on a recent drive over this route, at modern Interstate highway speeds, Fort Ord (now CSU Monterey) is separated from Fort Lewis (now Joint Base Lewis-McChord) by at least 14 hours. At military truck convoy speeds on the two-lane highways as they existed in 1941, especially in December when heavy snow was probable in the Siskiyous, the journey, if a shift of personnel was deemed necessary, would have taken several days. The Japanese would have known of this bottleneck and would have made it a high priority for sabotage.

Had a Japanese sabotage campaign launched immediately before the invasion been successful, it would have sown confusion among the defenders and the residents of the Pacific Coast. It also would have prompted demands from politicians at every level as well as the press that DeWitt disperse his forces to prevent further sabotage—at a moment when the concentration of forces would have been of paramount importance.

In 1942, in historical fact, the Japanese 16th Army defeated an Allied force of equal size in Java within a week. In Malaya and Singapore, the roughly thirty thousand men of the IJA 25th Army defeated a British Empire force of more than one hundred thousand. These facts effectively dispel the notion, coined by Voltaire in 1770, that "God is always on the side of the big battalions."

For DeWitt, his powerful, well-manned Coast Artillery organization would have been a blessing and a curse. Has the Japanese attempted to move directly against any of the major Pacific Coast ports, for example, trying to force the Golden Gate, they would have faced formidable firepower. At the same time, however, the fixed coastal batteries tied down a sizable number of troops, and they could have been easily outflanked. If, as Lieutenant General Tomoyuki Yamashita would do, famously and successfully, at Singapore in February 1942, the invaders had avoided a direct attack on the harbor entrances guarded by coastal guns, they could have made successful landings. DeWitt probably would have brought more field artillery to the battlefield than Terauchi would have had, at least initially, but, by all estimates, the American stocks of ammunition would have been spent within a few days at best. The tanks available to the two sides were evenly matched. The M3 Stuart light tank and the Japanese Type 95 were similar in size and armament (both had a 37 mm gun as their main armament), but, according to Stilwell in his diary, maintenance issues had reduced the number of M3s available at Fort Ord to just six.

For the sake of this "What If...?", let's assume that D-Day would have been Sunday, December 14, and arbitrarily assign the field armies to specific locations. The 14th Army under Lieutenant General Masaharu Homma would land in Washington and/or Oregon; the 15th Army under Lieutenant Shojiro Iida would land at San Francisco; and the 16th Army under Lieutenant General Hitoshi Imamura would land at Monterey Bay. Meanwhile, commanded by Lieutenant General Takashi Sakai, the 23rd Army would land north of San Diego. The attack on Los Angeles would fall to Hideki Tojo's old friend and professional rival General Yamashita and his 25th Army.

A surprise attack might have been achieved as it was at Pearl Harbor, but it is likely that at least some of the Japanese invasion forces would have been detected by American patrol planes a day or two ahead of the landings. However, their exact destinations would have been open to speculation, and there would have been little that the U.S. forces present at the time could have done to stop them.

Arrayed against the Japanese thrust into the Pacific Northwest would have been the forces of the Northwest Sector of the Western Defense Command, under Major General Kenyon Joyce whose headquarters were at Fort Lewis. Within this organization, Joyce two coastal artillery regiments at Fort Worden, which guarded the approaches to Puget Sound, and the 3rd Infantry Division under Major General John Porter Lucas and the 41st Infantry Division under Major General Horace Fuller, the latter a National Guard unit.

When he received word of an impending Japanese invasion deemed likely, Joyce might have deployed his two divisions to the area of Grays

Harbor and Willapa Bay to stop the amphibious invasion, and he certainly would have kept at least part of the force back to protect the U.S. Route 99 approaches to Seattle and Tacoma. Knowing that he also had responsibility for protecting Portland, he might have sent troops south to that city.

General Homma would likely have concentrated his full force at Willapa Bay, but he may also have availed himself of the opportunity for an unexpected landing at Newport for one of his three divisions. When he learned of this, Joyce would have perhaps sent his 41st Infantry Division to Portland to defend the city, and possibly to drive south on Route 99 to meet the Japanese before they could reach Portland. In any case, Homma would have had the initiative, and Joyce's deployments would have been based on no small amount of guesswork.

Even with some opposition, the Japanese, landing in the predawn hours of December 14, would have consolidated their beachhead at Willapa Bay by the middle of the day. By that time some of the troops on the tip of Homma's spear could have been on their way to capturing Aberdeen, adding a second port at Grays Harbor at which to unload transport ships. By that time, the troops that landed at Newport would have been ready to begin their drive on Portland.

In Malaya, the Japanese famously used bicycles to transport their troops on the excellent paved roads built a few years earlier by the British. In the United States, where automobiles were more common than in the Far East, the Japanese might have preferred to use purloined motor vehicles. Indeed, as in Malaya, the Japanese might well have limited the number of motor vehicles in the invasion force, deliberately planning to rely heavily on stolen cars. The Japanese probably also would have brought bicycles to the Pacific Coast, and, given the availability of fuel, they might have included motorcycles for reconnaissance.

As a precursor to any landing, the aircraft from the *Akagi* and *Kaga* of the Rear Admiral Chuichi Nagumo's 1st Carrier Division would have launched dawn attacks against the USAAF at Paine Field, McChord Field (adjacent to Fort Lewis), and Portland Airport. If things had played out as they actually did at Pearl Harbor and in the Philippines, many American aircraft would have been destroyed on the ground, and any aircraft that rose to meet the enemy probably would have endured heavy losses as well. Among the second wave targets would have been Fort Lewis itself and the Bremerton Navy Yard on Puget Sound, where the battleship USS *Colorado* was being refitted.

The distance from Aberdeen to Olympia was only about an hour at highway speeds on U.S. Route 410, with Tacoma and Fort Lewis less than an hour beyond on Route 99 northbound. The pace of any Japanese advance would have been much slower because, after securing a beach-head, the force would have paused to allow for the unloading of vehicles, such as tanks, and supplies. Furthermore, given that the top highway speed of the Type 95 tanks was around thirty mph, and that the tanks would have slowed down in order to allow supporting infantry and artillery to keep pace, the Japanese spearhead might have taken a couple of days to reach Olympia.

Assuming that he would keep most of Lucas's 3rd Infantry Division in reserve, Joyce would probably have been forced into a race to Olympia with Homma's spearhead. Any American forces advancing to meet the invaders, however, probably would have been slowed by streams of refugees escaping north toward Seattle, and probably clogging the south-bound lanes that Lucas needed to move troops.

As soon as a landing force at Newport, Oregon, had been able to round up a sufficient number of vehicles, it could have made their way to Oregon's state capital Salem, by way of Albany, in a few hours against little or no organized resistance. Perhaps, Homma would have ordered a motorized *coup de main* to seize the city.

In any event, as they would have for American forces, northbound refugees on Highway 99 and other roads probably would have slowed the advancing the Japanese between Salem and Portland. While they could not have stopped the Japanese advance because of their lack of heavy weapons, as well as effective command and control, home guards, state and local police, and self-generating group of guerrillas also might have hindered it, if only slightly. It is probable, therefore, that the invaders would not have reached Portland until December 16 or later.

D➡

Shifting south, it would still have been dark on the morning of December 14 when the first troops from Shojiro Iida's 15th Army began to disembark into landing barges for their assault on Ocean Beach in San Francisco. Although General DeWitt probably would have ordered a blackout as soon as he had received warnings of an approaching invasion force, there is every reason that it would have been as spotty and ineffective as it actually was that week. In fact, had advance Japanese raiding parties been able to attack the electrical grid, their actions would have been more effective in imposing a blackout than any public efforts to do so. In any case, there probably would have been sufficient light to orient the barge operators and the troops could land with relative ease. These initial landings would have been largely unopposed, and any opposition from home guards and, police would have been brushed aside. Behind the advance elements of the invading force, heavy equipment, such as tanks and artillery, would be unloaded after daylight.

At his headquarters at the Presidio, General DeWitt would have faced a dire situation. Probably, Japanese aircraft would have targeted his headquarters and, if their strikes were successful, DeWitt's ability to keep up with events and exercise effective command throughout the theater and the more immediate area of San Francisco would have been severely curtailed.

Furthermore, the military police and a few infantry troops assigned to the Presidio would have been too few in number to intervene effectively in the Battle of San Francisco. The best they could have done was to protect the Presidio itself.

The majority of the soldiers then in the San Francisco area would have been those who manned the forts protecting the Golden Gate. The good news, as DeWitt would have been informed, would have been that the enemy had not tried to pass through the Golden Gate. The bad news, of which DeWitt need not be reminded, would have been that his big coastal guns—especially the casemated sixteen-inch rifles—could not engage the invasion fleet located south around Point Lobos.

Once the first Japanese regiment or two were ashore, they would have begun to march or drive, depending on how many motor vehicles they could have seized, toward the heart of the city—and the Presidio. The only thing that would have slowed the Japanese advance, besides improvised roadblocks, would have been the thousands of San Franciscans attempting to flee the city.

The forces on the ground would have been supported by naval gunfire from battleships and cruisers and the aircraft of the *Soryu* of the 2nd Carrier Division, then commanded by Rear Admiral Tamon Yamaguchi. The Japanese naval aviators would have struck at first light throughout the Bay Area. Their initial targets would have been the Mare Island Naval Shipyard and Hamilton Field in Marin County, both north of San Francisco. The naval air station at Moffett Field, thirty-five miles south of San Francisco, which had been a major center of rigid airship operations in the 1930s, was now only lightly used as a USAAF training facility. Meanwhile, at Alameda Naval Air Station across the Bay from San Francisco, facilities for a major future presence were still under construction, and there were only a few patrol planes based there.

If some of the P-40s of the IV Interceptor Command were in the air that morning, they might have enjoyed some success against the attackers. Over time, however, Japanese attacks on American airfields would have denied the fighters the ability to operate in an effective manner. It might have taken more than a day or two, but it might have happened as quickly as it did at Clark and Nichols Fields in the Philippines, and the USAAF would have lost the air battle over San Francisco.

On the ground, the Japanese would have probably reached the city's huge *beaux-arts* City Hall, the dome of which is taller than the U.S. Capitol's, sometime on the first day. Iida's forces also could have bypassed City Hall in order to capture a far more valuable prize, the Port of San Francisco. If those facilities had been captured intact—and there is little reason to think that such would not have been the case—any follow-on build-up of Japanese forces would have been fast and efficient.

What would have—could have—General DeWitt done on that first day? He might have tried to call his subordinate commanders—Joe Stilwell in San Bernardino, Major General Walter Wilson, the commander of the III Corps at the Presidio of Monterey, and Major General Charles White, who commanded the 7th Infantry Division at Fort Ord.

As soon as patrol planes detected and confirmed Japanese ships offshore a day or so earlier, DeWitt would have huddled with Fourth Air Force commander Major General Jacob Fickel and Brigadier General William Ord Ryan of the IV Interceptor Command, who both had their offices inside the Presidio. DeWitt would certainly have been in touch with Admiral John Wills Greenslade of the Twelfth Naval District, who maintained his office in San Francisco.

On that first day, DeWitt would have contacted local officials, such as Mayor Rossi and Chief Dullea. He would have tried to get in touch with the state governors, although both Olympia and Salem would have been in danger of imminent ground attack. If Japanese saboteurs had managed to cut telephone lines and Japanese air attacks had damaged his headquarters, his attempts to contact these men would have been fruitless. If he had been able to reach any of his ground commanders and officials, they probably would have told him that their hands were full and that they would have been unable to lend him any assistance in the defense of the immediate San Francisco area. At sea, Greenslade's entire available force at Mare Island consisted of three destroyers, which might have put up a valiant defensive action against the invasion fleet, but one that was doomed from the outset.

Almost certainly, his commanders and public officials would be calling DeWitt, begging for assistance that he could not give. Almost certainly, reports of real and imagined (and exaggerated) Japanese actions would have flooded his headquarters, denying him the ability to get a hold of the actual situation. Columns of smoke rising from the city and in the direction of Hamilton Field and Mare Island would only have heightened his anxiety. Perhaps, the best he could have done was to hold the southern approaches to the Golden Gate Bridge long enough to allow some civilians to evacuate the city, and for he and his headquarters staff to escape into Marin County in hopes of organizing future resistance.

As DeWitt dealt with an increasingly chaotic situation in San Francisco, his subordinate commanders in the Monterey area would have been dealing with their own problems. As elsewhere in the theater, the day would have begun with Japanese air attacks in the early morning. Aircraft from the *Hiryu*, the other 2nd Division carrier, would have attacked Fort Ord, bombing and strafing barracks, tank and artillery parks, and headquarters facilities.

It is doubtful that Lieutenant General Hitoshi Imamura would have landed his 16th Army in Monterey Bay, as doing so would have thrown out his forces directly against the 7th Infantry Division. More probably, he would have mounted a diversion to draw Wilson and White southward. Perhaps the IJN could have bombarded the picturesque little town of Carmel, and the entrance to the Carmel Valley, four miles south of Monterey. If Wilson and White believed that this bombardment was the preliminary to landings in Monterey Bay, they would have moved troops into position to thwart it—and left the actual beachhead, forty miles to the north, between Santa Cruz and Watsonville, undefended.

The mobility that unchallenged sea power would have granted Imamura would have provided him many options for action. He might have sent two divisions ashore in order to meet Wilson and White and landed his third one hundred miles farther south on the coast near San Simeon with the purpose of engaging and defeating the 40th Infantry Division, commanded by Major General Ernest Dawley and based at Camp San Luis Obispo, as early as possible in the campaign.

Alternatively, Imamura could have kept his entire command intact to ensure the defeat of the 7th Infantry Division before turning his attention to the 40th Infantry Division. Assuming that he had prevailed in the Battle of Monterey Bay, Imamura would have moved his army, minus a force to garrison Monterey and nearby Salinas, south, down Route 101, through the broad and level, Salinas Valley, to San Luis Obispo, 150 highway miles away. Just north of the city, however, the highway reaches a roadblock of rugged mountains and crosses the very steep Cuesta Grade, a choke point and an ideal defensive position. Dawley almost certainly have established a defensive line there before a battle that probably would have taken place around December 21. Confronted by such a situation, Imamura might have sent his army into a head-long frontal assault against the Americans or, as occurred in the Southeast Asia campaign in 1941 and 1942, mounted an amphibious assault in regimental strength north of Morro Bay, roughly thirty miles to the rear of Dawley's roadblock. Confronted by the possibility of being surrounded, Dawley might have ordered a retreat, and, considering that breaking contact with an enemy and conducting an orderly retreat is a challenging task even for regular army troops with combat experience, this retreat could have turned into a rout for the National Guardsmen.

In Southern California, there would be a vast air-land-sea campaign, with battles spanning nearly 200 miles of the California coastline.

As noted in the previous chapter, the opening gambit would have been the naval Battle of San Diego, for which Yamamoto would have set aside the world's most advanced aircraft carriers, *Shokaku* and *Zuikaku* of the 5th Carrier Division commanded by Rear Admiral Chuichi Hara. This battle would be aimed at finishing—or at least continuing—the destruction of the U.S. Navy's Pacific Fleet.

Alternatively, Hara might well have positioned one of his carriers farther north of the other so that its aircraft could have struck the USAAF's main facility in the area, March Field in Riverside, California. Such a strike would have done much to prevent American airpower, such as it was, from influencing future operations.

Japanese strikes against the U.S. Navy in San Diego probably would have delayed the amphibious operations for a day in order to ensure that they could be supported by the aircraft from both *Shokaku* and *Zuikaku* without distraction. The 23rd Army under Lieutenant General Takashi Sakai would have begun with predawn landings on the coast near San Clemente, whereupon the Japanese would turn south toward San Diego, only fifty miles away. After having secured San Diego, Sakai could then have pivoted his army northward and headed toward Los Angeles and Long Beach, acting as the southern side of a pincer movement with the 25th Army that would have been driving from the north. That would have been the plan. However, in his assault on San Diego, Sakai's army would have been met by the 2nd Marine Division, based at Camp Elliot and commanded by the imperturbable Major General Charles Price. Price may well have dispatched his Marines to meet the invaders as they moved south from San Clemente. If he had, there is no doubt that the Marines would have inflicted serious casualties on the Japanese and disrupted whatever timetable Sakai had set for the 23rd Army's operations. Yet, given Japanese air supremacy and the limited stocks of ammunition and other supplies available to his division, Price could not have held the Japanese back for long. In the end, he probably would have ordered a fighting retreat toward the east, hoping to preserve as much of his unit as possible for a future counteroffensive.

The Battle of Los Angeles would have been an enormous undertaking in urban combat. While the cities of the Bay Area were densely populated and highly concentrated in 1941, the population centers of Southern California were already showing the evidence of suburban sprawl for which they would became famous after World War II. Within the 4,058 square miles of Los Angeles County alone, there were 2.8 million people, 40 percent of the California total. By December 1941, the largest city captured by the Japanese had been Shanghai with a population of 1.5 million. It took the Japanese Army two months to take Shanghai in a costly and destructive battle.

An unopposed landing on the broad strawberry fields of Oxnard would have had a strong appeal to Yamashita. However, it would have taken two days or more to reach downtown Los Angeles, so a direct assault against Los Angeles on Santa Monica Bay might have had the appeal of expedience. As in San Francisco, the bulk of U.S. soldiers in Los Angeles were assigned to Coast Artillery forts. Given this lack of substantial U.S. Army maneuver forces in the Los Angeles area, therefore, Yamashita could have taken the same direct approach used by Iida in San Francisco. Like Iida, Yamashita would have emphasized swift movement in the first few hours, knowing that, after the initial shock of the invasion had worn off, refugees would have clogged the local roads and highways. Therefore, a landing at Santa Monica Bay would have been considered the best option.

Of course, a landing within full view of the homes of movie stars in the Hollywood Hills would have been, dare we say it, cinematic. Likewise would have been the sight of Type 95 tanks on Hollywood Boulevard, though the actual invasion routes would have probably followed such parallel boulevards as Beverly, Pico and Santa Monica.

The city of Santa Monica, at the north end of the bay would have provided the threshold for a direct push toward downtown Los Angeles, as well as an opportunity to capture the Douglas Aircraft Company headquarters at Clover Field inside the city.

At the center of the bay, Los Angeles Airport was a literal stone's throw from the beach and within sight of the factories of Douglas Aircraft in El Segundo, Northrop in Hawthorne, and North American Aviation in Inglewood. Capturing these intact would have been desirable and probably a high priority for the Japanese. It is hard to say if the Americans would have been able to seriously damage these factories before the Japanese reached them. Attempts might have been made to destroy the factories to keep them from being used by the enemy, but considering how quickly the Japanese would have reached them after coming ashore, it is doubtful that there would have been time for extensive sabotage.

Additional landings at the southern end of San Monica Bay, between Manhattan Beach and Redondo Beach, would put the Japanese at the doorstep of strategically important petroleum facilities, and provide troops of the 25th Army a southbound gateway, via the Pacific Coast Highway and Hawthorne Boulevard, toward the ports. Once those were in hand, a great stream of ships from Japan would flood in, carrying reinforcements and the civilian technicians and administrators who would run California's most populous region as a virtual Japanese colony.

TWENTY-SEVEN

Beyond the First Contact

Napoleon is famously, though erroneously, credited with saying that "No plan survives contact with the enemy." In fact, it was Field Marshal Helmuth von Moltke who said in 1871 that "no plan of operations extends with any certainty beyond the first contact with the main hostile force."

It is hard, therefore, to write a hypothetical narrative of a hypothetical military campaign beyond its opening days, just as it is hard for a commander to prepare for all contingencies. Often things go as planned, but almost never exactly, and frequently not at all.

There are unexpected moments of failure and cowardice, just as there are unexpected moments of heroism and improbable successes. The best that a commander can hope for is that he has covered, or at least considered, the possible as well as the probable.

Had the Japanese invaded the West Coast, the United States might have lost most if not all of the opening battles. Masaharu Homma's 14th Army might have defeated John Porter Lucas' 7th Infantry Division in a battle between Olympia and Tacoma. If Joyce had committed Horace Fuller's 41st Infantry Division, the Americans might have prevailed, since one of Homma's divisions was south of Portland.

In actual history, Homma defeated the U.S. Army's Philippine Division and 26th Cavalry Regiment in a 140-mile, week-long drive from Lingayen Gulf to Manila in December 1941. It is therefore reasonable to assume that he could have successfully made a sixty-mile drive from Olympia into Seattle via Tacoma in the same length of time.

Would Tacoma have been destroyed to intimidate Seattle into surrender? Would the 110,000 civilians in Tacoma have fled? What then of 370,000 people of Seattle? Certainly, the employees at Boeing and the shipyards of Seattle would have had time—more than would have been available in Southern California—to destroy their facilities and any completed aircraft to keep them out of Japanese hands.

Would Portland have been captured, and how soon? Would the U.S. Army or civilian personnel have been able to destroy the Route 99 bridge and the railroad bridges across the Columbia River, thus, isolating Oregon from Washington?

In history, Takashi Sakai's 23rd Army captured Hong Kong in about two weeks during December 1941, though five days in the middle were spent in the preparation for crossing the harbor from Kowloon to Hong Kong Island. Once on the island, it took seven days to subdue a city with a population of 625,000 swelled by innumerable refugees. At San Diego, Sakai would have found a city with a prewar population of around 200,000, and many of these people would have fled inland before the Japanese closed in. From Hong Kong, there was nowhere to escape.

At San Diego, Sakai would have had a straight drive of fifty miles on a good highway without the interruption of a ten-mile water crossing. However, Hong Kong was defended by a collection of British battalions of less than division strength. In San Diego, Sakai would have found himself facing a Marine division augmented by a large number of sailors from the naval base. As the Battle of San Diego would have taken place a day or two after the invasion, there would also have been time for the U.S. Army to redeploy coastal artillery troops as infantry.

Tomoyuki Yamashita's incredible campaign in December 1941 and January 1942 earned him the nickname "Tiger of Malaya." Then, he captured "impregnable" Singapore in a week, even though he was outnumbered by more than two-to-one. If he had instead been auditioning for the role of "Tiger of Hollywood," how would he have fared in Southern California?

With 2.8 million people, Los Angeles County alone had five times the population and fifteen times the area of Singapore. Beyond that, while Singapore is an island, Southern California stretches into the distance for hundreds of miles.

Yamashita would certainly have taken the airfields and the aircraft factories, and, if he possessed a flair for the dramatic, he could have staged an elaborate surrender ceremony at City Hall, though perhaps not until as late as December 18 or 19. In the ensuing days, he would have sent his army up the Arroyo Seco Parkway and through the Hollywood Hills into the vast San Fernando Valley, where he probably would have found the sprawling Lockheed facilities in Burbank ablaze. After that, he would have turned his army eastward toward the USAAF base at March Field in Riverside and Joe Stilwell's Southern Sector headquarters at San Bernardino. Capturing the runways at March, and perhaps other facilities, would have been extremely useful, though Stilwell would have long since abandoned the California Hotel for a new headquarters in the mountains farther north and east.

◗━

Back in San Francisco, inside the Presidio, had he not managed to escape from the Presidio and reestablish his headquarters in the Sierras or elsewhere, General DeWitt would have faced the bitter humiliation of surrender, probably in a ceremony on the great Presidio Parade Ground which slopes down to its spectacular view of the Golden Gate Bridge. Had he done so, DeWitt would have the distinction of being the highest-ranking

United States general to surrender his command, a distinction that in actual history would go to Lieutenant General Jonathan Wainwright after the fall of the Philippines in May 1942.

What exactly would DeWitt have surrendered? Theoretically, because he commanded the Fourth Army and the entire Western Defense Command, he would have surrendered all United States forces in California, Washington and Oregon, as well as in Alaska. There is little doubt that General Count Hisaichi Terauchi, commander of the America Expeditionary Army Group, would have demanded exactly this.

In the Philippines, prior to his own surrender, General Wainwright had anticipated this demand and had transferred the forces in the southern Philippines under Major General William Sharp to the command of General Douglas MacArthur in Australia. When Wainwright surrendered to Masaharu Homma, he intended to surrender only the forces under his immediate command on Corregidor. In turn, Homma refused his surrender and insisted that Wainwright surrender *all* American troops in the Philippines, including Sharp's. Unless Wainwright did so, Homma told him, the Japanese would consider all captured American troops from Corregidor, Bataan and elsewhere, not as prisoners of war, but still as combatants—or essentially as hostages—subject to being killed. Faced with the prospect of a massacre, Wainwright complied with Homma's demands and ordered Sharp, who was still fighting, to give up.

DeWitt could have transferred command of the Fourth Army and the Western Defense Command to Stilwell in Southern California, assuming that Stilwell could rally enough troops to continue to resist. Furthermore, there is every probability that President Roosevelt might have relieved DeWitt and ordered that any unit still capable of fighting do so and refuse any order to surrender. It is also hard to believe that, faced with an invasion of their home soil, American forces would have ignored any order to surrender and implacably avenged any massacre of captured American fighting men.

What might have happened in the days and weeks that may have followed the Pacific Coast invasion are open to speculation.

How would General Terauchi have ruled the Pacific Coast? As a nobleman, a former governor general of Korea and the ninth prime minister of Japan, he was a politician first, and a soldier second, so he may have erred on the side of conciliation. Faced now with ruling nine million Americans who did not want to be ruled by Japan, and who were well-armed and independence-minded, he almost certainly would have faced a long and intractable guerilla war that could not be won.

Would it have come to this at all? Would the Pacific Coast invasion and occupation plan have succeeded?

There were an enormous number of moving parts, and therefore a myriad of opportunities for it to go wrong. Still, it would have probably taken until January for Marshall to start sending reinforcements from the east, ample time for the Japanese to prepare their defenses.

The USAAF might have used bases in Spokane, Sacramento and Fresno to begin launching air attacks on the Japanese, but these bases were within range of Japanese medium bombers flying from the Coast. The next line would have been bases at Missoula, Salt Lake, and Phoenix, but these were around 1,500 round trip air miles from the targets and could be used only by heavy bombers. In December 1941, the USAAF had only about 200 B-17 Flying Fortresses and fewer than one hundred B-24 Liberators. With Boeing in Seattle and Consolidated in San Diego under Japanese control, there would be no more of either.

The U.S. Navy would have rushed battleships and carriers from the Atlantic Fleet. Via the Panama Canal, they would have arrived in strength by Christmas, but what if they had been intercepted by aircraft from the *Shokaku* and *Zuikaku* of Chuichi Hara's 5th Carrier Division when they emerged from the Canal? If the canal locks were put out of action, the Atlantic Fleet would have had to spend more than a month traveling around Cape Horn. Had the fleet made it through to the Pacific, they *might* have won a Midway-style victory over the 5th Carrier Division, but they would still have other battles to fight, and they were far from home. Whereas the U.S. Navy at Midway was about 1,300 miles from its base at Pearl Harbor, the Atlantic Fleet operating off California would have been roughly 15,000 miles from Norfolk via Cape Horn.

If, by some measure of luck, the later land battles on the Pacific Coast would have been won by Americans, there is a big question whether World War II in the Pacific would have happened as it did, or whether, having thrown the invaders into the sea at great cost, the Americans would have been content to concede the South Pacific and Southeast Asia to the Japanese Empire.

Inside the Pacific Coast, the battles would have continued, with or without immediate reinforcements. The U.S. Army would have regrouped, and throughout the mountains of the West, well-armed civilians would have made life difficult for the invaders. In the Philippines and Southeast Asia the Japanese ruled though a combination of intimidation and currying favor with local populations fed up with colonial rule, but on the Pacific Coast, they would have faced an almost universally hostile population unwilling to submit easily to occupation. The situation would have required more carrot than stick, and even then, managing nearly 10 million independence-minded Americans would have been impossibly difficult.

Whether Terauchi chose to rule as a beneficent monarch or as a monster, the whole enterprise would probably have been doomed to failure on many levels. The Japanese would have been at the end of a supply chain that stretched over thousands of miles, and it would have consumed much of the available Japanese shipping, creating shortages and logistical nightmares throughout the Japanese Empire. Given that food shortages existed in Japan itself, the occupation would have needed to exploit the natural resources of the Pacific Coast states. To take over the vast agricultural lands, they would have faced the same labor shortages as the Americans did, something that might have been resolved by attempting to use slave labor, but this would have backfired.

They would have occupied the aircraft factories, oil fields, refineries, and shipyards, but the Japanese would have had to import management and technical personnel, and even factory labor, or face threats of sabotage. Then, of course, there would also have been the subtle impediments to using American industrial plants, issues ranging from non-metric calibration to English-language documentation.

Although a great deal of American manufacturing would have been lost, the industrial powerhouse that stretched from Chicago through Detroit and into the Northeast would have been untouched. Likewise, all the great shipyards of the Atlantic and the Gulf Coasts, and the oilfields and refineries of Texas, Oklahoma, and Louisiana would have still been in American hands. Most of the biggest plane makers would have been gone, but steps had already been taken to move some of their production inland, and manufacturers such as Bell, Curtiss, Grumman, Martin, and Republic would have been among those that remained. Also still available to the American industrial machine was virtually all of its aircraft and other vehicle engine manufacturing. History shows that American industry did rise to the occasion during World War II, and that it achieved a production miracle of unprecedented proportions.

Most important, the sole focus of the United States armed forces and the American people would have been the reconquest of the West Coast. *Everything* would have been directed toward this purpose.

The American fighting spirit would have been galvanized as never before. Having shed so much blood in the creation and preservation of an independent union in the wars between 1776 and 1865, there remained in 1941 and 1942, an unwillingness in the American spirit to surrender when that spirit did not perceive itself to have been defeated—and indeed, that spirit is something which cannot be defeated—and, therefore, America would ultimately have triumphed.

EPILOGUE

"Where is the Jap fleet?" General DeWitt crowed rhetorically, as he looked out to the cold and empty North Pacific from a west-facing cliff. His choice of words was an obvious reference to the broadcast from Radio Tokyo after the Pearl Harbor attack, which asked sarcastically, "Where is the United States fleet?"

"The Jap navy is in hiding, dispersed," DeWitt said, answering his own question to Eugene Burns of the Associated Press. "Part of it is on the ocean floor...part of it is in the South Pacific to counter Admiral Halsey's forces...part of it is at home to meet any threats from Admiral Nimitz's forces...and part of it is in the North Pacific."

The date was August 21, 1943, and DeWitt was stomping across the rugged black volcanic rubble of the Aleutian island of Kiska—though when Burns was finally able to file his story two days later, it would be datelined merely as "an Advanced Aleutian Base." DeWitt's censors obfuscated the obvious for dramatic effect, just as his spokesmen had continually exaggerated the unverified for the dramatic effect.

DeWitt rambled on and on about how "we" had held the Japanese at Midway, Guadalcanal and New Guinea, and that "now we have driven him out of the Aleutians... As Kiska fell when Attu was reduced, so too will the enemy's other bases fall when with strength we can attack and split him further."

The figurehead theater commander who had done little to plan, execute or even command, the operations at Attu and Kiska, spoke of American strength and an inevitable American victory, but in fact, the reality in the Aleutians had been more nuanced. Though technically a victory, the fight on Attu had gone so poorly at first that the 7th Infantry Division commander had to be sacked and replaced. The victory had been so difficult that the invasion of Kiska was delayed two months until August 15, when a ground force of nearly 35,000 American and Canadian troops had been assembled.

George MacGarrigle of the U.S. Army Center of Military History wrote of the attack that "surprise was achieved, but it was not the Japanese who were surprised."

Despite continuous American surveillance, the entire Japanese occupation force had slipped away undetected on July 28. The 313 American casualties during the invasion were from friendly fire, accidents, and an exploding mine left behind by the enemy.

DeWitt told Burns that the Japanese had escaped by submarine. In fact, surface ships had done the job. Attu, the only land battle fought in the theater of the Western Defense Command, was a costly success. Kiska was an anticlimactic embarrassment for the Americans and, to an extent, DeWitt, who had let the enemy get away.

Nevertheless, during that week on windswept Kiska, DeWitt imagined that the Aleutian campaign was only the beginning of something bigger, much bigger. A few days later, Burns caught up with him. This time, the general was ready to speak about his ideas as to how to prosecute the war against Japan. As General Douglas MacArthur was leading American forces through the South Pacific, Lieutenant General John DeWitt would lead them against Japan across the North Pacific. In the summer of 1943, MacArthur stood 3,200 miles from Tokyo. From where DeWitt spoke so emphatically, Tokyo was a relatively short 1,950 miles away.

"We are now on the offensive in the Pacific," he insisted. "The Jap is on the run. We must retain the initiative now in our hands…We must carry the war to the Japanese Empire. We must wade in and dynamite and gut her with incendiaries. We most hold the initiative we have gained and press it."

That "advanced Aleutians base" was, however, as close as the old soldier would ever get to Japan. A week after he pontificated his North Pacific strategy to Burns, he was back in San Francisco, but he would not be unpacking his bags. The end of his tenure as the commander on the Pacific Coast, rumored in May, had become official in September.

President Roosevelt and General Marshall had decided as early as May to let DeWitt stay on through the conclusion of the Aleutians campaign, but that was it. DeWitt was to be brought back to Washington, D.C. as the figurehead of the newly created Army and Navy Staff College (ANSCOL), envisioned as a training program for officers destined for command and staff duties in joint operations.

In the meantime, Roosevelt had authorized a parting gift for DeWitt: an Oak Leaf Cluster for the Distinguished Service Medal (DSM) he had received at the end of the Great War, which effectively constituted his second DSM. The citation mentioned his "exceptionally meritorious and distinguished service in a position of great responsibility." The effusive language continued, "inspired and animated by his outstanding leadership, American troops in the Aleutians expelled the invading Japanese from American soil." Unmentioned was that the occupation had lasted a full year or that most of the occupiers withdrew on their own.

DeWitt received the medal in a private ceremony at the Presidio and from the Fourth Army's chief of staff, Brigadier General James Barnett. None of the troops whom he had "inspired and animated" were present to see him honored, though in a conversation with William Flynn of the *San Francisco Chronicle*, who reported on the event, DeWitt did praise the men of the Aleutian campaign. He then turned to a familiar theme, insisting that saboteurs remained a threat to the Pacific Coast. He told Flynn that "successful sabotage now would do more damage than it would have at the initial stage [of the war] because of development of our production facilities."

On September 15, DeWitt delivered his parting remarks to San Francisco, insisting to a Chamber of Commerce luncheon that there was *still* plenty to fear because "the enemy still had capabilities that will not disappear until we have landed in Northern Japan and MacArthur has reached the Philippines."

When DeWitt arrived at ANSCOL in Washington, he was out of the limelight, and the scope of his authority reduced from 886,000 square miles of territory and millions of soldiers and civilians to a suite of offices and a small staff.

The Army waived the mandatory retirement age for DeWitt, as it did for many generals during the war, and so he remained on duty, at his Washington desk until August 1944. On August 6, the Associated Press reported that DeWitt had been mysteriously relocated to England, having been summoned to Europe to take up an "undisclosed command of great importance." The fact of the matter was that from the command of much, to the command of little, DeWitt's new assignment called for the command of *nothing*. The First U.S. Army Group (FUSAG) was a fictitious force that had been created under the "command" of General George S. Patton as a deception prior to the Allied landings in Normandy in June. "Secret" information was leaked to the Germans about an immense fighting force preparing for a cross-channel invasion in the vicinity of Calais, the nearest French port to England.

The ruse was immensely successful. The Germans kept substantial forces at Calais even after the Normandy invasion, convinced that *this* was the diversion. Indeed, FUSAG was so successful that it was decided that the hoax should continue. After Patton was placed in command of a real army, the Third Army, which entered Normandy after the invasion, Lieutenant General Lesley McNair, commander of U.S. Army Ground Forces was reassigned to head FUSAG. When he was killed by misaimed USAAF bombs in France on July 25, the War Department scrambled for a lieutenant general to fill in as a successor and they settled on DeWitt.

Both the imaginary FUSAG and the extraneous ANSCOL were eventually terminated without fanfare. The man who commanded them soon was overshadowed by others who were doing so much to win the war. DeWitt's departure from the Presidio of San Francisco had been front page news. His retirement from the Army in June 1947 went unnoticed in the press. He lived his final years at The Norwood, an apartment building in Washington, D.C., died of a heart attack in 1962 at the age of eighty-two, and was buried at the Arlington National Cemetery. Except in the collective memory of Japanese-Americans, who still speak of him with scorn, the once formidable military governor of the Pacific Coast is little more than an obscure footnote to World War II.

The fear that DeWitt had articulated in December 1941 and nurtured thereafter, was shared and felt across the Pacific Coast until late in the war. In January 1945, Jack A. Hayes, the Acting Administrator of the Oregon Defense Council, wrote to Colonel Joe Leedom of the West Coast field office of the Office of Civilian Defense in San Francisco "Here in the northwest we have never lost our fear that the enemy would attempt to utilize our forests and unfavorable periods of weather as a means of attacking us here at home, in spite of the developing feeling the war was largely over and that Civilian Defense could be relegated to an almost inactive status."

However, by the late summer of 1942, especially after the Battle of Midway, the powers that be at the War Department were moving away from such concerns. Attacks on the Pacific Coast, while theoretically possible, seemed more and more improbable.

In their study of the defense of the Coast, Stetson Conn, Rose Engelman, and Byron Fairchild remind us that the Army understood a Japanese carrier force "could have executed its mission and been out of bombardment range before any of the reinforcing planes were ready to attack it. It is therefore evident that from June 1942 on, the [W]est [C]oast lacked the air power to forestall a carrier raid, although its close-in air defenses for combating one were in good shape. In practice, the Army had already begun to apply the policy of 'calculated risk.'"

That calculated risk involved a gradual dismantling of DeWitt's command.

One by one, the four infantry divisions that had been the core of the Western Defense Command's combat strength left the Pacific Coast. The 7th Infantry Division never returned from the Aleutians. Instead, it headed farther west, to the opposite side of the Pacific, eventually taking part in the campaign to liberate the Philippines in 1944 and 1945. Likewise was the case of the 40th Infantry Division and the 41st Infantry Division, which also headed west. The former would leave in April 1942, first to serve in Hawaii and then to fight in the Southwest Pacific and the Philippines. The latter was sent to Australia in September 1942 and, after training, fought in New Guinea and helped liberate the Philippines. The 3rd Infantry Division left Fort Lewis to take part of the Operation Torch landings in North Africa in November 1942, and went on to make its name in the Italian campaign, the invasion of Southern France, and the final push into the Third Reich in 1945.

▷●

Joe Stilwell, who had commanded the Southern Sector of the Western Defense Command, moved on to the China–Burma-India Theater, where he achieved a great deal of notoriety and became perhaps the best known to history of the men who had been in DeWitt's chain of command—and the only one to reach four-star rank. Late in the war, he was given command of the Tenth Army for the invasion of Japan after its commander, Simon Bolivar Buckner was killed on Okinawa.

In February 1946, Stilwell found himself in DeWitt's job and office at the Presidio of San Francisco, as commander of the U.S. Army in the western United States, now designated as the Sixth Army. It was his last assignment. Stilwell died of stomach cancer at the Presidio eight months later.

Speaking of wartime Army units and the ironies of wartime on the Pacific Coast, we cannot ignore the 442nd Infantry Regiment, comprised of young *nisei* men who volunteered to serve, despite the treatment they had endured, in order to prove the loyalty of Japanese-Americans. Originally, the unit was expected to have remained small, but eventually fourteen thousand men passed through its ranks, and the support organizations that transformed it into the 442nd Regimental Combat Team. Operating in Italy, France, and Germany, the 442nd became the most decorated regiment in U.S. Army history in relation to its size and length of time in combat, coming home with six Presidential Unit Citations (originally Distinguished Unit Citations) and receiving a seventh from President Harry Truman in person on the White House lawn. Its men received more than a dozen Distinguished Service Crosses, the Army's second highest award for valor, more than 550 Silver Stars, and nearly 10,000 Purple Hearts.

The Medal of Honor, the highest award for battlefield valor, was awarded posthumously to the 442nd's Private First Class Sadao Munemori, who had sacrificed his life to save others in Italy. His mother, Nawa Munemori was still in Manzanar when she got the news of Sadao's death, but she was back at home in San Pedro when the medal was authorized in 1946. In 2000, the Army upgraded the Distinguished Service Crosses awarded to men of the 442nd to the Medal of Honor.

Much less heralded than the men of the 442nd because of the classified nature of their work were the Japanese-Americans who had served as linguists with the U.S. Army's Military Intelligence Service (MIS) in the Pacific Theater, monitoring Japanese radio traffic, translating captured documents, and interrogating prisoners. Because of the sensitive nature of their operations, few details of the MIS activities were known during the war, and the full breadth of the *nisei* contribution to victory in the Pacific would not be known until after the government began to declassify World War II intelligence documents in the 1970s.

By the spring of 1944, the cabinet level departments, including the Justice Department and the War Department, that had actively implemented internment, were taking the first steps toward unwinding it, and DeWitt's successor, Delos Emmons, was authorized to issue individual exceptions to internment. In December 1944, President Roosevelt, under Public Proclamation 21, finally rescinded the 1942 exclusion orders.

Early in 1945, Japanese-Americans began returning to the Pacific Coast. It was a slow process given that the pendulum of public opinion had not yet followed that of public policy. This meant difficulty in finding jobs and housing, as well as incidents of violence. Many returnees found their prewar homes and property vandalized or foreclosed upon. Business owners and farmers lacked access to capital and credit. Large numbers had nowhere to go and found themselves confined to barracks and trailer parks while they sorted out their postwar lives. Between September and December 1945, the internment camps were closed and, with them, the War Relocation Authority.

Of the governors who once hovered metaphorically around DeWitt like cherubim and supplicants in a Renaissance painting, Culbert Olson of California and Charles Sprague of Oregon were gone before the general left the Pacific Coast. Both of them were turned out of office in 1942, and neither would hold public office again.

In Washington, Arthur Langlie was not on the ballot until 1944, but he lost for the same reasons as Olson and Sprague. Despite all three having stood with DeWitt in insisting on a complete removal of Japanese-Americans from the Pacific Coast states, voters felt they had not done *enough* for civilian defense. To oppose Langlie in 1944, the Democrats picked Monrad Charles "Mon" Wallgren, Washington's junior U.S. Senator, who had been among the first and loudest Congressional voices urging Japanese-American expulsion, and who vocally opposed repatriation, commenting in a July 1943 *Los Angeles Times* interview that Japanese-Americans should be kept in the internment camps indefinitely for their own "protection."

According to Amy Lowe Meger in a National Park Service Historic Resource Study of the Minidoka Internment Camp, citing an article by Roger Daniels in the Fall 1997 issue of *Pacific Northwest Quarterly*, Governor Wallgren "opposed the return of [Japanese-Americans] to the Coast until after the war, and U.S. Senator Warren G. Magnuson [appointed as Wallgren's successor] called for a mass deportation of any *nisei* "who have indicated by act or implication their loyalty to Hirohito." Langlie had the ultimate revenge, however, successfully defeating Wallgren in a 1948 rematch for the governorship.

◗▬

In the West's major cities, civil defense shortcomings were a nagging political issue. In January 1942, San Francisco mayor Angelo Rossi managed to withstand a short-lived recall campaign before it reached the ballot box, but four months later, the man who'd been mayor for more than a decade was implicated in a State Assembly investigation spearheaded by Los Angeles Democrat Jack Tenney, where the California-born Italian-American was accused of having links to Italian fascists.

"No one dares question my wholehearted loyalty to my native land," he told Tenney, referring to the United States, not Italy. He vehemently denied ever having given a fascist salute in public, but admitted that he had an autographed picture of Italian dictator Benito Mussolini. He was, he told Tenney's committee, an autograph collector, and he had taken his Mussolini picture off the wall before the war. When asked whether he had attended any fascist meetings, Rossi replied "not recently," but quickly corrected himself to say "not ever."

Rossi survived Tenney's accusations, but was defeated for reelection in 1943 by businessman Roger Lapham, the president of the

American-Hawaiian Steamship Company and an industry representative on the National War Labor Board.

San Francisco police chief Charles Dullea, remained in his post until 1947. Ironically, his most serious wartime challenge came not from Japanese troops, but from American ones. As tens of thousands of young men passed through the congested city, frequenting its bars, night clubs, and dens of iniquity, all sorts of crime naturally followed. The climax came with the end of the war in early August 1945, when the four-day "Peace Riot" left eleven people dead, and Dullea and his department seemed unable to handle the mayhem.

In Portland, Mayor Earl Riley, who also wore the hat of director of the Portland and Multnomah County Civilian Defense Council, won reelection in 1944, though he was dogged by charges that he had failed to control the drunkenness and vice that proliferated across his fiefdom during the war. Indeed, it was widely rumored that he ran a prostitution protection racket out of his own office. In 1948, he was challenged by city councilwoman and former state legislator Dorothy McCullough Lee, who promised to "enforce the law." She took nearly 80 percent of the vote.

In Seattle, Earl Millikin, who was elected as mayor in 1941 to serve out Arthur Langlie's term after he went to Olympia, served only fifteen months before being defeated by William F. Devin in March 1942. In office, Devin seemed incredibly out of touch with the question of Japanese-American internment, which was one of the most intense local issues on the Pacific Coast in 1942.

In a September 22 reply to Gertrude Apel of the Council of Churches and Christian Education, who had asked for a statement in support of the WRA's plan to relocate Japanese families outside of the internment camps, Devin protested, "I feel that I am not sufficiently well informed upon the work that is now being done to comment, and I cannot say that I knew any Japanese well enough to make the statements which you request. In fact, practically the only Japanese I knew were tried in Federal Court for being Japanese agents."

Devin served as Seattle's mayor for ten years, and, after the war, he was the first American mayor to visit Japan.

Among the Pacific Coast's big city mayors, Los Angeles' Fletcher Bowron was probably the most outspoken when it came to an advocating the removal of Japanese-Americans. With one-third of the Japanese-American population of the continental United States in his city, his fear of imminent sabotage had propelled him into a virtual crusade against them.

Meanwhile, Bowron faced other problems for which the removal question would provide a convenient distraction. He was implicated, though not charged in February 1942, when a county grand jury indicted Police Chief Clemence Horrall, Deputy Chief Ross McDonald and six other Los Angeles Police Department officers for felony wiretapping. By the time that charges were dropped, the Japanese-American evacuation was virtually over. Both Bowron and Horrall survived various attempts to oust or recall them, and Bowron went on to be the city's longest serving mayor to date, being reelected twice before finally being defeated in 1952. Horrall's demise came in 1949 after he became embroiled in a sensational protection scandal involving the infamous Hollywood madame Brenda Allen.

The Pacific Coast politician whose career survived most magnificently was Earl Warren. Having defeated Olson in 1942, Warren became an incredibly popular governor, winning the nominations of both major parties in 1946. As governor, he used the Golden State's postwar prosperity to finance major infrastructure expansions, from the university system to the freeway system. In 1948, Thomas Dewey chose him as his vice presidential running mate. In 1953, President Eisenhower appointed him as the Chief Justice of the United States Supreme Court. Here, he joined another wartime advocate of Japanese-American internment, Tom Clark, who had served as the U.S. Attorney General from 1946 to 1949 when his longtime friend Harry Truman appointed him to the Supreme Court in 1949. During Warren's sixteen years as Chief Justice, the man who had won the governorship of California by running as a full-throated supporter of

Japanese-American internment, completely reinvented himself—and his historical legacy—as a champion of civil rights.

D━

After the war, the fears and worries of wartime were washed away by the exhilaration of victory, and memories of them were buried beneath the wave of prosperity which swept across the nation—and especially across the Pacific Coast states. Far greater tragedies and triumphs than anything seen on the Home Front had been experienced by young Americans on far-flung battlefields across the globe. There were heartbreaks to be commemorated or forgotten, achievements and victories to be celebrated, and worries to be put aside as millions of men and women built new lives.

As the leaders who had defined the wartime experience moved toward the twilight of their careers, the returning GIs and the women who had worked the swing shift, shoulder to shoulder with Rosie the Riveter, settled down to raise the children who came of age in the '60s. In turn, these children of the Baby Boom learned of World War II largely in the abstract. They could not remember the anxious early days of the war, and they did not know what it was like to live in a time of blackouts, dimouts, rationing, and sacrifice.

In the decades since, generations have come and gone, generations who have been able look out across the Pacific without that wartime sense of foreboding. Just as it is now possible to stand atop the White Cliffs of Dover without imagining a potential Nazi invasion, it is possible to stand atop a bluff at Cape Flattery or Point Concepción and not to think of the great battle, once so fearfully expected, that never came.

However, as we do admire that view, perhaps with a pair of fishing boats and a line of pelicans silhouetted peacefully against the setting sun, it is important for those of us of later generations to reflect upon that distant time when things could easily have been so different, and to be thankful that they were not.

About the Author

ill Yenne has lived in San Francisco, less than five miles from the Pacific Ocean, for the better part of four decades, and has traveled extensively on the highways and coast-hugging byways of the Pacific Coast from Washington's Olympic Peninsula to the sandy beaches of San Diego County. He has walked the streets of the towns and cities that are the setting for this narrative, and he has researched and written about them. He has gazed often at Pacific sunsets, contemplating the events that took place, and might have taken place, here during World War II.

He is the author of more than three dozen non-fiction books, mainly on military and historical topics, as well as ten novels. Among his works is *Rising Sons: The Japanese American GIs Who Fought for the United States in WWII*, in which he examines the strange and difficult lives and times of the young *Nisei* men of the Greatest Generation who had to fight the system *in* their country before they were allowed to fight *for* their country.

General Wesley Clark called Yenne's biography of Alexander the Great, the "best yet," while *The New Yorker* wrote of *Sitting Bull*, his biography of the great Lakota leader, that it "excels as a study in leadership." His dual biography of Dick Bong and Tommy McGuire, *Aces High: The Heroic Story of the Two TopScoring American Aces of World War II*, was described by pilot and bestselling author Dan Roam as "The greatest flying story of all time."

Mr. Yenne has contributed to encyclopedias of both world wars, and has appeared in documentaries airing on the History Channel, the National Geographic Channel, the Smithsonian Channel, and ARD German Television. His book signings have been covered by CSPAN.

He is on the web at www. BillYenne.com.

Acronyms

ANSCOL	Army and Navy Staff College
AWS	Aircraft Warning Service
AWVS	American Women's Voluntary Services
FCC	Federal Communications Commission
FUSAG	First U.S. Army Group
HMCS	His Majesty's Canadian Ship
IJA	Imperial Japanese Army
IJN	Imperial Japanese Navy
JG	Junior Grade
MIS	Military Intelligence Service
MISLS	Military Intelligence Service Language School
NAS	Naval Air Station
OCD	Office of Civilian Defense
OEM	Office of Emergency Management
ROTC	Reserve Officer Training Corps
UCLA	University of California at Los Angeles
USAAF	U.S. Army Air Forces
WCCA	Wartime Civil Control Administration
WRA	War Relocation Authority

Bibliography

Bancroft Library Regional Oral History Office: Earl Warren Oral History Project, Earl Warren's Campaigns: Volume II; West Coast Defense During World War II. Victor Hansen Interview Conducted by Amelia R. Fry. Berkeley: University of California, 1977.

Bland, Larry, with Sharon Ritenour Stevens, and Clarence E. Wunderlin, Jr.(editors). *The Papers of George Catlett Marshall.* Lexington, VA: The George C. Marshall Foundation, 1981.

Boyd, Carl and Akihiko Yoshida. *Japanese Submarine Force and World War II.* Annapolis: Naval Institute Press, 1995.

Brock, Jacobis, with Edward N. Barnhart, and Floyd W. Watson. *Prejudice, War and the Constitution.* Berkeley: University of California Press, 1954.

Bywater, Hector. *Great Pacific War: A History of the American-Japanese Campaign of 1931–33.* New York: Houghton Mifflin, 1925.

California Military Department. California Military Museum System. http://www.militarymuseum.org/

Carter, Kit and Mueller, Robert. *The Army Air Forces in World War II: Combat Chronology.* Washington, DC: Office of Air Force History, 1973.

Commission on Wartime Relocation and Internment of Civilians. *Personal Justice Denied: Report of the Commission on Wartime Relocation and Internment of Civilians.* Washington, DC: Government Printing Office, 1982.

Conn, Stetson with Byron Fairchild and Rose C. Engelman. *United States Army in World War II: The Framework of Hemisphere Defense.* Washington, DC: Center of Military History, 1960.

———. *United States Army in World War II: The Western Hemisphere: Guarding the United States and Its Outposts.* Washington, DC: Center of Military History, 1964.

Coyle, Brendan. *War on Our Doorstep: The Unknown Campaign on North America's West Coast.* Surrey, BC: Heritage House, 2002.

Craven, Wesley Frank and James Lea Cate, editors. *The Army Air Forces in World War II, Volume One: Plans and Early Operations.* Washington, DC: Office of Air Force History, 1947.

Cressman, Robert. *The Official Chronology of the U.S. Navy in World War II.* Annapolis: Naval Institute Press, 2000.

Daniels, Roger. *Concentration Camps North America: Japanese Americans and World War II.* New York: Holt, Rinehart and Winston, 1972.

———. "The Exile and Return." *Pacific Northwest Quarterly.* Vol. 88, No. 4. Fall 1997.

de Nevers, Klancy Clark. *The Colonel and the Pacifist: Karl Bendetsen, Perry Saito, and the Incarceration of Japanese Americans during World War II.* Salt Lake City: University of Utah Press, 2004.

Densho Encyclopedia. http://encyclopedia.densho.org/

Fourth Air Force Historical Study No. III-2. *Defense Plans and Operations in the Fourth Air Force, 1942–1945.* Washington, DC: Office of Air Force History, 1947.

Greenfield, Kent Roberts, with Martin Blumenson and Stetson Conn. *Command Decisions.* New York: Harcourt, Brace and Company, 1959.

Grodzins, Mortin. *Americans Betrayed: Politics and the Japanese Evacuation.* Chicago: The University of Chicago Press, 1949.

Hackett, Bob and Kingsepp, Sander. Sensuikan. http://www.combinedfleet.com/

HistoryLink.org, the Online Encyclopedia of Washington State History. http://www.historylink.org/

Irons, Peter. *Justice at War: The Story of the Japanese American Internment Cases.* New York: Oxford University Press, 1983.

Lea, Homer. *The Valor of Ignorance.* New York & London: Harper and Brothers, 1909.

Maurer, Maurer. *Air Force Combat Units of World War II.* Maxwell AFB: Office of Air Force History. 1983.

McCash, William. *Bombs Over Brookings.* Corvallis, Oregon: McCash, 2005.

Meger, Amy Lowe. *Historic Resource Study, Minidoka Internment National Monument.* Seattle: National Park Service, U.S. Department of the Interior, 2005.

Morison, Samuel Eliot. *History of United States Naval Operations in World War II, vol. IV, Coral Sea, Midway and Submarine Actions: May 1942–August 1942.* Boston: Little, Brown and Company, 1950.

Oregon Encyclopedia. http://www.oregonencyclopedia.org/

Oregon State Defense and the Oregon State Archives. *Life on the Home Front.* http://arcweb.sos.state.or.us/pages/exhibits/ww2/index.htm

Robinson, Greg. *By Order of the President: FDR and the Internment of Japanese Americans.* Cambridge: Harvard University Press, 2001.

Starr, Kevin. *The Dream Endures: California Enters the 1940s.* New York: Oxford University Press, 1997.

———. *Embattled Dreams: California in War and Peace, 1940–1950.* New York: Oxford University Press, 2002.

———. *Endangered Dreams: The Great Depression in California.* New York: Oxford University Press, 1996.

———. *Material Dreams: Southern California through the 1920s*. New York: Oxford University Press, 1990.

Stilwell, General Joseph W. *The Stilwell Papers*. New York: William Sloane Associates, 1948.

Thomas, Dorothy and Richard S. Nishimoto. *The Salvage*. Berkeley: University of California Press, 1952.

———. *The Spoilage*. Berkeley: University of California Press, 1946.

Tuchman, Barbara. *Stilwell and the American Experience in China, 1911–45*. New York: The Macmillan Company, 1971.

United States Department of the Interior, War Relocation Authority. *WRA: A Story of Human Conservation*. Washington, DC: U.S. Government Printing Office, 1946.

United States Strategic Bombing Survey (USSBS). *Interrogations of Japanese Officials, Interview 97, Comdr Masatake Okumiya*. Washington, DC: United States Strategic Bombing Survey, 1946.

United States War Department. *Final Report: Japanese Evacuation From the West Coast, 1942*. Washington, DC: U.S. Government Printing Office, 1943

Watson, Mark Skinner. *War Department, Chief of Staff Prewar Plans and Operations*. Washington, DC: U.S. Government Printing Office, 1950.

Webber, Bert. *Retaliation: Japanese Attacks and Allied Countermeasures on the Pacific Coast in World War II*. Corvallis: Oregon State University Press, 1975.

sWhite, G. Edward. *Earl Warren, a Public Life*. New York: Oxford University Press, 1987.

Appendix

United States Army Order of Battle in the Continental United States (December 1941)

First Army

Headquarters: Fort Jay, Governors Island, New York
Commander: Lieutenant General Hugh Drum
(co-headquartered with the Eastern Defense Command)

First Corps Area (ME, VT, NH, MA, CT, RI)
Second Corps Area (NY, NJ, DE)
Third Corps Area (PA, MD, VA, DC)
Fourth Corps Area (NC, SC, GA, FL, AL, MS, TN)

Corresponding Coastal Frontier area: North Atlantic
Corresponding U.S. Navy Command: Third Naval District

Second Army
Headquarters: Memphis, Tennessee
Commander: Lieutenant General Ben Lear
(co-headquartered with the Central Defense Command)
    Fifth Corps Area (OH, IN, KY, WV)
    Sixth Corps Area (IL, MI, WI)
    Seventh Corps Area (MO, KS, NB, CO, IA, MN, ND, SD, WY)
Corresponding Coastal Frontier area: Great Lakes
Corresponding U.S. Navy Command: Ninth Naval District

Third Army
Headquarters: Fort Sam Houston, Texas
Commander: Lieutenant General Walter Krueger
(co-headquartered with the Southern Defense Command)
    Eighth Corps Area (AR, LA, TX, OK, NM)
Corresponding Coastal Frontier area: Southern
Corresponding U.S. Navy Command: Sixth Naval District

Fourth Army
Headquarters: Presidio of San Francisco, California
Commander: Lieutenant General John DeWitt
(co-headquartered with the Western Defense Command)
    Ninth Corps Area (WA, OR, CA, ID, MT, NV, UT, AK)
Corresponding Coastal Frontier area: Pacific
Corresponding U.S. Navy Commands:
    Eleventh Naval District (San Diego)
    Twelfth Naval District (San Francisco)
    Thirteenth Naval District (Seattle)

U.S. Army Air Forces Order of Battle in the Continental United States (December 1941)

First Air Force (formerly Northeast Air District)
Headquarters: Mitchel Field, New York
Geographic Jurisdiction: (MN, IA, MO, WI, IL, MI, OH, KY, WV, ME, NH, VT, MA, CT, RI, NY, NJ, PA, MD, DE, DC, VA)
Commander: Major General Herbert Dargue
(Brigadier General Arnold Krogstad after December 10)

Second Air Force (formerly Northwest Air District)
Headquarters: Fort George Wright, Washington
Geographic Jurisdiction: (WA, OR, ID, MT, NV, UT, CO, ND, SD, WY, NE, KS)
Commander: Major General Millard Harmon
(Major General John Brooks after December 19)

Third Air Force (formerly Southeast Air District)
Headquarters: Tampa, Florida
Geographic Jurisdiction: (AR, LA, TN, AL, MS, FL, GA, SC. NC)
Commander: Major General Walter Frank

Fourth Air Force (formerly Southwest Air District)
Headquarters: Hamilton Field, California
Geographic Jurisdiction: (CA, NV, AZ, NM, OK, TX)
Commander: Major General Jacob Fickel

U.S. Army Order of Battle on the Pacific Coast
(December 7, 1941)

Western Defense Command (Presidio of San Francisco)

California
Presidio of San Francisco
>Fourth Army
>Ninth Corps Area

Presidio of Monterey, Monterey California
>III Corps

Fort Ord, Monterey
>7th Infantry Division
>35th Infantry Division HQ (KS, MO, NE National Guard)

Camp Haan, Riverside County
>101st Coastal Artillery Brigade, MN National Guard

Camp Roberts, San Miguel
>30th Field Artillery Regiment
>40th Field Artillery Regiment

Camp San Luis Obispo, San Luis Obispo California
>40th Infantry Division (California National Guard)

Camp Seely, El Centro
>11th Cavalry Regiment (Horse)

Fort MacArthur, San Pedro (Harbor Defenses)
Fort Rosecrans, San Diego (Harbor Defenses)
Fort Winfield Scott, San Francisco (Harbor Defenses)

Oregon
Fort Stevens, Warrington
>(Harbor Defense of the Mouth of the Columbia River)

Washington

Fort Lewis, Tacoma
    IX Corps
    3rd Infantry Division
    41st Infantry Division (WA, OR, ID National Guard)
Fort Worden, Port Townsend (Harbor Defense of Puget Sound)

USAAF Order of Battle on the Pacific Coast
(December 7, 1941)

Second Air Force (Fort George Wright, Washington)

Fourth Air Force (Hamilton Field, California)

California

Fresno Army Air Base, Fresno
    47th Bombardment Group (Light)
Hamilton Field, San Rafael
    7th Bombardment Group (B-17)
    20th Pursuit Group (P-36, P-40)
March Field, Riverside (IV Interceptor Command)
    14th Pursuit Group (P-40)
    51st Pursuit Group (P-38)
McClellan Field, Sacramento
    62nd Transport Group

Oregon

Pendleton Army Air Base, Pendleton
    17th Bombardment Group (B-25)
Portland Army Air Base, Portland
    55th Pursuit Group (P-36, P-40, P-43)

Washington

 Fort George Wright, Spokane
  HQ II Bomber Command
 Fort Lawton, Seattle
  HQ II Interceptor Command
 Geiger Field, Spokane
  39th Bombardment Group (B-17)
 McChord Field, Tacoma
  12th Bombardment Group (B-18, B-23)
 Paine Field, Everett
  54th Pursuit Group (P-39)

Major U.S. Navy Warships on the Pacific Coast (December 7, 1941)

Aircraft Carrier (of a total of 8 in the U.S. Navy)

USS *Saratoga* (CV-3), San Diego

Battleship (of a total of 17 in the U.S. Navy)

USS *Colorado* (BB-45), Bremerton, Washington (being overhauled)

Heavy Cruisers (of a total of 18)

None

Light Cruisers (of a total of 19 in the U.S. Navy)

USS *Concord* (CL-10), San Diego (being overhauled)

Destroyers (of a total of 171 in the U.S. Navy)

USS *Crane* (DD-109), San Diego
USS *Rathburne* (DD-113), Mare Island Navy Yard
USS *Talbot* (DD-114), San Diego

USS *Waters* (DD-115), San Diego

USS *Kilty* (DD-137), San Diego

USS *Kennison* (DD-138), San Diego

USS *Hatfield* (DD-231), San Diego

USS *Gilmer* (DD-233), at sea off Puget Sound

USS *Fox* (DD-234), Bremerton, Washington

USS *Kane* (DD-235), Seattle

USS *Humphreys* (DD-236), San Diego

USS *King* (DD-242), San Francisco

USS *Cushing* (DD-376), Mare Island Navy Yard (being overhauled)

USS *Perkins* (DD-377), Mare Island Navy Yard (being overhauled)

USS *Smith* (DD-378), Mare Island Navy Yard

USS *Preston* (DD-379), Mare Island Navy Yard

Submarines (of a total of 112 in the U.S. Navy)

SS-123 S18, San Diego

SS-128 S23, San Diego

SS-132 S27, Mare Island (being overhauled)

SS-133 S28, Mare Island (being overhauled)

SS-139 S34, San Diego

SS-140 S35, San Diego

USS *Nautilus* (SS-168), Mare Island (being overhauled)

USS *Cuttlefish* (SS-171), Mare Island (being overhauled)

USS *Gar* (SS-206), en route to San Diego from Canal Zone

USS *Grayling* (SS-209), en route to San Diego from Canal Zone

Index